Ensign to Admiral

Line Officer Albert E. Jarrell's Life of Adventure, War, and Diplomacy

Henry Jarrell

Independently Published by Henry Jarrell

ISBN: 9798610928364

DEDICATION

The seafaring men of the olden days, and the modern-day ocean travelers who put themselves up against the relentless dominance of the elements, all deserve our respect and gratitude. Particularly the men and women of the United States Navy, Forged by the Sea since 1775

CONTENTS

PREFACE

This book would not be possible without Nick Reed, Bob Anderson, Lewis Jarrell and Joan (Jarrell) Williams. But most of all, Albert Edmondson Jarrell.

Nick Reed is a radio talk show host for KSGF Radio in Springfield, Missouri. His ability to analyze and explain any world situation in a manner that I could not even imagine made me a devoted listener. His Thursday show always featured the "Author of the Week" segment and I enjoyed listening.

Bob Anderson was the author being interviewed on one particular Thursday in April, 2017. He had written the thirty-fourth book in a series of action novels originally started by author Jerry Ahern. At the end of Nick's interview, Bob offered a free copy of the book to one randomly selected listener who would place their email address on his web site. The action apocalypse genre was to my liking so I submitted my information. I was soon notified by email from Bob that "You are a winner." I, being somewhat of a jokester, replied with a witty comment and soon a series of email dialogs ensued. In these I mentioned that I had an article that my dad had written about his involvement in the battle of Okinawa that I was considering publishing in a magazine, and Bob offered to help me in the process. Bob was a local Springfield, Missouri author and we soon met and discussed my project. After looking at what I had, he told me that my dad's story is much more than just an article, and that a biography, or maybe several books, could be written about his life and experiences. Bob was very encouraging in pushing me to start this project.

Lewis and Joan, my dad's two other children, provided immeasurable insight on details of living in the Jarrell family from a perspective not seen by me. Joan, in particular, had written her own memories in a piece that she called, "I Remember." She included writings from our Uncle Henry about his growing up with his brother, Albert.

In September, 2017 I started accumulating the boxes of writings and records my dad had saved including his early school work, letters he had written home, Navy orders for reassignment, awards and commendations – boxes full of papers. I sorted them by date and started writing. Much of the material in the book is directly from my dad's writings, letters he wrote, and articles he published. Five months later I had completed the first draft. Because of the volume of his original writings, Dad is the primary contributor to the book. All the while, Bob Anderson gave me positive encouragement to keep going.

Serendipitously listening to Nick Reed, who interviewed Bob Anderson, who offered a free book, who happened to live near me, led me to organize the troves of information that resulted in this biography.

This is a biography – more a semi-autobiography – unlike most that you will find. It is a first-hand adventure story with the personal, sometimes shocking opinionations of an outspoken observer. You will discover unpublished insights to the life of a naval officer. Enjoy it for the unique history lesson that it is!

AUTHOR'S NOTE

It is difficult for someone living in the twenty first century to have the faintest clue of what the world was like in the first half of the twentieth century. No one had air conditioning. Forced air heating for homes was almost unheard of. Many homes did not have telephones and those that did were on party lines where a number of houses shared the line. If the line was clear, the operator would ask you who you wanted to talk to – no dialing. No ball point pens, Velcro, credit cards, or Nike shoes. Gas was ten cents a gallon. Public assistance was friends and neighbors helping you overcome a problem, probably though a church group. People helped other people.

When the Japanese attacked Pearl Harbor the American People became enraged. We were attacked! It was not like today where conflicts are addressed in far away places by a non-descript military that is available to do that sort of thing. The Japanese had attacked us and every American citizen was aware of it and every American citizen wanted to do their part to defeat the Japanese. Young Americans volunteered for service by the thousands. School children would collect scrap metals for the war. Everyone reduced their consumption so that food and materials were available to support the war effort.

Because we were attacked, there was great enmity toward the Japanese. This was reflected in how the public referred to the Japanese with the slur, "Jap." I think that the word was used in reference to the Japanese military who were fighting America, and not the population of Japan in general. A soldier, sailor or marine charging up Mount Suribachi certainly wouldn't refer to the enemy as the Imperial Japanese Army soldier I need to kill, but could very well use the word Jap. A defending Japanese soldier probably would not say he needs to kill the attacking United States Marines, but might say that he needs to kill the *kichiku* (Devil). Even the American Press bought into the Jap moniker:

Following the war, the peoples of both countries, military and civilian, cultivated a fondness for each other that remains today. You will see this as you read the book. The animus of battle and the angry words slung about are no longer in common use today. A good portion of this book is written by the hand of Albert Edmondson Jarrell. He died before most readers were born. Please keep in mind that the words he chose, and the phrases he used, and the opinions he expressed, are not of today's politically correct, sanitized society, but of a time when such usage was more tolerated and accepted. To change his words just to please a reader who might be offended today would be a disservice to the memory of the man who lived a century ago, and it would effectively change history. The world is no longer thought to be flat, the earth is not believed to be the center of the universe, and we no longer use the lexicon of 1941. But let's understand that those things are a part of history.

ILLUSTRATIONS

Cover design and creation by Henry Jarrell. Components of the cover art are from the files of Albert Jarrell or are from official United States Navy photographs.

Pages 4, 82:
Thanks to Wikimedia.
Roel Balingit (https://commons.wikimedia.org/wiki/File:Ph_fil_tawi-tawi.png), „Ph fil tawi-tawi", Size, text, colors by Henry Jarrell, https://creativecommons.org/licenses/by-sa/3.0/legalcode.

Pages 33, 49, 65, 79, 89, 156, 159, 164, 170, 180, 243, 324:
The most gracious permission by d-maps.com to use their map data bases to create these images is greatly appreciated. Final map format created by Henry Jarrell.

Pages 217, 245:
Thanks to Wikimedia. Wikimedia open source or public domain images.

Pages 11, 12, 21, 22, 48, 105, 142, 163, 166, 167, 172, 222, 225, 226, 234, 251, 281, 286, 291, 312, 328, 336, 351:
Photographs and images are the personal property of the Jarrell family and were taken by members of the family or other non-commercial entities.

Official U.S. Navy photographs, U.S. Army photographs, Marine Corps photographs, and Republic of Korea photographs are individually attributed in the book.

Ensign to Admiral

CHAPTER 1

<u>What I Hope To Do and Be</u>

When I grow up to be a man,
I'll do something dandy,
I'll buy a carload of nuts
And a whole ton of candy.

I'm going to be President someday,
'Cause Mama says I am,
I want to be a rich man
And rule old Uncle Sam.

I want to be a poet,
Like that of Longfellar,
Who was a mighty fine man
And also a story-tellar.

I'd like to be a rich man
And have a lot of money,
And have a fine horse and buggy
And eat bread and honey.

Albert Jarrell

c. 1910

My dad, Albert Jarrell, even at the tender age of 9, had a prescient sense of what the future may hold in store for him. The confidence he displayed in this short poem remained with him for his entire life and served to propel him to accomplishments reserved for few people. Not only did he proudly serve with distinction in the United States Navy for thirty eight years, he became very involved in community organizations and political causes. He was a prolific writer of articles, and his opinions were often seen in the Letters section of various newspapers and magazines.

His drive, however, was not unique to just him. His mother traces her ancestry to Parmenas Haynes, a Captain who served in the Virginia Continental Line during the Revolutionary War. His father's ancestry traces back to the grandparents of Meriwether Lewis, who became one of the leaders of President Thomas Jefferson's Corps of Discovery – the Lewis and Clark Expedition.

Meriwether Lewis was a tenacious leader during the nearly two and a half years of the Expedition, and the success in making it all the way to the Pacific Ocean and back is a testament to his focused drive. My dad must have inherited this drive. His various challenges and obstacles were met with a determination to succeed, regardless if the task was to fulfill his duty assignments or prosecute battles against an enemy. This determination and his leadership capabilities resulted in his being awarded the Navy Cross during World War Two, an honor bestowed upon some 6,900 people in the last one hundred years. The only award higher is the Congressional Medal of Honor.

Dad had a long career as a line officer in the United States Navy, from graduation from the Naval Academy in 1925 as an Ensign until retirement in 1959 as a Vice Admiral. In those 34 years, and afterward as a civilian involved in community endeavors, my dad proceeded with a focus and drive that would become a constant measure of his being.

Early in his career, Dad, Lieutenant (junior grade) Albert Edmondson Jarrell, displayed his venturesome heritage while serving as Gunnery Officer on his fourth ship, USS Pruitt. The Forty-fifth Division, to which it was attached, sailed for the island of Tawi Tawi in the Sulu Archipelago, off the northeast tip of Borneo. The various islands had not been surveyed and each ship in the division was tasked with noting the navigable waters, adjacent islands, rivers, and other prominent features.

In early February 1929 Pruitt was anchored off the town of Balimbing (in today's municipality of Panglima Sugala), the largest town on Tawi Tawi. Lieutenant (jg) Jarrell was given orders to conduct a survey expedition on the island. Much like Meriwether Lewis and the Corps of Discovery, some things didn't go according to plan. (It is interesting to note that many early writings of Balimbing used the spelling "Balambing," which is what my dad used in his journals.)

Here, in his own words, is my dad's story:

> Early in the morning of the second day after our arrival I received orders to land with a party of three men at Madanni, on the north coast, then proceed overland to Gadang, on the south coast, where I was to find a canoe or vinta [traditional sailed canoe with outrigger] and proceed twenty miles east to the Pruitt's anchorage off the east coast of Tawi Tawi. I was to complete the journey by midnight if possible.

> We landed with a guide at midday and immediately commenced the journey overland. A light trail was followed for half an hour but then it vanished and we had no guide except the sun, for our ship carried no pocket compasses. In another hour we could not even use the sun because the undergrowth was so thick it could not be seen.

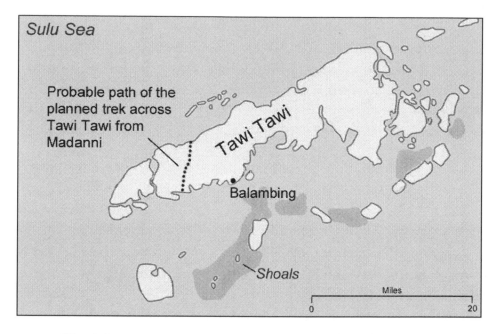

The Island of Tawi Tawi - South of the Philippine Islands
(Attribution on Page xiii)

I learned during this trip a valuable lesson about the food that should be taken on a hike in the tropics. Nothing but canned food should be carried. Within an hour after we started all of our food had become saturated with our perspiration and we had to discard it.

Whenever an opportunity afforded, one of us would climb a tree to get a glimpse of the sun. We had few chances of doing this, however, because most of the trees were too heavily guarded by undergrowth. The guide seemed to be completely lost. I am sure that he had not penetrated the interior of the island before and, to make matters worse, he could not speak a word of English. We did make him useful, nevertheless, by sending him ahead with a bayonet to hack a trail for us. After four o'clock we didn't make over two hundred yards an hour.

About one hour before sunset one of the men climbed a tree and said that he thought he could see water about a mile distant. We pushed ahead as rapidly as possible, but soon struck a mangrove swamp that was impenetrable. It was rapidly getting dark and I began to search for higher ground, where I hoped we could find a dry spot to spend the night.

We could find nothing better than a spot where wild hogs had been rooting. The mud was ankle deep, but we cut some tree branches and laid them in rows and then placed other branches at right angles across these. The result was a bed that would be very uncomfortable under most circumstances, but we found that we could sleep soundly on it.

It had been raining all afternoon, but after an hour's effort we got a fire started and prepared to dry our clothing. When it was almost dry the rain began falling again in torrents, and we decided to devote the rest of our time to sleeping. One man was on watch all through the night to guard against the possibility of our guide going jao mentada.

The expression "jao mentada" means "insanely murderous." It is not uncommon for a Filipino or a band of Filipinos to go jao mentada, especially in the southern islands. Frequently, armed forces have to be used against them. I believe that when one goes on a killing craze he is seldom mentally deranged, however, because he usually chooses an opportune moment to commit his murders. The victims are seldom Mohammedans, but the murderer kills both sexes and all ages with equal delight.

There is an old story about a Spanish captain who took his ship to the southern islands. The Spanish governor of one of the provinces called on him and told him that he had been having a lot of trouble with the natives going jao mentada. When the native Datu [Leader or Chief] was asked to put a stop to it, he would merely reply, "Well, what can I do? They are not criminals, just jao mentada."

The captain told the governor to let him know the next time a native went jao mentada, and he would see what he could do to stop it. The next time one did, the captain was notified. He immediately fired a broadside into the center of the native settlement and followed this with others, scattering them at random so that the natives would have no idea where the next would fall.

The Datu went terrified to the governor and asked him to have the firing stopped. "Well, what can I do? He has only gone jao mentada," answered the governor with amusement in his voice.

We awoke early the next morning and again headed in the direction the sea had been seen. All day we walked, taking advantage of the beds of small streams when we could, to make the going easier. Finally, in the early afternoon, we struck a brook larger than the others and I decided to follow it to the coast. We had not had a glimpse of the sun all day and our bearings were very doubtful, but I thought the stream was our best bet.

We had been forced to drink local water since our canteen supply had given out and, although I had a supply of quinine, I was a little uneasy about the possibility of malaria.

The stream rapidly became deeper and wider and we took to the banks. After several hours of rough going, we came across a large canoe. We were delighted with our find. We boarded it and paddled about 3 miles down stream when, to my great chagrin, we emerged in the late afternoon at Madanni, where we started the journey. I was so greatly disappointed that, had we had food, I would have set forth back into the jungle.

There were two houses in the small settlement of Madanni. I approached the occupants of one of these and finally got the idea across that we wanted a boat to proceed east in. They brought out a heavy vinta and manned it themselves, apparently not wishing to trust it to our care.

We made slow progress in it until about ten o'clock that night when a brisk breeze sprang up. This worried the Moros, but I kept urging them to continue. Finally their mood became so threatening that I directed them to land us and return to their village. I sent the guide back with them because I didn't want to worry about him another night, and besides, I felt that he should have assisted me in urging the continuation of the journey.

The part of the island where we landed was a sand beach, and it was the most comfortable spot we had yet found. We built the fire and immediately went to sleep.

It seemed like only a few minutes later when I was awakened by the sound of paddles. In reality it was two o'clock; I had been asleep nearly four hours. The sound came from 2 canoes approaching the shore. In a few minutes they were beached, and I discovered to my surprise that one of the occupants was our guide. Upon his return to Madanni he had prevailed on two young Moros to bring their outrigger canoes to our camp for the purpose of carrying us closer to our destination.

We were all very tired, but I was anxious to get closer to our ship as soon as possible, so we broke camp and headed eastward. The moon was very bright and I enjoyed the ride. I soon forgot my soreness when the Moros began singing their native songs while they paddled.

They possessed remarkably musical voices. It seemed almost like they sang to a stringed accompaniment. The air was dead calm and the sky was so clear that the stars were as bright as planets. The shoreline was silhouetted in black contrast to the sky's glare and the bright reflection of the moon on the water. Everything seemed bustling with life except the island, which looked somber and bare.

The Moros became tired after about two hours, for they had already traveled seven miles, and we landed at a coral beach to stay the rest of the night. The beach was very hard and jagged, without a soft spot on it. After a long search, we found pieces of drift wood which served as mattresses.

Early the next morning we started again, but after an hour or so a brisk breeze sprang up so suddenly that our boats were swamped in about four 4 feet of water. We had removed our shoes to rest our feet and the coral bottom was hard to walk on, but we rescued the boats and most of our equipment before we waded ashore.

We walked about five miles before we came to a small settlement where we found half a dozen Moros. The leader was Hadji Efrem Haud, an enormous person, which is unusual among Filipinos. He spoke English well and possessed a license to carry firearms, which meant that he was a man of trust.

In spite of his good recommendation, Haud took advantage of my predicament by charging me ten pesos before he would consent to take us to our anchorage. Before we began this leg of our journey we found some coconut palms and obtained a few coconuts. This was the first food we had eaten since we left the Pruitt. We were offered some native rice, but we couldn't quite stomach it.

Haud and three men manned a large covered vinta which had a capacity of twenty persons. When we boarded the craft, all of us immediately fell asleep. We were awakened in the middle of the afternoon by Haud, who pointed out a ship on the horizon. When she came closer we made her out as the U.S.S. Noa, one of the ships of our Division.

We signaled to her and she stood over to pick us up. It was a great relief when we got aboard but, except for our fatigue, the trip had certainly been interesting enough.

CHAPTER 2
THE EARLY YEARS

Born in Rome, Georgia, on August 1, 1901, Albert Edmondson Jarrell spent very little time there, as within a year or two the family moved to LaGrange, Georgia, the town where he was to grow up. My dad had two brothers and a sister. Albert was the middle of the two brothers, William (Bill), born 1892 in Athens, Georgia, and Henry, born 1903 in LaGrange, Georgia. Sister Corinne, the eldest sibling, was born 1889 in Athens, Georgia.

Dad's father, Henry Franklin Jarrell, owned LaGrange Hardware Company, an old-style hardware store with nails and screws in revolving bins, where the customers could grab the fasteners they need and stuff them into paper bags to be weighed at the cash register. Nearly every item necessary to maintain a farm was available on the shelves behind the counters. Mother Lola Corinne was a stay-at-home mother, as was the norm in that day.

In the early 19th century, LaGrange was incorporated and named for the country estate of the wife of the Marquis de La Fayette near Paris, France. La Fayette had visited the Georgia area in 1825 and had commented on how similar the Georgia landscape was to the area near Paris. Half a century later, shortly before the end of the American Civil War, a battle took place near LaGrange led by a Union Colonel named La Grange, an odd coincidence which may today lead to confusion over the derivation of the town's name. When the Union troops entered LaGrange the Confederate defenders negotiated a surrender, and Colonel La Grange spared the town the destruction that so often happens during war. In gratitude, the LaGrange defenders hosted a dinner for Colonel La Grange and he reciprocated by pardoning a number of prisoners of war. It turns out that the Colonel had been wounded in an earlier battle and Confederate doctors had treated him with great care, a kindness that most likely played a role in his decision to spare the town.

Albert with Great Uncle

c. 1904

In 1910, when my dad was growing up in LaGrange, the population was about 6,000. Located on the western border with Alabama, it was considered an important city for industry, railroads, and textiles. Opportunity was so great that the city expanded to a population of 17,000 by 1920, when Albert was nineteen years of age.

LaGrange Hardware Company

Albert's younger brother Henry, my uncle, told me that he – Uncle Henry – claimed the dubious distinction of being the first person in LaGrange to be run over by an automobile. The car hit him and he lay in the dirt road crying his eyes out. The driver, wanting to ameliorate the situation, offered to buy Uncle Henry two one-cent pieces of candy, which he immediately accepted and the incident was over.

Dad and Uncle Henry spent many hours in their daddy's store playing with the hardware and, on occasion, helping clean up.

Their brother Bill was a decade older and worked in the store when he was not at school or doing other things. Uncle Bill, who had a degree from a Pennsylvania Technical School, would eventually take over the store.

Albert, who went by the nickname Al, and Henry were best of friends. Al, being older, watched over Henry and made sure no one took advantage of him. Henry, however, was very able to take care of himself but appreciated Al's support. Henry had many memories of their times together and wrote of them in the late 1980s at the request of my sister, Joan.

Here is Uncle Henry's recollection of growing up with his older brother, Al:

When two kids, two years apart, grow up together, the language they use, the games they play, their appraisal of the present, and imaginary plans for the future, are always those of the senior team-mate, who contributes all – and to the advantage of the junior partner who receives everything. I know, because I've lived through it. I wish every American kid could grow up in the shadow of an older brother.

Al was born on August 1st, 1901, and I came along 22 months and 22 days later. During the 75 years of his life, Al's goal was to be a good family member, a good friend, and a good American citizen; he felt that it could all be summed up in the latter phrase, and I've often heard him say that his ambitions and expectations for his children and their children would be met if they just "grew up to be good citizens."

One of my earliest childhood joys was Grand-Pa Edmondson's approval of requests from Al and from me that we spend a night with him and share the luxury of his broad bed and comfort of an eiderdown quilt. Grand-Pa agreed to oblige us on a one-on-one basis, and Al, because of seniority, was Grand-Pa's first guest. Sometime between midnight and dawn Al confided to Grand-Pa that he wanted to whisper. "Alright Albert," came a sleepy response, "whisper in Grand-Pa's ear." Albert did! What Grand-Pa didn't know, or had forgotten, was that Al's mother and Aunt Mell had taught him to use the secret code "whisper" rather than the direct and customary three letter repeated word, pee pee, when guests or strangers were present. I never got my chance to sleep with Grand-Pa.

Al had his likes and dislikes and seldom, if ever, did one find him halfway between two choices. He was a macho kid, and he was thumbs-down on everything feminine. He would assure the entire family – and then re-assure us – that three pivotal points in his future were already resolved: (1) I will never marry, (2) if I do marry, we will have no children, and (3) if we do have children, none will be named "Junior," or after anyone in the family. Those were the only promises I know of that Al didn't keep. His word was as solid as any guarantee.

When I was pre-school age, I wore "knickerbockers" – a knee-length trouser, buckled or button-closed below the knee. These were the "uniform of the day" for teen-age boys. But knickerbockers were not for Al, whose bottom line was, "they are bloomers – and for girls!" He would wear only straight, knee-length boy's trousers, and they were not available in small town LaGrange's shops. Our mother tried to keep some on hand, because re-stocking involved a round-trip on the daily "local" train that stopped at every cross-road on the 70-mile run between the Troup County capital and Atlanta.

In those days we lived less than a mile from the center of town – the Town Square, with its County Court House and monument, in Georgia marble, of a Confederate Soldier. But we had all the comforts and luxuries of a self-sufficient farm – a huge vegetable garden, a fruit orchard of peaches, pears, grapes, and supporting two horses, a sow or two, plus a cow. Al would have nothing to do with "that female cow," so the milking job was mine while Al, by choice, took on the far more demanding job of feeding and grooming two horses and attending to the wood, coal, and kindling needs of six fireplaces in the six-room house.

Both of the horses were named "Sam!" Why? Names are so expensive! But their similarities began and ended with their names. Big, docile, Black Sam's weekly chore was to haul our Mother, sister Corinne, and maiden-aunt Mell to early Sunday School and morning Church in the family surrey. We males walked. Our mother saw to it that Al and I had perfect attendance records at Sunday School but during summer I was able to escape the later 11:00-to-12:00 o'clock "Brimstone and Hell" warnings from the Southern Baptist pulpit due to the popularity of my homemade fresh-peach ice cream. Both the Reverend's message and my ice cream filled about an hour's time, and, my Mother couldn't have both unless I was set free after Sunday School.

Al and I were in the same Sunday School class, and at roll call our teacher required the pupils to answer with a verse from the Bible rather than "Here," or "Present." Al searched the "Good Book" for its shortest quote and came up with "Jesus wept" for me, and "God is love" for himself. Al always chose the "shortest way home."

Little Sam's intended year-round duty was to pull the family's open buggy (forerunner to today's pick-up truck), meet the local train with Atlanta's afternoon paper, and deliver the newsprint to our subscribers – six days of the week. The daily operation took about two hours. After two weeks of this, Al and I had been paid nothing by the local agent, and our Father suggested that we bring the paper's account up-to-date. The "agent," who was also LaGrange's Fire Chief, deducted "unpaid subscriptions" (not our responsibility) and paid us 48 cents – 12 cents a week for Al; 12 cents for me; nothing for Little Sam. We were advised to quit our first job. We followed the Fatherly advice.

Big Sam balked at pulling a plow, so our Father had to call in a man-and-mule team to do the heavy work. The three or four acres beyond the vegetable garden produced a bountiful supply of "feed corn" for the livestock, and before winter's arrival, our ample corn-crib was filled to the rafters – enough to feed horses, hogs, and cow until the next harvest. Corncobs were plentiful around the barnyard.

Soak a dry corncob overnight in the livestock's watering trough and you have ideal ammunition for a corncob battle; it can deliver a nasty sting to a bare arm or leg. Al loved corncob battles – and he never lost one. Why? The battle would end when one side or the other surrendered, and armies usually surrendered when they ran out of ammunition. Al seldom expended all of his ammunition, and he <u>never</u> surrendered.

During summer months we played baseball in any available pasture, but cold weather best benefitted corncob warfare. All of the other kids in the neighborhood had a standing invitation from Al to assemble after school at 344 Hill Street, for whatever the season had to offer. Often there were six or more of us. Al and the second toughest guy in the neighborhood would be named "Captains," and would choose their teammates. I was always "still available" when Al started to pick his team, and I was always his "first choice" – not for my offensive wallop, but because Al wanted his Kid Brother to be on the winning team.

During the "No School" summer months, my six-days-a-week morning contribution to the family effort was to harvest the vegetable garden's surplus production – our black cook of 30 year's service always looked after her kitchen's needs – and deliver it to my regular customers (mostly boarding houses) in time for mid-day "dinner." Little Sam and the open buggy were indispensible in this. Fresh-from-the-stock roasting ears were 15 cents-a-dozen; today [1980-90], in the supermarkets, last-week's-refrigerated-harvest are "two ears for 99 cents."

In those days "cholesterol" and "Low Fat" was in no one's vocabulary, and on none of the grocery shelves, but we lived well. Three of our grandparents died in their 80's, and our Mother reached 92 before she left us.

When I was about five years old, I had below-the-shoulder length blond curls which were my mother's "pride and joy." One afternoon when our Mother returned home after visiting a neighbor, she found me hard to recognize; I looked like just another kid in the block. A few days earlier my long hair had snarled on the crooked handle of an umbrella, and getting the locks freed was no easy assignment. With adults absent and Al in charge, my curls were again conveniently snarled by the umbrella handle and Al felt it was time to take precautions. Our Mother's dressmaker scissors were handy and helpful. No longer would passers-by think that Al was playing with a GIRL!

My dad was a very athletic young man, but also had a quick wit. He participated in most sports and competitive activities, and somewhere along the line became known by the nickname, "Ditty" or "Diddie." Al's participation, drive, and success are best summarized in *The Clarion*, LaGrange High School's yearbook of 1919.

"Diddie" Albert Jarrell Scientific

"With too much quickness ever to be taught;
With too much thinking to have common thought"

What student of L.H.S. does not know Albert Jarrell?
A witty yet argumentative person, who is probably one
of the smartest pupils who ever attended our school.
Indeed, while Diddie is by no means a hard student he
has a brilliant mind and enters into all the class and
school contests and activities. From an athletic stand-
point, Diddie was decidedly the best player of the Football Team this year, and his work in '17 and '18 was
excellent. He is also one of our best debaters while the
medal won at the High School contest in Newman (1918)
shows his ability in writing.

Varsity Football Team '16, '17, '18; Class Basketball
Team '19; Captain Baseball Team '19; Sub Basketball
Team '19; Baseball '18, '19; Business Manager Clarion
'19; Class Historian.

At graduation in 1919, Dad enrolled for the freshman year
at the University of Georgia, but concurrently began the process
for entry into the United States Naval Academy in Annapolis,
Maryland. He tried for two years to secure an appointment but it
wasn't until February 1921 that he received word from
Congressman W. C. Wright, 4th Georgia District, that appointment
to the Academy was imminent. In looking back years later, Dad
said, "I was twenty years old on entry, and I know that if I had
been accepted two years earlier I would not have passed the
course."

Jarrell entered Annapolis as a Midshipman (Naval
Academy student) on June 22, 1921. As with all United States
military academies at the time, the appointment was made by
direction of the President, and was signed by the Acting Secretary
of the Navy, Theodore Roosevelt, Jr.

Soon after beginning his Plebe year (Freshman) at
Annapolis, he and many classmates went to New York City to
attend the 1921 Army-Navy football game at the Polo Grounds.
Travel to the game was only allowed for Midshipmen in good
standing, with passing grades and no demerits. Jarrell wrote to his
parents that his marks were all above 3.0 (with 4.0 being perfect)
with the exception of the class on Steam, which was 2.95. The trip
to New York was well choreographed, as the trip was a repeat of
five earlier games played at the Polo Grounds. The Midshipmen
marched to the stadium from the ferry landing and arrived ten

minutes before the start of the game. Navy won, 7-0. Jarrell later wrote his parents, "I saw the best game of football I have ever seen last Saturday in New York."

Following the game the Midshipmen stayed the night in the Commodore Hotel, eight miles from the Polo Grounds. Jarrell commented in his letter that New York is very big. "I was certainly surprised at the size of the place." Many Middies went to the comedy show, *Six Cylinder Love*, which they thought was pretty good. The next morning the trip back to the Naval Academy started at 9:30 and they arrived in time for the meal formation at 5:00 pm. The Academy routine recommenced. In the letter to his parents he mentioned that part of the ten dollars they had recently sent him had been used for the trip to New York.

My dad had a love of sports his entire life. Baseball was of particular interest to him and he played on the Annapolis team. He also was the Manager of the Fencing Team. He continued to follow baseball, and actively played tennis for the rest of his life. I remember the many annual cross-country trips the family made when he was reassigned to a new duty station. He would have my mom scan the radio frequencies looking for a baseball game, and if she found one we all had to keep quiet until the game was over or the car moved out of range of the station. The chit-chat of the announcers would bore him, and on one occasion they were comparing the condiments they preferred to have on their hot dogs. Dad told us that a baseball announcer should stick to baseball and leave the food to the chefs.

Jarrell graduated from the United States Naval Academy in June 1925, and became a commissioned officer as described in the Presidential Decree:

CALVIN COOLIDGE

President of the United States of America

To all who shall see these presents, Greeting:

Know ye, That, reposing special trust and confidence in the patriotism, valor, fidelity, and abilities of .... ALBERT E. JARRELL, ... I do appoint him an Ensign in the Navy, from the 4th day of June, 1925, in the service of the United States. He is, therefore, carefully and diligently to discharge the duties of an Ensign, by doing and performing all manner of things thereunto belonging. And I do strictly charge and require all officers, seamen, and marines, under his command, to be obedient to his orders as an Ensign. And he is to observe and follow such orders and directions, from time to time, as he shall receive from me, or the future **President of the United States of America**, or his superior officer set over him, according to the rules and discipline of the NAVY. This Commission to continue in force during the pleasure of the President of the United States for the time being, and until the end of the next session of the Senate of the United States.

Done at the City of Washington, this 3RD day of June, in the year of our Lord one thousand nine hundred and twenty-five and in the one hundred and forty-ninth year of the Independence of the United States.

By the PRESIDENT:

Secretary of the Navy.

Registered No.............. { The lowest number of { same date takes rank

Registrar.

21

Ensign Jarrell

Ensign Jarrell's service was as a line officer, meaning that his education, training and experience qualified him to command a ship. Other navy professions would be legal, medical and clergy, for example, but officers in those fields would not command ships. Each profession had a distinct symbol worn on the uniform and the line officer symbol was a single star on the shoulder boards or sleeves. The term "line officer" goes back to the time in history when warships would form a line (ships of the line) prior to a sea battle so that the maximum number of cannon could be fired at the enemy. The officers manning the ships were "officers of the line" or, simply, line officers.

Somewhere along the way my dad developed a fondness for cigars. The full-sized cigars, not the little slim cigarillos that a woman might be seen puffing. In his travels he picked up humidors that became a common sight in his home and office. Dad's affection for a good cigar led him in 1951 to place a standing order for one hundred premium Admiral Cigars per month from Swann Products, Inc., Tampa, Florida. They must have been good, as they were nearly nine cents apiece after his 10% discount for having a standing order. He smoked cigars until well after retirement, when he found that the cost and quality of available cigars no longer met his standards.

*   *   *   *   *

His first assignment after graduation was to the battleship USS TEXAS (BB-35). Jarrell's billet was Gunnery Officer, but Texas was in the Norfolk, Virginia, Navy Yard undergoing overhaul and modernization so he didn't get to practice his trade.

It was common for a newly commissioned officer to be assigned duty as a Gunnery Officer. Typically, a gunnery officer is in charge of all aspects of munitions aboard ship including training, maintenance, storage, fire control, and supervision of men. Fire control in the Gunnery Department refers to the ability of a gun to track and hit a target, not the fighting of fires. On a battleship such as Texas, the gunnery officer may be directed to supervise a subset of the Gunnery Department such as a Battle Station or Torpedo Control.

Assignment as a Gunnery Officer allows the newly commissioned officer to practice the academic training he received at the Naval Academy and apply it to real-world practice aboard ship. He also receives on-the-job training in gunnery and in the supervision of men, a talent needed for career officers.

Texas entered the Norfolk Navy Yard at the end of July 1925 and underwent extensive changes, which included conversion from coal-fired boilers to oil-fired, upgraded anti-aircraft guns, and relocation of her 5-inch deck guns. Ensign Jarrell was kept busy supervising and inspecting the work as it progressed. The shipyard work would be completed in November 1926, but Jarrell did not get the opportunity to sail with Texas, as she was in the Navy Yard for the five months he was attached.

Texas was a New York-class battleship, the second of only two in this class, and was the second battleship to be named for the state of Texas. Texas was commissioned in 1914 and served honorably until 1948, when she was decommissioned. The Lone Star State honored her by making U.S.S. Texas the first permanent battleship museum, mooring her in La Porte, Texas.

*　　*　　*　　*　　*

In November 1925, change of duty orders were issued ordering Ensign Jarrell to report to the Edgewood Arsenal, Edgewood, Maryland, where he was to attend classes at the Army Chemical Warfare school. The schooling took place from November 16 through December 24, 1925, and focused on the history of the use of chemical weapons in the World War (WWI), moral and strategic aspects of being prepared to use chemical weapons, the folly of trusting adversaries who promise not to use chemical weapons, and chemical weapon tactics both offensive and defensive.

The Chemical Warfare School came within the purview of the Chemical Warfare Service (CWS), founded near the end of World War I in 1918. At the time Jarrell attended the school, the CWS held a stockpile of chemical weapons in its arsenal despite great pressure in favor of disarmament. The second commander of the CWS, Major General Amos Fries, viewed chemical disarmament efforts as being a Communist plot and through his efforts was able to stop disarmament. He was even able to block an effort to prevent ratification of the 1925 Geneva Protocol, which would have allowed chemical weapons to be used only in retaliation for an attack, not for first use.

In the December 15, 1925, issue of *Chemical Warfare - A Magazine devoted to the activities of the Chemical Warfare Service,* General Fries is quoted as saying, "Every development of science that makes warfare more universal and more scientific makes for permanent peace by making war intolerable." The magazine included articles addressing the humane aspect of chemical weapons, and the humanity of chemical warfare. In 1925, chemicals used in warfare were relatively new and studies of the effects during the World War led military leaders to believe that "...of all the means of so-called civilized warfare, the use of chemical agents is the most humane." The author of that statement,

Lt. Col. H. L. Gilchrist, Chief of the Division of Medical Research at Edgewood Arsenal, goes on to clarify that no killing or maiming of a human being is humane, just that relative to other weapons chemicals are more humane.

Although Ensign Jarrell was taught the history and future of chemical warfare as it was understood at the time, the focus of the class was naval aspects of chemicals which, to a large extent, would be defensive.

*   *   *   *   *

On December 15, 1925, Jarrell received orders that upon completion of the Chemical Warfare School he was to make his way to Norfolk, Virginia, to obtain passage to the Panama Canal Zone aboard U.S.S Bushnell (AS-2). Bushnell was a submarine tender that operated both in the Atlantic and the Pacific. After a short leave he reported aboard Bushnell on January 12, 1926. Upon arriving in Balboa, Canal Zone, Ensign Jarrell's orders were to report aboard the battleship U.S.S. Mississippi (BB-41) as Gunnery Officer, which he did on February 22, 1926. Although she was part of the Pacific Fleet, during Jarrell's tenure aboard Mississippi she would be conducting normal winter training exercises in the Caribbean and Atlantic. Mississippi would return to her home port in Washington State later in the year.

U.S.S. Mississippi was the second of three battleships built to the New Mexico-class specification, which had an improved hull design and better 14-inch naval guns and turrets. Battleship design was progressing so rapidly that the New Mexico-class production was limited to three ships. Further changes to naval gun design, and other improvements, produced the Tennessee-class battleships, of which three were produced. The most well known battleship feature, the 16-inch gun, was found on the next class of ships, the Colorado-class. All of the newer battleship classes, beginning with the New Mexico-class, had similar operating characteristics of speed and maneuverability, which allowed for efficient battle planning without the need to take into account the speed or maneuverability capabilities of individual ships.

Mississippi had a long career, serving from 1917 to November 1956. She had been through a number of modification programs including propulsion and armament improvements, but eventually was sold for scrap.

*   *   *   *   *

The Navy Department, Bureau of Navigation, issued orders on June 22, 1926, directing Ensign Jarrell to detach from duty aboard Mississippi and report for duty aboard U.S.S. Sumner (DD-333) as Gunnery Officer. Both ships were at Port Angeles, Washington, and Jarrell departed Mississippi July 12 and reported aboard Sumner July 16.

U.S.S. Sumner was a Clemson-class destroyer, also known as four-stackers because of their four distinctive exhaust stacks. She had a length of 314 feet and her 26,500 horsepower steam turbines could drive her at a published speed of 35 knots (40 mph).

During the ten months Ensign Jarrell was aboard her, Sumner conducted training and patrols in the Pacific. Sumner transited the Panama Canal to the Atlantic in March 1927 to participate in fleet maneuvers, and Jarrell departed Sumner soon after.

Sumner was the fourth billet for Jarrell since his graduation from the Naval Academy one year prior. All graduates were required to serve in the United States Navy as repayment for the education and training received, and in order to see if they "fit in" with the strenuous life and responsibilities of a career officer. In those years of service, the officer and the Navy would evaluate each other to see if a naval career is the proper course of action. Jarrell's multiple assignments and increasing responsibilities were a part of that process. From graduation on, naval officers were trained and groomed for command, part of the process being to see how they performed in a variety of challenging positions. At each billet Jarrell would be evaluated for his performance and, as he rose in the ranks, would evaluate his own subordinates.

CHAPTER 3
CHINA AND SOUTHEAST ASIA

Ensign Jarrell received orders April 30, 1927, detaching him from duty aboard Sumner and instructing him to proceed to San Francisco for passage aboard the Steamship President Cleveland for travel to Manila, Philippine Islands. He arrived in Manila July 21, 1927, and was ordered to proceed to Cavite, P.I., where he reported to the Commandant, Sixteenth Naval District, for duty. The next day, Jarrell was ordered to report aboard U.S.S. Pruitt, DD-347, which was located at Cavite. Pruitt, like Sumner, was a Clemson-class destroyer sporting four stacks. Ensign Jarrell would serve aboard Pruitt for the next 34 months.

Assignment to U.S.S. Pruitt as a Gunnery Officer was the first real duty assignment for my dad, Ensign Jarrell, and he would thoroughly enjoy it. He kept an account of this in a journal he titled "An Asiatic Cruise," which was found in one of the boxes my sister, Joan, had saved.

U.S.S. Pruitt (DD-347)
(Official U. S. Navy Photograph)

Following is my dad's record of his arrival in the Philippine Islands:

> If you like excitement, go to the orient. Go to China if you can, but anywhere west of Hawaii and east of Russia will do. You will find the best in everything, and the worst. It is a place of extremes. There is no moderation because none is wanted.

> When I arrived at Manila I was surprised to find the city rather pleasing in appearance, which is unusual among oriental cities. The Luneta Park is situated on the waterfront and on the north side of this park is the Manila Hotel. On

the opposite side are the Army and Navy Club and the Elks club.

At the Army and Navy Club I was told that my ship, the U.S.S. Pruitt, was in the Navy yard at Cavite undergoing her annual overhaul. Cavite is only seven miles by water from Manila and I caught one of the small boats that operate between the two cities and reported for duty on the Pruitt, a destroyer which was to be my home for the cruise. A happy home she proved to be.

One day while we were in the Navy yard I called on Mayor Brown. He has recently died, but while he lived he was one of Manila's best known citizens. He was a resident of the city when Dewey captured it, and was its first American mayor. He possessed a remarkable memory. It was said that he never forgot a name. At any rate, the second time I saw Mayor Brown he remembered my name, rank, and the ship to which I was attached. He owned a chimpanzee that had a passion for cocktails. The beast was kept in a small room adjoining the reception room and I have seen it become quite drunk. It was amazing how insane it seemed to become when it saw a cocktail.

Sometimes in the evenings we would visit Louis Cox's bar in Cavite to have a beer. Louis had been in the Philippines too long and had "gone native" which means that he had married a Filipino woman. He had, I think, seven mestizo children. Louis said that he never wanted to visit the United States again. He was more Filipino, mentally, than American. I could never understand an American "gone native." I met several while I was on the station, and they all impressed me as being mentally unbalanced. Their "going native" is not the result of any magic tropical spell, as novelists would have us believe. It is the result of deliberately following the line of least resistance.

One night in Louis' bar I saw a Marine Sergeant, who was weeping as if he was in great trouble. When I questioned him, he said that he was afraid his courage might fail him at some time when he might need it. The sergeant had been decorated five times during the World War. He could handle his rifles, but not his beer.

Navy ships all have a home port where they return for restocking of supplies and for maintenance, but they spend very little time there. Pruitt was coming out of overhaul and was preparing for her next cruise, which would be to ports in China and Southeast Asia. As with all Navy ships, time would not be wasted and a constant regimen of training and naval exercises would be undertaken. This was to be Ensign Jarrell's first extended cruise and he continued to describe his remarkable experiences in his journal.

Pruitt began the eleven-week deployment by sailing into the South China Sea, past Taiwan and into the East China Sea on a northerly heading. The destination was Chefoo (now named Yantai), the summer base for gunnery exercises. Chefoo is on the north coast of China's Shandong peninsula in the Bohai Strait. To the east is the Yellow Sea and Korea.

On the first of August, 1927, the Pruitt finished her overhaul and sailed for Chefoo, China, our summer base. We spent an active six weeks there firing our gunnery and torpedo practices. In the afternoons, we would go ashore for either tennis or riding.

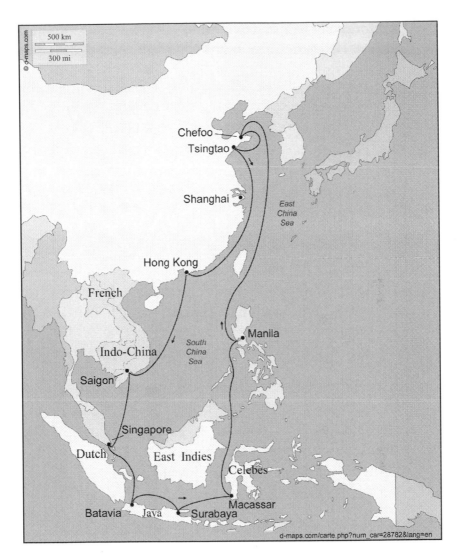

Pruitt's Asia cruise, August 1 – October 20, 1927

When in Chinese ports we always had to exercise great care with our food, because dysentery and cholera were continuingly prevalent. All food was either thoroughly cooked, or dipped in a solution of potassium permanganate followed by dipping it in boiling water. We never drank shore water, but only the ship's distilled water.

Chefoo, like all Chinese ports, has a large population of white Russians. They have fled Russia for political reasons, and all experience much difficulty in making a living. Most of them are cabaret dancers, and few ever go higher than hostess in a cabaret. Theirs is a pitiful plight. They belong to the peasant class and are not trained for any occupation.

The first impression one gets of them is distasteful. They appear to be leeches whose sole idea is to get everything they can out of every man they meet. They play their sex skillfully, attempting to rouse enough interest to obtain an extra book of dance tickets or a bottle of champagne. They receive a commission on everything sold.

But this first bad impression soon changes to a sympathetic tolerance for these exiled people. They are parasites because they have no chance to be anything else. Many are ambitious and attempt to reach a better station by studying English and stenography, but I never heard of one who was successful at office work.

It is remarkable how these Russian women keep their health and beauty. They are up every night until about four o'clock, and they have to begin at about four thirty in the afternoon. Most of them consume quite a lot of alcoholic beverage every night. In fact, the quantity that some consume is astounding. Of course some will be found who abstain, even though it hurts their profits. These are rare, because few cabaret proprietors will accept them. In spite of the strenuous life they lead, these Russians far surpass our American professional cabaret dancers. But the terrific pace they have to keep wears them down before they reach old age. There are not many aged Russian women in China. And there are few Russian men of any age, probably one to every ten women.

Early in September, we went to Tsingtao, which is about two hundred miles from Chefoo, on the southern side of the Shandong peninsula. This was a German colony until the World War, and still has many German residents. It is the most beautiful city in China, and the only one that has an adequate sewage system. The climate is bracing, and many people from southern China and the Philippines spend their summers there. The best surf bathing in China is found there. The country around Tsingtao is thickly wooded. There are numerous bridle paths and any day during the summer months many little Chinese ponies can be seen with their foreign riders.

The city was under Japanese control, and remained so until the summer of 1929. The Japanese maintained an army corps in the vicinity on Tsingtao, and occasionally a man-of-war would come into port for a few days visit.

In spite of the large number of Japanese, both military and commercial, residing in Tsingtao, the German influence could not be entirely removed. It was rather amusing to see Chinese with German manners and dressed like Germans, even to the extent of wearing short cropped hair. The Tsingtao Chinese were always clean, courteous, and orderly. I liked them better than any other Chinese that I met, but I can't say that I ever met any Chinese that I didn't like. They are an intelligent, industrious, well mannered race. I have seen a Chinese waiter take correctly, without using a memorandum, dinner orders for nine people. In the Chefoo Club, the number one boy has for years called each morning about fifteen or twenty members at the correct time and filled their orders for breakfast, given the night before. I have gone into the club at all hours and I always found him awake. He seemed to never need sleep, for he showed no effect of strain.

I have seen Ricksha boys pull their vehicles 24 hours a day, in four inches of snow, without shoes of any description. Sometimes they would squat between the shafts of the Ricksha and catch a few winks of sleep, but not often, because a customer might be lost.

The Tsingtao Russians are a lower class of those in Chefoo. They are more honest, however, but this is not surprising because they have not been in China long. They have had little experience with the outside world, but they are gradually learning to become mercenary like their brothers and sisters in Chefoo and Tientsin and Shanghai.

When one enters a cabaret in Tsingtao, he will usually find the orchestra quiet and the dancing partners seated at the tables. But the moment he enters all becomes a scene of activity. The orchestra, consisting of a piano, a violin, and a drum begins to make a loud tinny noise from which keen ears can sometimes distinguish a few notes from "Stenka Razin." The dancers are no longer stolid, sleepy creatures, but are transformed into starry eyed nymphs, each trying to out-ogle the other. Little effort is spared by these girls to inveigle a man into buying them a book of dance tickets or a bottle of wine. Almost invariably, they try to coax him, one by one, to take them home. Their tactics are crude. Often the hostess will stop at a table and say "If you see a girl you would like to know better, let me know."

Many of the Russians have Jewish blood in them, and they live up to the letter of their religious customs regardless of their occupation. I have seen them get hilariously drunk on the anniversary of the feast of the Passover, yet they would eat only unleavened bread which they professed had been shipped from Jerusalem.

On the fifteenth of September, we got under way for Saigon, French Indo-china and a six weeks cruise of the Dutch East Indies. There were with us five other destroyers which, with the Pruitt, composed the 45th Destroyer Division. There was also the U.S.S. Blackhawk, tender for the 15th Destroyer Squadron.

We had not been out of port a day before the signs of an approaching typhoon became evident. On the second day the sea was so rough that we had to eat only sandwiches and canned food, it being impossible to set a table or use the range. A typhoon is always accompanied by a very heavy rain. On the second and third days we had difficulty in distinguishing the other ships in the column because the rain was so blinding. About noon of the third day the division commander signaled a change of course to take us into the harbor of Hong Kong, where we could remain until the typhoon had passed. As we changed course we caught the wind and the sea full on the beam, and for half and hour the ships rolled through an arc of 120 degrees.

Hong Kong has one of the most distinctive harbors in the world. The depth of water is adequate, but there is so much shipping that two or three vessels frequently have to secure to a buoy. About a quarter of a mile from the waterfront the island rises abruptly to a height of about half a mile. Private dwellings of foreigners are scattered over this high section, and at night the place seems like a huge Christmas tree.

Half a mile directly abreast Hong Kong is Kowloon, a railroad terminal. Ferries frequently ply between the two places, but in spite of the congested traffic and the military protection afforded, these ferries are not safe from attack by Chinese pirates. While we were in port, pirates obtained tickets on one of the boats and forced the helmsman to leave his course and steer for a group of small islands to the northeast of Hong Kong. There they quickly looted the ship and passengers and departed. As a reprisal, several days later a British gunboat demolished one of the numerous pirate hangouts.

Hong Kong, like all British towns, is very quiet. There is no nightlife because there are few Americans in the place. Americans require excitement, while Englishmen detest it. Wherever you find a large number of Americans, you are certain to find much noise and activity.

A strong garrison is maintained on the island, but the soldiers apparently seldom go on liberty, for the uniform is not frequently seen. Hong Kong would be a difficult station for an American soldier.

There are two distinct social cliques, the military and the commercial. Both are cool toward transients, but many friendships have been made in Hong Kong between British and American Naval officers. The civilians, both British and American, are so loath to accept strangers, however, that it is a relief to leave Hong Kong.

After two days in port, we stood out to sea again, and two days later arrived at Saigon, where we spent four pleasant days. The natives of Indo-China are of smaller stature than those of China. And the southern Chinese are smaller than the northern, but more energetic.

The French have a happy gift of making their surroundings beautiful. Saigon has few natural attractions other than commercial, but industrious French architects and horticulturists have made of it one of the loveliest towns in the Orient. Located in the center of town is a quaint opera house surrounded by open air cafes and lace and perfume shops. Radiating from this center, paved streets, lined with tropical trees whose foliage is so thick that the sky can hardly be seen, extend for several miles.

On the twenty-fourth of September we shoved off for Singapore, and the expression "shoved off" may here be taken literally. Saigon is situated on the banks of one of the tributaries of the Mekong River, and the stream is so narrow that large vessels have difficulty in turning around. There is deep water right to the banks, however, which makes it possible for ships to shove their bows into the soft mud and spin around.

The trip to Singapore was uneventful and, I can almost say, so was our visit there. Except for the interest which a mingling of many races always causes, Singapore has nothing to offer. I suppose there are representatives of every race and every station there. The waterfront is said to be the home of half the criminals of Asia at one time or another of their careers. One street has been nicknamed "Death Street."

During our stay, we visited a rubber plantation. The natives make no effort to keep the sap clean, but instead they appear to take keen delight in seeing how polluted the rubber can be made. Many of the impurities are later removed by punching holes in the rubber and forcing water through.

Crossing the equator for the first time is a big event in the life of a mariner, and requires a ceremony to mark the event. Overseeing the initiation is King Neptune and his Royal Court, represented by senior seamen. Those who haven't crossed the equator are called Pollywogs and those who have - the Shellbacks - summon the Pollywogs to court and perform the initiation ceremony. The initiation puts the Pollywogs through a series of embarrassing and distasteful actions culminating in the transformation of the Pollywog into a Shellback. On September 27, 1927, Ensign Jarrell was about to become a Shellback.

On the same day that we left Singapore we crossed the equator. About one-third of the crew had previously crossed, and they had spent about two weeks planning an adequate initiation for the remainder into the Kingdom of Neptunus Rex, ruler of the Raging Main.

I had never crossed the line before and, together with the other neophytes, was sent to the forecastle about noon to await the ceremonies. When my turn came, the starboard door to the forecastle was opened and I was told to crawl through a windsail [a canvas sheet rigged like a tunnel] that had been stretched on deck from the forecastle to the foot of the ladder leading to the galley deck-house. I did this as quickly as possible, because a steady shower of paddle blows was falling on me, and very little time was required for it to have a telling effect.

When I finally got through the windsail, I scrambled up the ladder to the top of the galley deck-house, where I was met by the court photographer and the Royal Sheriff. The sheriff forced me with an improvised pitchfork, which was connected to an electric circuit, to stand in front of the camera and be saturated with mercurochrome. Then I was led over to the Royal Baby and told to kiss his ring. The part of the baby was played by the largest sailor on the ship. The stone in his ring was a turtle shell. When I leaned over to kiss it, I received a jab from the electric pitchfork and several blows from paddles in the hands of the sheriff and photographer.

Then I was taken before King Neptunus Rex, where various charges against me were read. These charges included annoying the crew at reveille, carrying a tennis racket ashore with intent to deceive my shipmates into believing me a player, and playing the phonograph after nine o'clock in the evenings. The king told me that although the charges were very serious, he would mitigate my punishment if I could please him with a song. My song not only failed to please him, but made him furious, and he ordered me to report to the Royal Barber. As I sat in the barber's chair, the Royal Sympathizer came over to weep over me and bemoan my sad fate. Anyone who sang as I did, in his opinion, was already punished sufficiently.

The Royal Barber first cut a streak through my hair and then he began to give me a shampoo and massage with gun grease. Just as he finished, the chair in which I was sitting was tipped over on its hinges and I fell about eight feet into a large canvas bag of water. There is a steel deck where this bag was placed, and I got a real shock during the fraction of a second that I was falling, because this part of the program could not be anticipated. After I was dunked a few times, I was dragged out and told that I was no longer a landlubber, but a full-fledged member of the Royal Order of Shellbacks. I was greatly relieved to know that my initiation was completed.

The trip from Singapore, at the Southern tip of Malaysia, to Batavia (now named Jakarta), the capital of the Dutch East Indies (Indonesia), would take Pruitt from the South China Sea, through the Karimata Straight and into the Java Sea. The destination was the city's main port, Tanjung Priok, located on the northwest coast of Java.

From Batavia (Jakarta), Pruitt would make stops at Sarabaya, also on Java, and Macassar (more commonly spelled Makassar) on Indonesia's island of Sulawesi. Return to Manila would take Pruitt on a northerly route into the Celebes Sea and Sulu Sea, then into the South China Sea. Ensign Jarrell noted in his journal a number of things that he found particularly interesting.

Dad's story continues as Pruitt sails for Jakarta:

Two days later, we arrived at Tanjung Priok, the harbor of Batavia. Batavia is located about six miles from its harbor, but fast automobiles driven by native Javanese carried us this distance in eight minutes. The Javanese are the fastest drivers I ever saw, but they are very good.

Batavia is a very clean city and a beautiful one. The principal residential street runs parallel to a narrow boat canal, and on both sides is a luxuriant growth of tropical flowers whose perfume is distinguishable over most of the foreign area.

The Harmonie Club has never had its doors closed. "Never let it be said," one hospitable Dutchman told us, "that a man suffering from thirst at any hour could not quench it in this club." When several Dutchman get together for a drinking bout, the drinks are not paid for until the contest is over. A record of rounds ordered is kept by piling saucers on the table, one saucer for each round. The size of the stacks often reaches prodigious proportions.

Javanese men do not wear shoes and, as a consequence, they always have large feet. It is ludicrous to see a waiter in a spic and span dress uniform hustling from table to table dragging his incongruous, frog-like feet behind him. One is often tempted to drop a bottle on them to see if he would notice. He probably wouldn't.

One evening three of us were invited to dinner by three Dutch naval officers. We met them, with their wives, at the Harmonie Club and to my surprise, every wife was a half-caste. I learned later that it is not uncommon in the Dutch East Indies to marry a Eurasian, especially if she has material assets.

These Dutch wives were the ugliest three women that I ever saw in one group. I have seen single women, suffering from cancer or elephantiasis, who was worse on the eyes, but I never saw three women together whose average was so low. They were perfectly charming hostesses, however, and we all had a delightful evening.

After 5 days in Batavia we departed for Surabaya, Java, where we arrived two days later. The Dutch East Indies fleet bases at this port and we were royally entertained while there. I did not remain in Surabaya, however, but visited Borobudur, an old Buddhist shrine about 150 miles inland. This shrine was recommended by the Black Hawk's [USS Black Hawk, AD-9, a destroyer tender] Chaplain to be the most interesting place in the East Indies, and one world traveler in his writings said that it is more marvelous than the pyramids.

The visit was a disappointment to me. When my party arrived at the shrine, we were met by the manager of the only hotel in the vicinity, who complained because our party was not larger. He said that he expected better patronage from the American Navy. He then asked me if I would not pay the price for two guests, since he had a large supply of food on hand and expected to suffer a financial loss. I told him that the only reason he was getting even one price from me was because I objected to sleeping in the jungle with the snakes.

He then carefully explained to all of us that he was a teetotaler, but that he sold liquor because he liked to afford his guests all the privileges possible. His prices proved to be nearly twice as high as those of other hotels.

I suppose I am prejudice against teetotalers and reformers, but it is because I have never met an interesting one. Such people find so much fault with their neighbors that they frequently develop a chronic grouch. They are never original or amusing. And I never saw one that I did not believe would change his tactics for a profit.

The shrine at Borobudur is a pyramid of rock about 150 feet high. Several hundred stone statues of Buddha are spaced at equal intervals over the structure, and all around the base are inscriptions depicting the life of the man. The exact date of building is not known. The island was visited by Mohammedans in the twelfth century and has remained principally Mohammedan since. It is believed that the Buddhist shrine was built during the eighth and ninth centuries.

From Surabaya we went to Macassar, Celebes. There is nothing of interest there except the shops, most of which are run by Chinese. There are thousands of Chinese on the island, although it is governed by the Dutch, and the natives are Malayan. Pieces of gold and silver filigree of good quality can be bought from the Chinese, and some amber and silk shipped from China. Birds of Paradise are still plentiful, although they are slowly being exterminated. There is a law prohibiting the sale of their feathers, but foreign visitors offer such attractive prices that most of the shops carry a few feathers hidden behind their shelves.

From Macassar we returned to Manila, our winter base, where we arrived on the 20th of October, 1927. Manila is pleasant in the winter, there being no rain and little oppressive heat. But during the summer months it rains almost every day, there are frequent typhoons, much heat, and many insects!

Being at home port doesn't mean it is time to relax. There was plenty of work to be accomplished, preparation for sea duty, and practice exercises to keep the ship's battle readiness up to par. As a Gunnery Officer, Ensign Jarrell seems to have found the perfect occupation. However, there was ample time ashore in which to become familiar with the local territory and the culture of the people. My dad thoroughly enjoyed the sea duty, but also liked to understand the local culture and politics.

At this time there was considerable agitation throughout the islands, and especially in Manila, for Philippine independence. Manuel Quezon, who was speaker of the senate, was champion of the cause, but he was supported by Sergio Osmena and Manuel Roxas, two politicians with considerable power. [The Philippines were never self-governing during their colonial period beginning in 1565. After the Spanish-American War, in 1898, the Philippines had a legislature but the United States maintained control of the government through a Governor-General until 1935, at which time the transition to Philippine governance began.]

Shortly after we arrived at Manila a bill was proposed which would prohibit the isolation of lepers. The only reason for it was to prevent families being separated. This bill actually was passed by the House of Representatives, but failed in the Senate after the acting Governor General made it clear that he would veto it if necessary. There was no excuse for ever giving the slightest attention to this bill. Leprosy is the most loathsome of all diseases, and isolation is the safest way to combat it. Governor General Leonard Wood made much progress in his fight against Leprosy, but he was never popular with the Filipinos. This was due, to a large degree, to his anti-independence tendencies, however.

While based in Manila Bay, we would go out for maneuvers on Monday morning and return Friday afternoon. This time was devoted to preparation for division practices. Occasionally we would anchor overnight in the closed harbor of Olongapo, where there was good fishing and hunting.

About the middle of December we fired the practices. There is no thrill equal to that given by a naval battle practice. Aviation and diving cannot compare with it.

As the word "Coming on the range" is received in the fire control station, the target, which seems to be about the size of a postage stamp, can be distinguished on the horizon. A few minutes later "Stand by" comes up from the bridge. Every man is intensely alert, every effort concentrated on hitting the target. Ranges and deflections are continually sent out to the guns as the ship, making 30 knots, closes on the target.

Then comes the order "Commence firing," and the scene changes instantly from quiet vigilance to bustling activity. A salvo goes out, and then two more before the first one lands. About 20 seconds after the first salvo, a splash is seen near the target, and the spotter calls down "Up two double-0." The salvos continue until all shots have been fired, which is usually not much longer than a minute. Four weeks of intensive training for a one minute practice. But it is worth it. The ship's reputation, her battle efficiency standing, depends to a great extent on her ability to shoot.

I don't believe any other sporting team requires as perfect coordination as a gunnery team. From magazine to gun there is perfect functioning of material and men. Not a second is lost. New ammunition is in the hands of the first loader the instant the gun is fired. All motions are performed like clock work. Each loading crew is trained to such a degree that all the guns are loaded almost simultaneously, which eliminates waiting to fire a salvo. Accuracy is not enough, speed being just as important in determining the score.

Good Shooting! Jarrell Is Far Right

All drills and exercises were stopped for about a
week during the Christmas holidays, and we spent this time
on leave or attending parties. But on the first of the year we
left for China, almost 3 months ahead of the regular
schedule because of disturbances along the Yangtze Valley.

CHAPTER 4
CHINA AND THE YANGTZE RIVER

On the first of January, 1928, Ensign Jarrell began his second major voyage on the U.S.S. Pruitt. The first stop would be Shanghai, where Pruitt would be docked off the Yangtze on the Huangpu River (often spelled Whangpoo by Anglos). From there, up and down the Yangtze to Wuhu, Chinkiang (Zhenjiang), and Hankow. Hankow, also known as Hangkow, was one of three cities that eventually grew together to become the metropolitan city of Wuhan.

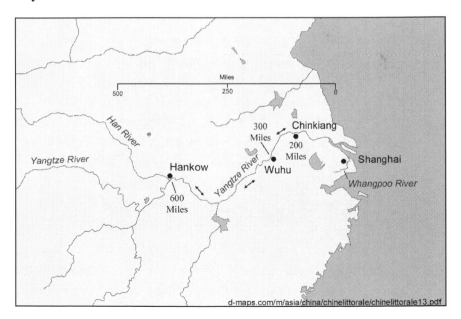

Cruises Up the Yangtze River

49

The journal my dad wrote, containing many of his unique personal, often insensitive opinions, continues as Pruitt begins the new year with another cruise:

> In three days we arrived off the mouth of the Yangtze River. This river collects so much sediment that it discolors the sea for about 25 miles from its mouth, making it a dark yellow hue. We steamed for about 15 miles up the Yangtze and then turned left into the Whangpoo River. About half an hour later we moored to the Dollar Dock at Shanghai.

> Shanghai has often been called the Paris of the East. This is no compliment because Shanghai is the most interesting city in the world. People of every nationality and creed may be found there. One may spend a pleasant evening at the French Club, the Russian Club, the American Club, the Shanghai Club (English), or the Columbia Club. There are about 35 Russian cabarets, numerous night clubs, night dog racing, and a regular season of horse racing. Shanghai, although essentially a commercial city, is one of the worlds foremost leaders of sport.

> A morning in Shanghai is rather quiet. In the afternoons, however, the traffic is congested with shoppers and sightseers from the steamers in the harbor. From seven until nine o'clock in the evening the sidewalks are almost bare, but the rickshaw and automobile traffic is heavy with people going to fulfill dinner engagements. From nine until eleven Shanghai is quiet again, but at eleven o'clock the diners move to the cabarets and clubs. From midnight until three the city is almost dead. Then comes the exodus from the places of amusement, and Shanghai is noisy with the

patter of rickshaw coolie feet and taxis taking the revelers home.

Shanghai is the best place in China to buy clothes. They are not only inexpensive, but the service is good. I have seen a Chinese tailor take orders for a hundred suits of clothes from the passengers of a steamer, make them according to measurement during the night, and deliver them the next morning. For the ladies, Shanghai offers "Lingerie Street," whose shops sell nothing but intimate articles of women's dress. Female tourists spend many hours there.

There is an old tailor in Shanghai named Sze Ching Chong. He has been known to the Navy for about 50 years, but now is almost blind in his old age. He has seen many changes in the Asiatic Fleet, and numbers many high officers among his acquaintances.

Sze was always a welcome guest on our ship. We would greet him with, "How is everything today Sze?" and he would answer "Oh, it's 7 coats cold today, sir." He was always a perfect gentleman. A misfit was a discredit to his profession. I don't believe that Sze ever overcharged or gave an article of bad quality to anyone.

There is a story about Sze that gives a good illustration of the practical nature of the average Chinaman. Sze was in a Sampan on the Whangpoo one day, when a passing steamer upset him. Like most Chinese, he was a poor swimmer and immediately called for help. The owner of a passing Sampan, hearing his calls, came close by and asked, "How much?" Sze answered "five dollars." The perspective rescuer said, "Not enough; one hundred dollars." Sze held out as long as he could and, just as he became exhausted, waived assent. He was dragged aboard a limp mass but paid his agreement price. I had heard this story many times before I met Sze, and doubted it, but he corroborated it when I questioned him.

Americans have been accused of having a gross sense of humor, but the Chinese are even more noisy and unrestrained. They will laugh at a man who slips on a banana skin, or is sprayed with mud by a passing automobile. Their favorite actor is Charlie Chaplin. One day, while I was on a ferry in the harbor of Shanghai, I heard a large volume of laughter on the opposite side of the boat. I walked over, and found about a hundred Chinese laughing uncontrollably. The cause of their amusement was a sailor who had fallen from a boat boom on the French cruiser, "Jules Michelet," into the Whangpoo River. He was fighting desperately against the strong current to reach the sea ladder, which he finally succeeded in doing. Not many people who fall into the Whangpoo come out alive, however. This is because of the river having two currents, of different intensity, and sometimes opposite in direction. The undercurrent is the river's own current, which always flows towards the sea. The surface current is caused by the tides. The action of the two currents produces a suction, which makes it very difficult for a swimmer to stay afloat. An average of about five hundred drownings occur yearly in the Whangpoo.

All Chinese, from rickshaw boys to the Mandarins, are optimists. They expect more out of every transaction they enter into than can reasonably be expected. If a rickshaw boy is paid twice his regular fare, he is disappointed because it isn't four times as much. And if a general is given half the army to command, he is disappointed because he doesn't receive all of it.

Optimism, in my opinion, is a fault. Pessimists succeed because they have a truer sense of values. They recognize the possibility of failure and work to prevent it. They are more pleasing people to meet, because they seldom are despondent since they can anticipate a setback. Most suicides are due to either insanity or unwarranted optimism. Men commit suicide because of a failure in love or stocks, because they can't make the football team, and because of losing their jobs. Most of them have no reason for expecting better than they receive.

Orientals are the worlds champion suiciders. A highly valued Japanese admiral, very important to his country's defense, may slash his throat because of the loss of a ship or the death of a friend. The Chinese, as well as all Asiatic people, must learn to see facts without the use of their rose-colored glasses.

Census takers say that Shanghai has a population of nearly two million, but it is impossible for an accurate census to be taken. Thousands of people live in small boats in the Whangpoo River. A family of seven can live for weeks in a Sampan twelve feet long without setting foot ashore. They take their food from the water and rescue rags to make their clothes. We never dumped refuse into the slop chute when several of these boats were not waiting at the foot to retrieve it. When a ship coaled, Sampans would hang around like vultures, waiting for a few lumps to be dropped overboard. I have seen Chinese take soggy pieces of bread from the water, which would be dried in the sun and eaten. If a beef bone were thrown overboard, there was certain to be a mad rush for it.

There is no degree of poverty anywhere that can compare to the poverty of these "river people." Once, a steamer sank in the Yangtze River. An American survivor told me that many Sampans stood by, their occupants calmly waiting for passengers to drown so that they could be stripped of their clothes. No sympathy is given among the Chinese. What is one man's misfortune is another's good luck. They have no fear of death, anyway, so long as punishment does not accompany it.

A chief petty officer told me of an execution he witnessed in Peking. The victims were confined in a compound, and four of them were playing mahjong. As one was taken from the game to be beheaded in full view of the others, another would fill his place and the game would be continued.

This indifference toward death has caused the development of methods of torture to reach a high degree. Possibly the most distasteful of all is the "wicker basket" torture. The offender is placed in a wicker basket, with only his head on the outside. He is given all the food and drink that he desires. He eventually is killed by vermin.

The Chinese have a unique way of displaying hospitality to a guest that is apt to lead a foreigner into committing a social blunder. I have been invited to dinner at eight o'clock, let us assume. At about seven my host will send a vehicle for me. I must, under no circumstances, take it. Two or three times again, before the appointed hour, my host will send for me but I must not appear ahead of schedule, for he is merely trying to impress upon me his impatience to see me.

When I do arrive, I must express my regret at not being able to prepare myself in time to make an earlier vehicle. At dinner I must not restrain myself in the least. I must eat everything as if it were the most delightful food it is possible to prepare. I must accompany each gulp with snorts and grunts to show my pleasure. The more noise I make, the better my host is pleased.

I really believe that Chinese table manners are better than ours. One certainly feels at ease at a Chinese dinner. If I tip over a glass at an American table I must stutter an apology. But a Chinese host would be delighted, because he would attribute the accident to my hurried desire to stuff myself with his food.

We were in Shanghai only a few days before we were ordered to Wuhu, about three hundred miles up the Yangtze River. The schedule was arranged so that we would alternately spend two weeks up the river and two weeks at Shanghai. We required two days to make the trip because we anchored overnight, the river being too treacherous for night steaming except for steamers running a regular schedule. And even these steamers are often wrecked. The freight rate from Hankow to Chungking, a distance of about seven hundred miles, is higher than from San Francisco to Hankow.

Wuhu is a city of about a half million inhabitants, but only fourteen of these were American. All except three were missionaries, these three being Standard Oil Company employees. We relieved the U.S.S. Pope, which had been stationed at Wuhu for two weeks, and each officer familiarized himself with the new special landing force organization. Each officer was also given a list of names and addresses of Americans present.

We called at the various establishments of American and British subjects, but none of the missionaries ever returned our calls. I had an interesting time visiting some of the missionary headquarters, nevertheless, especially the Wuhu General Hospital, which is operated by the Methodist Episcopal Church. I was told by Miss Walters, the surgeon, that the hospital was always crowded with patients. It certainly was during our stay at Wuhu, for every time I stopped there I found every bed filled and some cots set up.

Many of the patients were bandit victims. Chinese bandits do not restrict their attacks on men, but will attack women and children as well. There was an eight year old boy in one bed. He was suffering from a rifle wound, deliberately inflicted by bandits. The bullet had pierced one side just above the hip and left the other side near the knee. Miss Walters said the boy was suffering intense pain, but he was never known to utter a sound of complaint. He had no chance to recover. His aged father, a destitute coolie, sat by his side night and day.

Bandit attacks were a nightly occurrence up the Yangtze. Every night, while we were at Wuhu, their rifle fire could be heard from our ship. They would frequently enter the city a short distance, in order to loot a dwelling or shop. We never went ashore at night except in groups of at least three, and then only when necessary to obtain or disseminate information.

During all of our stay at Wuhu the weather was quite cold. One day two old women paddled out to the ship in a large wooden tub, hoping to pick up a few scraps from the slop chute. In the tub with them was a small child, about one year old, I should say. While the tub was lying off the ship, they undressed the child and put some clean rags on him. The youngster remained perfectly expressionless, as indifferent as a Spartan or, to express it stronger, he remained a typical Chinese. I looked at the dry bulb thermometer. It read seven degrees below freezing.

Occasionally we would go hunting. Snipe, pheasant, and duck are plentiful everywhere along the lower Yangtze valley. Dogs were never used, because they were not needed. Chinese would volunteer to go along to carry the game, and when we finished we would give them some of the birds. They were always delighted.

The Country Chinese are a better type than the city people. City Chinese are dirty and rather mercenary, though I think they do well to be no worse than they are. But the country Chinese are clean, courteous, and honest. And the Country children are just about the most attractive youngsters that I ever saw. Every time we went hunting, they would flock around us smiling and wide eyed with interest. They never showed the least fear, although they must have seen some bandit attacks. It seemed incredible that these children were not perfectly safe from anyone, for they certainly impressed me as being capable of disarming the most hideous ogre of fairy tales.

From Wuhu we returned to Shanghai, where we remained for two weeks. Shanghai is always a delightful city to be in, but this time it was surpassed in novelty, at least, by the country we had just arrived from.

All the junks in the harbor had banners flying, beginning the celebration of the Chinese New Year. One New Year custom of the Chinese could be emulated advantageously by us. This is the custom they have of settling all debts on the birth of the new year. No good Chinese will allow the debts to carry over. They will sell the last rag on their backs, if necessary, to prevent it.

A junk is a queer looking ship. On the bow is painted, on raised hemispheres, two fish eyes. This is to enable the junk to see all rocks, shoals, and other hazards in time to keep clear of them. The stern is higher than the bow, so that a person conning the ship aft may see ahead. An enormous amount of sail is carried, which is usually a dirty tan color. Before a junk goes to sea, a quantity of fire crackers will be fired on it to scare the demons off. The Chinese never seem able to rid themselves of all demons, however. Whenever junks were encountered by us at sea, they try to pass very close astern. This was to give their demons a chance to board our ship. I suppose the idea that our own demons would want to visit them never occurred to the Chinese navigators.

It was lucky for us, while we were in Shanghai, that one dollar of our money was worth over two dollars of Chinese money, because we had many reasons for spending it. Besides being a gay city, Shanghai offers shops where pewter, silks, rugs, lacquer, lace, china, and furs may be purchased from huge stocks. A tea dance at the Astor House Hotel is always interesting, with many nationalities represented, and the orchestra playing strange music. The horse races are amusing, more than exciting. The horses are about half ordinary size, but the jockeys usually weigh between 150 and 170 pounds. They are called "gentlemen jockeys," for the same reason that we nickname a fat man "skinny," I suppose. In the evenings there are dog races, which hundreds of foreigners consider as good an excuse for getting tight as any other.

There are thirty-five thousand foreigners in Shanghai. They carry on most of the commerce of the East's greatest port. They have built a modern city on swamp land. They are a wealthy group. But they don't work in the evenings. And I never met one that worried about the shortcomings of anyone else.

Our next Yangtze port was Chinkiang, located about two hundred miles from the river's mouth. The only American industry there was a Standard Oil Company agency. There were only about twenty foreigners in all, but they had constructed a little club, which was all that saved them from fading away.

About one mile below Chinkiang is Silver Island, where a Buddhist monastery has been built. One afternoon a party of us went to the island, hoping that we would be allowed to enter the monastery. To our surprise, the Chinese Monks were delighted to see us. They insisted on showing us everything, and then served us tea. Such genial old fellows were they, that they probably could have won over a few Buddhist converts had they tried.

Chinkiang is the dirtiest and most disarranged city that I ever saw. There is not a street in the town, so of course there are no vehicles larger than rickshaws. It has a population of about a quarter of a million people and two million dogs, who live in such a jumbled mess that an observer unconsciously thinks of a stagnant pool of water covered with millions of bugs scooting aimlessly about.

In almost the exact center of Chinkiang are half a dozen large cesspools. I never got near those cesspools but once, and I shall forever remember the experience. The

Chinese built hundreds of shacks in this area, unmindful of its disagreeable character.

We were glad to return to Shanghai when our tour at Chinkiang was completed. This time we moored to the Standard Oil Company dock at the lower outskirts of the city. This dock is on the opposite side from Shanghai, and whenever we went ashore we had to cross the river first. We could seldom make the dock in our boat, because sampans were usually tied alongside, about ten deep. Almost every time I crossed over these sampans I could see many card and fan tan [Chinese gambling game] games in progress. I have seen Chinese gathered about a small box in these open boats at three o'clock in the morning, playing by the light of an oil lantern, oblivious of the cold.

Chinese are inveterate gamblers. The manager of the Shanghai branch of the Dollar Steamship Company told me that the boys, aged ten to twelve years, employed by him spent most of their lunch period gambling with their ten copper lunch allowance. I have frequently had to break up a poker game in a taxi office in order to get a cab.

On every Socony [Standard Oil Company of New York] boat is painted the word "Meifoo." In Chinese, this means "good luck." When the Standard Oil Company was beginning its activities in China, it was faced with the problem of educating the people to the use of kerosene oil. In order to expedite this education, oil lamps were sold at cost, and on each lamp was the word "Meifoo." So popular has the word become, that the Chinese know the company by no other name. And it is often used when referring to Americans in general, regardless of their business.

Our next trip up the river was to Hankow, six hundred miles from the coast. I received one of the great thrills of my life on this trip. The river is continually changing its bed and washing away or building islands, so that the chart cannot be trusted. At a point two hundred miles below Hankow the chart showed an island about four miles long and one mile wide. When we arrived at this point the island appeared as shown on the chart, but midway of its length the Chinese pilot suddenly called for hard right rudder and full speed. I was startled, because it seemed that we would surely crash headlong into the island. But the pilot understood his job. The river had washed a narrow channel through the middle of the island. The entrance was so sharply cut that it could not be seen until the ship was almost abreast. Full speed was called for in order to dash through before the current, which set strongly along the lower bank, could take hold of the ship. As we emerged from the channel the stern of the Pruitt cleared the bank by about one yard.

Hankow is second only to Shanghai in population. Some people have found it even more interesting, but I think it has quieted considerably since the return of the international area to the Chinese.

Our pilot decided to take all the officers to a Chinese dinner while we were there. Luckily for me, I had the duty and could not go. The day after the dinner every officer was ill except me. The pilot seemed very disappointed with American stomachs. He said that the shark fins and bird nest soup were delicious, but that none of the officers would touch the half-hatched eggs.

Hankow was rather quiet while we were there except for one parade. This parade was given by the

Chinese prostitutes of Hankow as a protest to the increase in taxation against members of their profession. As I looked at the huge mob I couldn't help but feel a little sympathetic, because with so many competitors business couldn't be very good. Almost every parader carried a large banner on which Chinese characters were painted. That was the only time that I ever regretted my lack of knowledge of the Chinese language. Those banners no doubt expressed some interesting ideas.

Every day while we were up the river we were besieged by vendors who taxed our sales resistance to its limit. Most of their wares consisted of brass, bronze, and pewter trinkets, and beads. These salesmen would always ask an exorbitant price to begin with, but the lower limit depended only on the buyer's stamina.

I was once offered a string of beads for three hundred dollars. The beads really were very attractive to me, but I managed to appear indifferent. After four hours of haggling I bought them for three second-hand pairs of socks and a five cent piece of candy from the ships canteen.

Food was cheap up the river, and the ships general mess flourished. Eggs were ten cents a dozen, beef seven cents a pound, pork nine cents, and chicken ten cents. The general mess had been without any surplus ever since the cruise to the East Indies, where food prices had been high, but it was never low again after the Yangtze patrol duty. An Asiatic destroyer is allowed sixty-five cents daily for each man in its compliment. Officers, on all ships, operate their own mess.

Although the Yangtze has a very dirty yellow color, it is probably the cleanest large river in the world. This is because of the lack of sewage systems in Chinese cities [sewage is not diverted into the river]. In Shanghai and Hankow, cities of about two million population, the situation is embarrassing.

But it is difficult to obtain money in China for public utilities, because the people in one part of the country care nothing about the welfare of those in other sections. Canton is indifferent toward Shanghai's lack of sewages, and Shanghai cares little whether Canton has adequate docking facilities. And the most indifferent people toward famine sufferers are the Chinese themselves. Millions die every year because the other hundreds of millions don't care.

This disregard is not due to barbarism, but to lack of communication facilities. China is far behind the rest of the world in the development of all methods of communication; roads, railroads, telegraphs, telephones, canals, airways, and radio stations are needed. Not much progress will be made, however, until China's political system improves.

A general of the Northern faction enters the city and levies a heavy tax. A few weeks later he is driven out by the Nationalist army and he seeks another town to replenish his funds. Taxes continually fluctuate, depending upon the military situation, which situation affects even our own trade to some extent. If a general decides to tax oil heavily, our oil sales to the Chinese people are certain to diminish.

The allegiance of a Chinese general is very uncertain. Feng Yu Hsiang has changed his three times. Feng is called "the Christian General." He has been an ardent Christian ever since a missionary treated him, in his youth, for a malady caused by over indulgence.

Chang Hsueh Liang, son of the late Chang Tso Lin who was warlord of Manchuria, professed Nationalism shortly after his father's death. His true adherence has always been doubtful, however, because he was hard pressed by the Nationalist Army when he accepted Chiang Kai Shek's terms.

Chiang Kai Shek appears to really have the interests of his country at heart. He is, without doubt, Chinas most capable leader. He may be able to eventually accomplish much toward the consolidation of the country. China needs leaders whose honesty can not be doubted. Many of Chiang's subordinates have, because of jealousy or selfishness, caused much dissention in the ranks of the Kuomintang (Nationalist Party), so that not much real progress has yet been made. There is an appalling lack of confidence among the leaders themselves, and solid support from the masses can hardly be expected.

Upon our return to Shanghai we moored, bow and stern, to buoys in the middle of the stream. This was to prevent the ships swinging around and obstructing traffic, which is very congested.

We lost one man before we left again. He went ashore on regular liberty and disappeared completely. He probably met with foul play because, had he merely intended to overstay his liberty, he would have returned when his money was spent. Most accidents to foreigners are due to carelessness; entering forbidden places or traveling alone are two of the principal causes.

Once the duties at Shanghai were completed, Pruitt sailed April 1, 1928, to Chinwangtao (now called Qinhuangdao) on the Sea of Bohai, in northern China. Pruitt later moved to Chefoo (Yantai), from where she made several forays to Tsingtao (Qingdao). Pruitt would remain in northern China until mid-September, when she would sail with the Asiatic Fleet for Guam.

On June 4, 1928, while at Chefoo, Ensign Jarrell received a promotion to Lieutenant (junior grade).

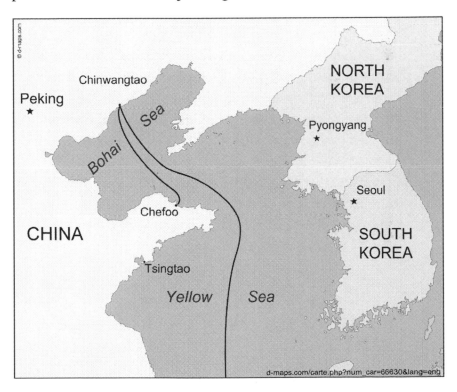

Pruitt's Operation in April in the Bohai Sea

On the first of April we left for Chinwangtao, the port of Peking. We stayed there for two weeks, but seldom went ashore because the water was so rough. The wind blew continually, and dust from the land was so thick over the harbor that the atmosphere appeared hazy. We spent most of our time preparing for short range battle practice and the annual inspection by the squadron commander. Two trips to the great wall and a few special leaves to Peking were the limit of our shore activities.

We were glad when we left for the sheltered harbor of Chefoo. Soon after we arrived there, two of our officers returned to the United States, and the rest of us were kept rather busy until they were replaced a month later.

On one of my first trips ashore I saw how justice is meted out to thieves. I was first attracted by the sound of a drum and cymbals and, upon investigating the cause, saw two men being paraded through the streets. They were stripped to the waist, and their backs had been beaten with bamboo canes until they were almost cut to shreds. The noise had attracted a large crowd which followed the culprits through the streets of the city until they were lodged in jail. The thieves took no notice of any of the proceedings, but many small children got much pleasure from teasing them and occasionally throwing a rock.

Chinese justice is swift, but not sure if the offender has money. The editor of the local native paper made a misstatement and public opinion forced him to quit his job. He was well liked, else he would have lost more than his job. On the other hand, the operator of a dope ring bribed himself free for one hundred thousand dollars, after he had been convicted. The penalty for trafficking dope is beheading.

The people of Chefoo own two sets of flags, one for use when the city is occupied by the Northern army, the other when the Nationalists hold the upper hand. Once it was rumored that Chang Tsung Chang was coming to Chefoo. He was detested because he always levied a tribute. In addition, he would allow opium traffic in order to tax the sellers of the drug. Chang did this in spite of the fact that an attempt was being made by the city to suppress the sale. The citizens erected a large arch of welcome at the waterfront, nevertheless, in hopes of putting their unwanted visitor in a good humor. They covered it with flowers and vines and banners. But, due to pressure from his enemies, Chang Tsung Chang never arrived. The arch was left standing a month before the people thought it safe to remove it.

One day the English paper told about the death of Chang Tso Lin. His death would probably not have occurred, it was stated, had the Chinese physicians attending him not insisted on old, superstitious practices instead of allowing capable Japanese doctors to prescribe for him. Chang was given doses of powdered tiger bone and pills made from dried, powdered human liver.

On the night of August 1-2 an attempt was made to loot the Bank of Communications. The disturbance broke out suddenly at about one o'clock, and became so general that all of our ships in the harbor were directed to send a landing force ashore to safeguard American lives and property.

When the Pruitt detachment arrived at the force headquarters Colonel Sze, who was commanding officer of the Chinese forces present, was explaining to the patrol officer that he had the situation well in hand. Just as he finished speaking, a volley of shots sounded from a point about fifty yards distant, in louder volume than before. The belief that a Chinaman is expressionless is erroneous, because the old colonel showed both stupefaction and chagrin on his face. He beat a hasty retreat. He did, however, suppress the disorders before daylight.

The disturbance was caused by a mutiny among part of Sze's soldiers, who were bent on looting the bank and as much of the city that they could. Some foreign naval officers expressed their opinion that the mutiny was arranged by a foreign power for the purpose of impressing upon other foreign powers a realization of the instability of Chinese military government.

We suffered one casualty during the fray. A sailor had the middle finger of one of his hands shot off. I still believe that he accidentally did it himself, but he claimed that one of the Chinese looters did the shooting. He admitted however, that no Chinaman can hit what he points at, so we agreed that whatever the cause, the injury was unintentional.

Several times during the summer we were ordered to Tsingtao to operate with the submarines. During one of these visits a race meeting [horse race] was held by the foreigners, but most of the bettors were Chinese. The racing was done on turf, as in England. Everyone was so silent, that it didn't seem like a race track at all to me. What little noise there was came from drinkers trying to find out if their horses had won. I don't enjoy a Chinese race meeting, because half the pleasure at a horse race is the amusement afforded by other people's excitement.

There was little social activity in Chefoo. Everyone played tennis in the afternoons, but the evenings were blanks except Saturday evening, when the USS Black Hawk band could sometimes be coaxed to play for a dance at the Chefoo Club. I used to go to some of the dances whether I had a partner or not. It was fun to watch the British women execute their commotions. They would work very hard moving their arm like a piston rod and covering the floor with giant strides.

The most interesting character in Chefoo was "Boats." No one ever knew him by any other name. He had held the slop chute privileges of the Pruitt for seven years, ever since the ship first arrived in China. Every time we dropped the anchor off Chefoo, "Boats" would be the first person on board. No scraps of food ever went over the side while he was around, for every particle left over went into a huge iron tub that "Boats" kept in a sampan alongside. He would use this swill in catering to the customers of his lunch stand ashore. While the Pruitt was in port, he obtained supplies from no other source.

"Boats" got his name because of his knowledge of seamanship. He was good at splicing and knot-tying as well, and sometimes he would do a sailmakers job for us, since we did not have a sailmaker on board. "Boats" would never accept money for any of his work, being contented with his inexhaustible supply of garbage.

He was a strict disciplinarian. If one of his assistants failed to work with enthusiasm or spilled food he would get a swift cuff on the ear, usually accompanied by a kick. But they liked "Boats." He was a little gruff, but never cruel. No one could resist his grin, which spread all over his face and was almost perpetually present.

CHAPTER 5
PHILIPPINES

The Asiatic Fleet, including Pruitt, sailed from northern China to Guam and conducted a variety of training exercises while en route. Life aboard ship while under way was never dull, and the training never ceased. Following a week in Guam, Pruitt was finally able to return to her home port, Manila.

My dad, now Lieutenant (junior grade) Albert Jarrell, ever the observant bystander, had much to say about his visits.

> The middle of September, 1928, we left with the Asiatic fleet for Guam, in the Marianas Islands, fifteen hundred miles east of the Philippines. Fleet maneuvers were held en route and a simulated attack on the island was made the morning of our arrival. It was a relief when we anchored in the quiet water of the harbor, for the trip had been very rough indeed. The sea had been hitting us broadside on ever since we rounded the Shantung Promontory [China], and we hadn't had a hot meal for a week.

> Guam is a beautiful island. It has several good drives through thick groves of coconut palms and teak trees. The water seems to change its color as the sun's rays strike it from different angles, but in several shallow coves it is always transparent. We went swimming in one of these

coves, wearing water-tight goggles in order to examine the coral growths, and tennis shoes to protect our feet.

Through careful supervision, social diseases have been completely eradicated from Guam. Every person who lands must first pass a physical examination. The total native population is only about fifteen thousand, and disease control would be rather simple if it were not for ignorance. Since ignorance is our own principal stumbling block to any kind of progress, Guam's success should provide an interesting study for our students of social problems. It doesn't seem improbable that, with our higher education, Guam's example may be emulated on a much larger scale.

Even leprosy has almost been eliminated. I visited the leper colony, located about three miles outside the town of Agana, and found only about half a dozen patients undergoing treatment. These worked in the fields and provided their own subsistence. I believe that with the passing of the present patients, leprosy will be banished from Guam. The disease is a result of filthy living conditions, and the natives are rapidly being educated to clean habits. The infection is often, if not always, transmitted by the bite of the bed bug.

Guam is subject to our prohibition law, but liquor is bootlegged in spite of an exorbitant punishment for the misdemeanor. The native alcoholic drink is called aguardiente, and is made from the juice of the cabbage-like top of the coconut palm. It has a disagreeable odor, something like formaldehyde.

The natives are called Chamorros. They belong to a mixed race, with the Polynesian strain predominant. Under

Spanish rule they were dominated by Catholic Priests, who gave them no opportunity for self expression, and even today a Spanish Catholic mission is maintained on the island. Many of the natives still believe that the mission bell must be tolled during funerals. One peso is charged for each stroke of the bell. There is very little wealth in Guam, but often a large sum is raised in order to have a noisy funeral. This money is almost a total loss to the island, since very little is invested by the mission in home industries.

In Guam lives the "tree climbing" fish. It grows to a length of about five inches, but I don't believe it has any food value. Schools of them can frequently be seen on the banks of small streams near the coast, just after low slack water when the banks are still wet from high tide. They never really climb a tree, but they do remain away from water for several minutes, propelling themselves about with two pointed fins located about one inch from the head.

After a week at Guam we left for Manila, and the next two months were taken up with operations in the Manila-Olongapo area. On one of our visits to Olongapo several of us accepted an invitation to a wild boar hunt.

Our hosts were two veterans of the Spanish-American War who had remained in the Philippines after the islands were taken over. One had been a merchant skipper for about twenty five years and the other had spent most of his time prospecting. Both had finally decided to try their luck at farming and so they formed a partnership. They cleared a small area on Subic Bay, opposite Olongapo, where they built a shack. They spent most of their time in this shack instead of among the potatoes and corn, with the result that one could tell only after careful scrutiny where their farm ended and the jungle began.

We were soaked from a tropical shower when we arrived at the shack, so we spent the day listening to the interesting lies of our friends while waiting for our clothes to dry. At dinner our host cooked some eggs and biscuits; at least I have an idea that they were eggs and biscuits. I decided that a cup of coffee and a banana would be sufficient for me, and later decided that the banana alone would do.

After dinner I asked if I could be of any assistance in washing the dishes, and was told washing was not considered necessary. They would just let them stay in the rain for a while. I congratulated myself on my choice of food while I enjoyed the sickly look on my companions' faces.

Wild hogs are hunted at night. A water hole or mud wallow that has been visited by them is first located, and the hunter then selects a nearby tree in which he sits to wait for the appearance of the game. We had found a promising mud wallow before dark so there was nothing more to do, except stay at the shack and talk, until the moon rose. Moonlight is necessary for an accurate aim.

The moon did not rise until about two o'clock and, when it did, I had been sound asleep in my chair for two hours. When I was awakened I felt so drowsy that it seemed impossible that I could ever climb a tree, and I didn't even try. I refused to move, so the others went without me, saying that I was afraid of pythons. Three hours later they returned, wet and sore and very disappointed.

That was my first and last wild boar hunt. The best part of it all was the conversation of the two old partners. Both had "gone native" twenty five years before. "What do you expect?" they would ask. "We ain't monks and we ain't iron hosses."

The younger of the two was named Pete. He was well liked by the natives around Olongapo who, to express their goodwill, one day gave him a present. It was presented to him in a large wooden box in which several small holes had been bored. After Pete had expressed his appreciation he removed the lid, but immediately replaced it, for inside the box was a twenty-five foot rock python.

Pete said that the snake was caught when it attacked one of the native's dogs. It was struck on the head with an iron spike, which stunned it, and then was easily captured before it recovered. I only half believe this story, but it was told to Pete by the natives in good faith. If true, it is another excellent example of familiarity breeding contempt.

When we returned to Manila I was ordered to shore patrol duty for two weeks. There was little to do during the day, but in the evening after the cabarets opened there was enough action to keep me busy until two or three o'clock. A sailor is no more boisterous than other young men, but all youngsters have surplus energy after having been cooped up for several days. A floating university came into Manila once and let loose several hundred wild young students. After comparing their shore activities with those of our bluejackets [Navy sailor], I would say that the average sailor's recreation is as mild as can be expected.

But of course they occasionally, often unavoidably, find themselves in embarrassing predicaments. One sailor had his uniform stolen from him while he slept. Another was chased into the Pasig River by two Filipinos because he engaged a caramedo [carabao – a horse-drawn carriage] and, when he dismissed it, found himself broke.

But the most interesting case I ran across was a little more serious than these. At about 1 o'clock one morning a sailor came into patrol headquarters in a most badly battered condition. His nose was flattened, both eyes were closed, one ear was about half severed, and there were numerous scratches and bruises all over him. In general, he seemed to be about as badly hammered as possible without being killed. Yet his first remark was so unexpected that I had to laugh in spite of the seriousness of the situation. It was, "I certainly have had one great liberty. Oh boy, what a swell time." He didn't think so while the medical officer was sewing his ear back to his face, however.

Shortly after Christmas 1928 I was relieved of patrol duty and I obtained leave to spend three days at Baguio, in the mountains of northern Luzon. Baguio boasts an almost perfect climate; always cool, but never cold. It is ideal for golf, tennis, and riding. An Army camp is located there, and about fifteen of us were quartered in one of the government cottages.

The Filipinos of the mountains are heartier than those of the lowlands, but they have made less progress. Fewer go to school and there are almost no native industries or business activities. They still perform their tribal rites and have not abandoned child marriages.

While we were there they gave a spear dance. A native drum was beaten continuously for about two days before the dance while a dozen pigs were roasted on spits.

The pigs were wrapped in banana leaves, which gave them an individual flavor. On the day of the dance the warriors, clad in an ounce of gee string and a pound or two of beads, pranced onto the field around which the spectators sat. They shook their spears furiously, sometimes in unison but more often not. They went thru jerky motions with their arms and legs, and carried a most ferocious expression on their faces. I couldn't see anything beautiful or instructive in the dance, but I did think it rather humorous, which was not the way the dancers intended their efforts to be received. The native audience remained quite solemn, but other American observers were impressed the same way as was I.

A small but attractive club is maintained by the army at its camp a few miles outside Baguio, and I had most of my meals there. The uniform of the native waiters always impressed me with its novelty. They wore a gee string and a narrow band around the waist, the ends of which dangled in front like a cravat. Nothing else was worn except an immaculate white jacket. The dress of the upper half of the body was a decided contrast to the undress of the lower half.

There was not much night life in Baguio. Whenever a dance was held at the hotel, which was not often, it stopped promptly at midnight. Most of the visitors were there for outdoor recreation and, even when a dance was given, it was not well attended.

We spent the month of January 1929 in the vicinity of Manila Bay rehearsing and firing gun, torpedo and depth charge practices. We were busy every day, but in the late afternoon we found time to complete many of the Asiatic Fleet athletic championship competitions. Our division baseball team won in the finals from the Cavite Marine team, and was selected to go to Japan in April to play the Keio University team, champions of the Japanese College League.

CHAPTER 6
THE SULU ARCHIPELAGO

During the period between World War I and World War II there were few nautical charts for the archipelagos in the South Pacific. Routine peace-time duties included acquiring data to update or create navigational charts. Not only were water depths and coastline shapes inaccurate, village names often had changed or the villages had simply disappeared. The island of Tawi Tawi is today known as Tawi-Tawi, a minor change. The main city that my dad mentions, Balambing, was renamed Panglima Sugala as per a Muslim Mindanao autonomy act in 1991. Balambing (Balimbing), however, still exists as a village, or barrio, of Panglima Sugala. Many early nautical charts used the spelling "Balambing," but official government documents use the spelling "Balimbing."

The "Discovery" trek my dad made, as described in the beginning of this book, was to take him from the village of Madanni overland to Gadang. It later was found that Gadang does not exist. It is easy to see that charts and maps made in the eighteenth and nineteenth centuries could easily be wrong.

Pruitt would begin the cruise in February and would return in March, 1929, with most of the time spent around Tawi Tawi.

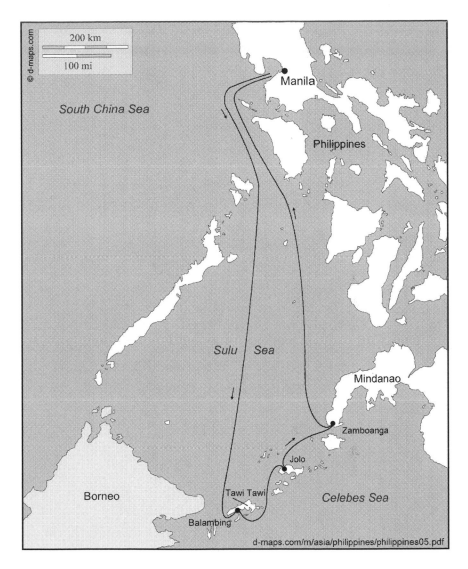

Pruitt in the southern Sulu Sea

Dad continues in his journal:

Early in February the 45th division went to Tawi
Tawi , the largest island in the Sulu archipelago, on a
surveying expedition. Tawi Tawi is about twenty miles

long and five miles wide. It is twenty miles due east of Cape Unsang, Borneo, and is the southernmost large island of our Philippine possessions.

No accurate chart of Tawi Tawi exists. A large portion of the chart we use was shown in dotted lines and we had to navigate with caution when close to land.

The ships of our division separated shortly after we arrived at the island, each to perform its separate task. The Pruitt's task was to make a rough survey of Tawi Tawi and the adjacent small islands, noting their relative positions and the location of mountains, rivers, and any other prominent features.

We anchored off Balambing, the largest town, which boasts a population of twelve hundred. A post of the Philippine constabulary was located at Bongao, near Balambing, and we immediately called to make our mission known and to get what information we could regarding the attitude of the natives.

The inhabitants of the southern Philippine Islands are called Moros because they resemble in dress and manners the Moors of North Africa. They are Mohammedans, and many fanatics may be found among them. We were told by the officers in the constabulary that many believe that a place in heaven is assured for any Mohammedan who slays a Christian. This belief differs from Mohammedanism as taught by the Koran, but the Prophet's followers have not tread the straight path any closer than Christians. They have their different sects, too.

The Moros continue to make pilgrimages to Mecca, however. When one has been to the holy city he becomes a

Hadji. Lifelong savings are spent unhesitatingly in realizing the ambition of acquiring this title. A Hadji always has much prestige among his less fortunate fellows.

After we left Bongao we visited Balambing. It is the most unique town that I ever saw. Built entirely on sticks driven into the sand near the shore, the need of a sanitary system has been eliminated. The streets consist of two poles, worn shiny from constant use, running between the houses. I tried to walk down one of these "streets" in my bare feet, but failed. The natives have no trouble at all. They can wrap their feet around the pole almost with the same ease that they can their hands.

The only person who could speak English was the school master. I visited the school house, and found the equipment fairly good. He said that his youthful students would show more promise of success if he could prevent their fishing through the cracks in the floor during classes. All of his efforts had failed, however, until he conceived the idea of allowing his pupils to use various colored crayons in working their arithmetic problems. Even this idea proved to be a failure when it was no longer a novelty, and the school master was at a loss for future schemes to create interest.

There was little leprosy in Tawi Tawi, but skin diseases were prevalent. Some of these were of such a violent nature that they looked to be as bad as leprosy. We always carried a bottle of alcohol ashore to wash our hands after meeting the natives, who always liked to shake hands at every opportunity. I have shaken some hands that almost turned my stomach with their scales and sores.

This is when, in my dad's story, he was ordered to survey a part of Tawi Tawi from the north coast to the south coast. It was to be an exploratory trip to take note of vegetation, trails, wildlife and any other items of interest. U. S. S. Pruitt had been at Tawi Tawi only a week or so when he took a crew of men on the "Discovery" trek overland from Madanni to Gadang. That event is presented at the beginning of this book. Modern maps show neither town, and Gadang, as it turned out, did not exist in 1929. From various bits of information in Dad's records the most likely route of the planned "hike" has been surmised.

Following Dad's unsuccessful attempt to hike from Madanni to Gadang, Pruitt and her crew sailed to islands neighboring Tawi Tawi to survey and record important and significant features.

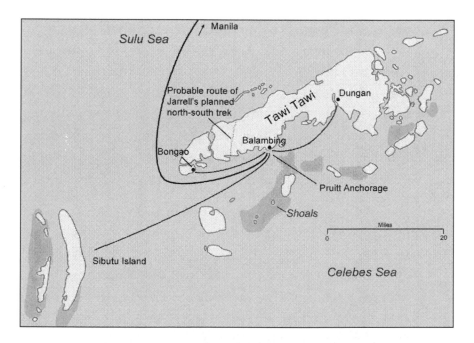

Areas Visited by Pruitt Around Tawi Tawi
(Attribution on Page xiii)

Dad's account of the cruise continues:

The next few days were spent surveying numerous smaller islands near Tawi Tawi. Most of them were similar in appearance. They were bounded by coral reefs and mangrove swamps, and the terrain was rugged. There was very little cultivation.

The island of Sibutu was the only one that differed in general description from the others. Sibutu is about ten miles to the southwest of Tawi Tawi. It is a long, narrow island, shaped like a banana, with the concave side to the west. All of the eastern side is very flat for a quarter of a mile inland, but there the land becomes rugged and vegetation wild. The flat area is only about ten feet above sea level, and is covered with unusually tall coconut palms. There is not a sign of a road on the island, but the earth is so firm and free from vegetation, excepting the palms, that any vehicle could be driven easily along the east coast.

All of Sibutu's trade is in copra [dried coconut meat], which is carried in Chinese junks because the value is not enough to warrant steamer visits. There is a village, containing possibly three hundred inhabitants, but it has no sheltered harbor. The coral fringe extends so far out that even junks have to anchor several hundred yards from the coast, and take on their cargos in minute quantities from canoes and vintas.

Two days before we left Tawi Tawi I made an excursion along the south coast in a motor whale boat. One of my discoveries was that the town of Gadang, which was the intended destination of my other trip, did not exist. There was not even a trace of human habitation where it was supposed to be.

Near the point where the south coast turns to the northward I found the village of Dungan, where I met Datu Mohammed Maulani, the highest official in Tawi Tawi. The word "datu" signifies prince, but Maulani's appearance was far different from what one would expect of a person with such a title.

He was a scrawny little man except for his flat, bare feet, which covered a tremendous area. He shook hands so long and so often that I became a little anxious about my limited supply of sterilizing alcohol.

He took me to his residence, a one room shack, and introduced me to his lieutenants, who forced me to undergo another handshaking orgy. I met the master of his household, the keeper of his boat, his secretary, and his personal advisor, all of whom said nothing. Their appearance was solemn and forbidding, but it apparently did not picture their real feelings, for soon Maulani and his staff began presenting me with gifts for some of the officers and crew.

The Datu would devote several minutes to oratory before handing me each article, and the entire ceremony lasted for two hours. Toward the end he gave me an article that looked like a hand-made brass cuspidor, which he said was for my wife. When I told him I had none, he was both amazed and amused. He couldn't understand how I could get along. "Why, even our fifteen year old boys," he said, "have three or four of them." I told him perhaps that was why they aged so early, and he laughed good-humoredly.

The village of Dungan is located on the right bank at the mouth of the Dungan River. The river is only about seven miles in length, but is half a mile wide at its mouth and is six fathoms deep. The water has a beautiful dark blue color, which makes a pleasing contrast with the bright green vegetation along the banks. Game fish are plentiful, but we had little time to try our luck.

I obtained two guides at the village and proceeded in a canoe as far up the river as we could go. During the trip some of my party let their hands hang over the sides, but the guides instantly cautioned them against crocodiles. The waters around Tawi Tawi abound with the reptiles, and the natives have a deadly fear of them. A few days before our arrival a Moro had been attacked by a crocodile. The beast caught the man in the right side of his chest, but his presence of mind saved his life. The native forced his arm down the crocodile's throat until the animal released him, and then made his escape before he was again attacked.

Toward the end of our journey up the river we had to lie flat in the canoe in order to pass under the heavy growth overhead. When we reached a place where the water was only a foot deep we left the canoe and spent several hours inspecting the surrounding country.

We returned to Dungan shortly after sunset and I spent another hour talking to Maulani. I found him to be strongly opposed to freedom for the Philippines. "It would be a breach of faith," he said, "if the United States gave the Philippine Islands their independence and left the two million Mohammedan Filipinos of the south to the mercy of the ten million Christian Filipinos of the north." The Moros had great confidence in General Wood because of his stand against independence.

I saw a few Moro wives at Dungan. They are not quite as unattractive as the men, but the beetle nut they chew stains their teeth and lips, making them black and ugly. They are ruled despotically by their husbands, and seem content with their fate. The Mohammedan religion requires that a man take no more wives than he can provide for, and it seemed to me that the Moros live up to this law. The women certainly look like they were better cared for than the men.

We left Tawi Tawi for Jolo the day after our return from Dungan. Jolo is the largest city on the island of Jolo. The palace of the Sultan of Sulu (or Jolo) is located just outside the city limits. I was much disappointed when I visited the palace, for I expected to find the highest ranking Mohammedan in the Sulu Archipelago residing in a magnificent dwelling. Instead, I saw a plank house, containing six or seven rooms, that needed paint badly. Outside of the palace was the Sultan's private shrine and, about 100 yards from this was the harem.

The dwelling for the ladies of the harem resembled very much the outhouses for servants that are seen on southern plantations, except that the harem was not as well kept. The Sultan had poor taste in selecting his ladies. There was not one to whom I would award a passing mark. But perhaps they delighted his sense of beauty.

Throughout the trip to the southern islands I found none of the things that fiction writers devote so much time to describing, excepting the musical nature of the people. And even this is greatly exaggerated. South Sea women are fat, dirty, and as uninteresting as a cigar store Indian. The towns and villages are dirty and disease-stricken. There are no beautiful native customs. The people are self-indulgent and lazy.

The country women of Jolo believe in being comfortable. The climate is always hot and they do not bother to wear anything above the waist. I do not approve of missionary reforms in clothing, such as the wearing of heavy flat shoes, long dresses, hats, and corsets, but I do believe that a few college-graduate school teachers could improve the Moro women's dress very much.

There is no cause for wearing more clothing than is comfortable, but a certain amount is necessary for maximum comfort. When a woman's breasts hang to her waist and dangle from side to side like a pendulum as she walks, she must be uncomfortable. She even makes an observer feel ill at ease. A shipment of reinforced brassieres to Jolo would not be amiss, especially if accompanied by a few high-pressure saleswomen.

The natural development of women just below the waist is accentuated in Moro women, but with the advent of radio perhaps more interest will be taken in early morning calisthenics. The Moro woman is an ideal subject for the impressionist painter, for he would not have to search long to find her common features. A large brown elliptical figure with two inverted parabolas hanging from each side near the top would depict her very clearly.

Jolo harbor is the only place where I ever saw diving girls perform. Large numbers of them would paddle out to the ships in the harbor and dive for coins. They were excellent swimmers and very modest, always wearing the same complete outfit of clothing that they wore ashore.

From Jolo we returned to Manila, but stopped at Zamboanga for a few hours en route. At Manila we spent a week taking on stores, provisions, and ammunition for a six month stay in China. We also gave the Pruitt her annual fumigation. On the twelfth of March, 1929, we left, steering a course almost due west across the South China Sea.

CHAPTER 7
THE FINAL CRUISE ON ASIATIC STATION

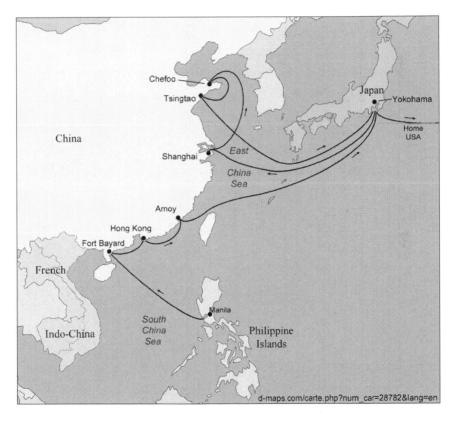

Pruitt's Final Asiatic Cruise

Dad's journal reports Pruitt's final cruise:

> We overtook the U.S.S. Pittsburgh off the entrance to the harbor of Fort Bayard, a French colony almost on the Indo-China border. The Commander-in-Chief came aboard and we continued the trip to the anchorage off the town.

> Only a few hours were spent there. Fort Bayard is a quiet, uninteresting town in Kwang Chow Wan province. The only American business that I noticed in the place was that of the Ford Motor Company. There was one Baptist missionary who was born in Louisville, but who had become a British subject. I remember him distinctly because he was the only missionary who visited our ship during my cruise on the Asiatic Station.

> He was not so cold in his attitude toward us as most missionaries. In fact, he seemed to really enjoy being in our company, and I am sure that we enjoyed having him with us. He was an exceptional missionary.

> After we left Fort Bayard we went to Hong Kong. The British fleet was present and we made some new acquaintances among their officers. I will never lose an opportunity to visit a British ship. Their officers always extend to us a warm welcome.

> I saw several Chinese funerals in Hong Kong, which were typical of any Chinese funeral. There are always present the hired mourners, the noise, and the colorful parade. It seems to me that the Chinese have a better viewpoint toward death than we.

> Instead of giving a beloved relative or friend a sad funeral ceremony, he is accorded a triumphant send-off to his heavenly home. Of course his departure is regretted, but

it is recognized as a victory for the deceased. He has gone to a better place.

Christians profess a belief in a heavenly life that is much better than any on earth, but Christian funerals are the saddest to be found anywhere.

Chinese and all Orientals commit a great error, however, in making the graves of their departed so magnificent when the cost cannot be afforded. Many an oriental resides in death in a more splendid abode than he ever did in life.

A Chinaman likes to feel that his memory will be revered long after his death. For this reason he has as many sons as possible. Sons are much more desired than daughters, and the number that a Chinaman will have is limited only by time and chance. This desire for perpetuation of memory is one of the causes for the overpopulation of China.

From Hong Kong we went to Amoy, about midway between Hong Kong and Shanghai. Amoy has the reputation, both among foreigners and natives, for being the foulest city in China, but I will state emphatically that Chinkiang has it beaten completely.

We spent about ten days at Amoy. The ships were given their annual inspection and the sailing and rowing races for the fleet championships were held. There was no activity ashore. Early in April we went to Shanghai.

Since my previous visit, the Chinese had taken over the management of the Majestic Hotel, the finest in Shanghai. I attended a Chinese benefit tea dance there and was particularly interested in a number on the program called "The Dancing Mothers." The dancers were six girls, about fifteen years old, and each was a mother. They were very attractive despite their youthful experience.

Child marriages and the subservience of women are the result of women's carelessness. Western women are the masters of men in only one subject, the men themselves, but this is enough. They have complete control over men.

I admire women's cleverness at the game of sexes tremendously. Men have learned to use to their advantage all of the elements. They have harnessed the tides, they have obtained electricity from the air, they have driven trains through mountains and ships through the clouds, and they have become the masters of all other animals with the one exception of woman.

Every day, women's literary clubs meet to discuss the work of men; they go to church to hear men preach and pray for their souls. Even the strictly feminine clothing they wear is designed by men and manufactured in men's factories.

Men are killed on automobile race tracks for the purpose of testing tires and steering knuckles so that automobiles will be safe for women. Men fight battles, and still lend an attentive ear while women press their claim for political recognition.

It is a good thing that women are the rulers, and it will remain a good thing so long as women demand much. If women did not create in men a desire to make life easier for the female sex, there would be no progress. We would soon go back to the jungle with the other animals whose feminine members are not so intelligent.

Woman's fight for equality in business and politics may hold up the march of progress until she has relinquished her leadership and finds herself working to please man just as man now works to please her. She doesn't seem to realize that no great general has ever raised a rifle and joined his troops on the firing line. He stays behind the front line and directs, as he should.

It seems that a few more years of the study of the western woman will be sufficient to liberate the eastern woman unless, as I have stated, the western woman continues to lose her grip. I am not sure who is behind the march of women into men's activities. Man himself may be the instigator. It seems incredible that woman would voluntarily give up her seat on the pedestal where she has forced man to place her.

I have no sympathy for the plight of oriental woman, but admiration for the men instead. And if our western women continue their present silly efforts for recognition, I am cruel enough to hope that they will be awarded the thorned crown of success.

We gave a luncheon on the Pruitt while we were in Shanghai and several Chinese women were invited. They were quite as interesting and attractive as the American women present, and this comparison does not discredit anyone. There were no uninteresting people at the party.

Early in April we went to Yokohama, Japan, to play the college champions a series of baseball games in the Meiji Shrine Stadium in Tokyo. Keio University beat our team badly, but much interest was taken in the games, nevertheless.

I made a visit, accidentally, to Kamakura while the ships were in Japan. A train that I thought was bound for Meanoshita, near Fujiyama, turned out to be headed in the other direction and I left it at Kamakura. I could not find anyone who could speak English, and the polite Japanese, seeing my embarrassment, directed me to a large tourist hotel. They did not even bother to collect for the railroad transportation.

At Kamakura is the Daibutsu, a gigantic hollow iron head of Buddha. It is about sixty feet high, and was formerly a shrine sacred to Japanese Buddhists, but now both the shrine and the surrounding grounds are cluttered with souvenir vendors, photographers, and tourists.

Some of us think that our younger generation is on its way to the dogs, and we may be half correct. But our younger people celebrate nothing so hilariously as the Japanese youngsters celebrate the cherry blossom season. I saw hundreds of boys from eight to sixteen years of age so inebriated they could barely stagger along. Many had been badly cut and bruised from falls, but their elders enjoyed their drunken antics very much. The youthful drinkers carried their bottles in their hands, taking drinks every few minutes from them. I saw many of these boys at every station between Kamakura and Yokohama.

Before we left Japan we visited a sukiyaki house, but I am sure that I shall not visit again. Japanese food is clean, but it's not cooked or served in a manner appetizing to western tastes.

Before we entered the house, we were requested to remove our shoes. It is an old Japanese custom to remove the shoes when entering a dwelling from outdoors. It is not a religious custom, but one developed to make housekeeping easier. Japanese houses are immaculate at all times.

We were led to a rather large room that was totally bare of furniture. The floor, sides, and ceiling were all covered with straw matting. Some cushions were brought in and we were told to wait a few minutes until the geisha girls arrived. A geisha girl lives in her own home. When she is wanted for an entertainment, she is telephoned or a messenger is sent. Frequently, especially when the party is composed of foreigners, she refuses to come.

In about ten minutes the girls arrived. They were very shy and when they were not eating or playing their stringed instruments they could not refrain from giggling. They possessed weak, shrill voices and their music did not help them. The instruments they played resembled ukuleles, but the sound from them was worse. This may seem like an exaggeration, but I am sure that anyone who has been in a sukiyaki house will substantiate my opinion of Japanese music and voices. Both are hideous.

Soon the mistress of the house brought in a large earthen bowl filled with hot coals. Into this she placed a skillet. Then she produced meat and vegetables, all uncooked.

Each person selected the food he fancied, cooked it, and ate it direct from the skillet. I thought the party was more suited to children's tastes than ours, but the Japanese like their sukiyaki parties very much. Some of them spend several thousand dollars on a single party.

I ate some rice and dried pickled peas, and nothing else. Saki was served in earthen pitchers. It was hot, and very weak. The whole affair was very weak, so it didn't continue late into the evening.

We left Yokohama late in April for Fusan, Korea. Before we arrived, however, despatch orders were received to proceed to Shanghai on a special mission.

Our mission was completed within a week and we proceeded to Chefoo, where daily training in preparations for the various battle practices was begun.

At about this time, so the newspapers stated, members of the Red Spear Order [A localized self-defense organization] began to take part in the military activities in the Shantung Peninsula. They apparently did not last long, because after a few weeks nothing more was heard of them in North China.

The Red Spear would be a strong organization if it had a large membership. Its members have no fear whatever. Before going into an engagement they spend many hours fasting and praying, thereby making themselves bullet-proof. Of course some are killed, but they are the ones who didn't prepare themselves properly. Whatever the merits or demerits of the Red Spear system, it at least sends its members into battle in a fighting, confident frame of mind.

I suspect that the Red Spear's practices are modeled after some of our own. We are continually talking ourselves into aggressive, optimistic, and prospective ways of thinking. After the recent market depression, confidence in business stability was expressed in newspapers and on billboards. Recently the governor of Virginia helped the situation by executing Old Man Depression, Old Lady Pessimism, and Miss Fortune.

The Red Spear method of thinking is by no means archaic.

A few days before our scheduled battle practice the Forty-fifth Division received despatch orders to proceed to the United States. All gunnery training was cancelled and preparations were begun for making the long trip. Officers who had been on the station less than two years were detached and others received. Stores were taken aboard. Training ammunition was turned over to other ships. Water-tight integrity was checked.

One week before leaving Chefoo I was ordered to duty as junior patrol officer. Among my duties was that of director of boat traffic at the city landing.

The first night that I was on duty a man from one of the destroyers rode to the landing in a rickshaw, apparently in a drunken condition. I directed one of the patrolmen to take care of him until his ship's boat arrived. About five minutes later the patrolman reported to me that the man appeared to be ill.

I made a quick examination. A quick one was all that was necessary because the man appeared to be dead. I sent him immediately to the tender, but the medical officers there could not revive him, although they worked all night. The sailor had been the victim of cocaine poisoning.

Whether he had deliberately taken the drug, or whether it had been secretly placed in his food by a person intent upon robbery, could never be positively determined. At any rate, no money or other valuable possessions could be found on him.

The patrol launched a campaign against bootleggers of narcotics, but its effectiveness was reduced because the senior patrol officer, myself, and half of the force sailed for Tsingtao with the ships a week later. We did succeed, however, in breaking up one large drug ring.

The Chinese police commissioner, Mr. Wen, agreed to assist us in our work. He was a great asset, too, but I never did like him personally. Once I informed him that a small Chinese boy, suffering from lack of food, was prostrated on the sidewalk only a few feet from him. He merely acknowledged my information and continued talking. I informed him again and he paid no attention. A moment later he walked outside and was passing the lad without noticing him. I became angry and asked if he intended to do anything at all for the boy. He then called a rickshaw and had him carried away.

On the day following the death of the sailor one of our patrolmen, playing the part of a drug addict, bribed a rickshaw coolie to take him to a large house about three miles outside the foreign section of Chefoo. There he purchased a small quantity of cocaine and returned to patrol headquarters.

The coolie who conveyed him was arrested by Wen. Wen beat the poor devil unmercifully with bamboo canes, trying to force him to give the names of the bootleggers higher up. Wen beat the man into unconsciousness, then revived him with cold water and continued the flogging. The coolie would never give the names of his bosses. He knew that they would torture and kill him if he did, more brutally than Wen.

Two nights later, shortly after midnight, we raided the house that our patrolman had discovered. Wen and his men did the actual raiding, because the Chinese wished to enforce their laws without foreign aid, but we stood by to see that those who caused the death of the sailor were punished.

The large house, which was the headquarters of a drug ring, was surrounded by about a dozen smaller houses and shacks. We passed through the circle of outhouses and looked at the occupants. Most of them were in a pitiful condition. Very few could even stand up. Several corpses were seen, a few of which were in the second or third day of putrefaction. The drug fiends paid no attention to these, possibly because they were there to end their own lives in a painless manner. Some of them showed horrible gangrene infections. The odor of decaying bodies was noticeable even outside the houses.

The Chinese policemen suddenly raided the large house and after a quick pistol duel, captured its four occupants. Wen said that they would be beheaded, but I later heard that all of them bribed themselves free after we left Chefoo.

Any kind of reform work is disagreeable because so many petty offenders suffer for the crimes of a few bosses. I was disgusted with Wen's method of extracting information, but Wen himself was rather boastful about his cruelty.

The coolie drug vendors have no sense of wrong. They find it very difficult to even exist, and if they find a person who wants drugs, they grasp the opportunity to earn a few extra coppers. If caught, they are helpless to bribe themselves free.

Opium drugs are subtle agents, but I doubt if a healthy person ever acquires the drug habit. The addicts in the outhouses all looked like deliberate suicides. They probably desired to end lives of misery and suffering. All white drug users that I ever saw gave me the impression that they would prefer to slowly kill themselves than suffer. There is something mentally or physically wrong with a dope fiend, even before he acquires the habit. No normally healthy person ever has the desire for drugs even after he has used them under the direction of a physician.

During one of my conversations with Wen, I asked him what effect the many military changes in Chefoo had on the police force. He said that it made no difference whether the Nationalists or the Northerners were in control; that both sides held the civil authorities of the police force inviolable.

Towards the last of June we went to Tsingtao, where I spent my final week in China. We completed the athletic championship contests there. The Pruitt was fortunate in winning the General Excellence Trophy, the President's Trophy for rowing, and the Soccer Trophy.

On the twelfth of July, 1929, we left Tsingtao for Yokohama, with our "homeward bound" pennants flying and the whistle of every man-of-war in the harbor sounding a shrill send-off.

When we arrived in Yokohama I was directed to organize a baseball team to play two games with Japanese teams. The newspapers gave us as much publicity as a team of professionals would have received. Reporters and photographers were constantly after us.

The first game was with a picked team from the ninety-odd teams in Yokohama. We lost, but the game was fairly good. I enjoyed playing against the Japanese, who were perfect sportsmen. The Japanese rooters gave us a cheer whenever we made a good play and kept calling to us to "hit it out of the lot." We won the second game which was played against a weaker team.

I think many Japanese sports writers study in America, because their style so closely resembles that of our prominent sporting editors. They are not yet adept in the use of slang, however, but this might be a point in their favor.

Japan has several excellent newspapers. The editorials are good and the news is accurate and prompt. The front page is not smeared with advertisements like the English-edited Chinese papers.

Advertisements are frank and brief, but not interesting. It is almost as pleasing to read the advertisements in an American newspaper or magazine as to read the news and fiction. The American advertisement writer is a master of exaggerative humor.

If I believe what our magazines say, I have a life of celibacy ahead of me. I can never remember to gargle my throat before engaging in conversation or to change my garters as frequently as I would if I wore them around my neck. I have never taken a French course and I can't play a piano. I have taken no course in personal magnetism. I have "Athlete's foot" and I seldom wear a bow tie.

Americans must be getting over-sexed. A few months ago I saw in one of our leading magazines a picture of a beautiful woman taking a bath. It was an illustration for a toothbrush advertisement. It's enough to put sex in our fiction. When we put it in our toothbrushes, that is going too far.

We left Yokohama on the twenty-fourth of July, 1929 for Honolulu and the United States. I left the Asiatic Station with some regret, but this was more than balanced by a feeling of anticipation. I wondered how much our country had changed.

I found the Red Sox still keeping company in the cellar and Al Capone still making money. Notre Dame was still winning football games and the Army and Navy were still refusing to play. But I made one astounding discovery. Everywhere big, brawny men, hairy-chested men, deep-voiced men were wearing silk underwear. American advertising had triumphed over American prejudice again.

CHAPTER 8
ANNA

The Pruitt made her way back to her home port of San Diego, California. Lieutenant (jg) Albert Jarrell remained attached as Gunnery Officer as Pruitt performed all the duties and exercises required of a United States warship.

In October of 1929 U.S.S. Pruitt visited Eureka, California, in celebration of Navy Day, which was held on the twenty seventh of October. The city welcomed the ship and held a dance. Jarrell had a reputation among the officers for not being the least bit interested in women, so it was a stroke of fate that he attended the dance. Anna Christine Holm, the daughter of a prominent Eureka doctor, was one of the hostesses at the dance. Shipmates reported that the minute Jarrell set eyes on her he was infatuated. One commented, "Al said that he was going to marry that girl."

Both of Anna's parents emigrated from Denmark. Her mother, Agnes Maria Marie (Nielsen) Holm was born in 1876, and her father, Edgar Holm, 1877. They were married 6 October, 1904, in Parsons, Kansas, and my mom, Anna, was born the next year, August 1, 1905, in Millbrook, Illinois.

My grandfather, Doctor Holm, took a position as chief physician and surgeon for Magma Copper Company in Superior, Arizona. My mom and grandmother told me stories about how, during that time, the Pancho Villa gang attacked the town to rob the bank and other establishments. They said the women and children hid under tables and the men stood at the windows firing guns and rifles at the gang, eventually driving them off. In 1916 the Holm family left Superior and moved to Chicago where Granddad studied to become an eye, ear, nose and throat specialist. They moved to Eureka, California, in 1920 and lived there until 9 March, 1941 when Dr. Holm died of cardiac arrest at age 63. Agnes would spend the rest of her life sharing her time between her two sons and our family. I remember her living with us, or in a close-by apartment, in many cities including Mexico City. We all called her Beste, which we were told was a Danish nickname for grandmother. She passed away in 1964 in Ramona, California, where my parents had retired.

My mom had been quite popular in Eureka, both with the boys and the townspeople. Being a well-known doctor, her father was involved in many civic functions and this meant that she was, too. She told me that there were many young men in Eureka who were interested in her, and things got very serious once but led to nothing. She graduated from the Eureka Junior College and then received her Bachelor's degree from the University of California, Berkeley. While at Berkeley she worked part time in the University Library and the Lange Library of Education on the campus. Following graduation, she became part of the staff of the Berkeley Library and subsequently went on to become a librarian at the city of Oakland library. Her degree and experience made her eminently qualified to join the staff at the Eureka Free Library in her home town, where she worked until she and my dad married in 1930. Anna would spend the rest of her life volunteering in libraries in the various cities where she would live throughout Dad's long Navy career.

Anna Christine Holm

Ann and Al became close and got to know each other while the Pruitt was in Eureka. Upon discovering that they shared the same birth date, August 1, they took it to be a sign that they were meant for each other. When the ship sailed with Lieutenant (jg)

Jarrell, a fifteen-month romance by mail ensued and a bond was formed.

* * * * *

Nine months after leaving Asiatic Station, on April 30, 1930, Jarrell received Orders from the Navy Department, Bureau of navigation, to detach from duty aboard Pruitt and report for duty aboard U.S.S. Oglala in Yorktown, Virginia. On 12 May Pruitt was at the Navy Yard, Brooklyn, New York, when the commanding officer relieved Jarrell of duty. Lt. Jarrell then reported to the U.S. Naval Hospital, New York, NY, for unspecified treatments. Following the treatments, on May 24, 1930, Lieutenant (jg) Albert Jarrell reported for duty aboard U.S.S. Oglala, (CM-4).

U.S.S. Oglala (CM-4)
(Official U. S. Navy Photograph)

U.S.S. Oglala was a 386 foot minelayer displacing 3,746 tons. My dad's billet aboard her was as Communications and Engineering Officer. After reporting aboard, Oglala returned to her home port of Boston, Massachusetts. In January, 1931, Oglala sailed for Balboa, the Canal Zone, Panama, but Dad was not aboard.

Earlier, in mid-1930, Jarrell had begun planning leave and travel to Eureka, California, to marry his first and only love, Anna Holm. On 22 July, 1930, he wrote to the Chief of the Bureau of Navigation requesting leave, and permission to miss Oglala's sailing to Panama. On 12 August permission was granted by his superiors. Jarrell traveled cross-country in January 1931 to Ann's home in Eureka. The wedding was held January twenty-fourth in Oakland, California. Following the wedding the newlyweds caught a steamship for Panama City, Panama, where they would set up their first home and Jarrell would rejoin his ship, the Oglala.

In a heartfelt letter home, Dad tells his parents about the wedding and about his love for my mom, Anna:

PANAMA PACIFIC LINE

ON BOARD S.S. CALIFORNIA

25 January, 1931

Dear Mama,

We arrived at Los Angeles about midnight tonight and leave tomorrow morning. After we see a few of Ann's relatives there we are going to forget everything except ourselves for a while.

We were married the 24th instead of the 22nd, and in Oakland instead of Eureka. Ann wanted to escape all the rice throwing and fuss that would have happened in Eureka. Only her family and relatives and the ministers were present.

Of course I don't need to tell you again that Ann is the only girl in the world for me. If I had never met Ann there wouldn't have been anybody. I love her, admire her, and respect her. So far as I am concerned, she is simply divine. I'm devoted to her and will stay that way, not because I have made up my mind to, but because it would be impossible to have any degree of affection for Ann less than devotion. She is a priceless jewel.

I had a wonderful time in Eureka. All of Ann's people are peaches, and Dr. and Mrs. Holm can't be beat. I think the world of them.

I want to thank you again for raising me so that Ann would look at me more than once. I love you

Your son,

Albert

My dad remained true to his promise and was devoted to my mom his entire life. Mom had some adjustments to make, as Dad's dietary peculiarities had to be accommodated. He did not like beef, seafood, chicken, or salads. She liked beef, seafood, chicken and salads. But she did like all the things that he would eat: ham, sausage, eggs, spaghetti, and various vegetables. So, when Dad was traveling or on sea duty, her diet would be those things that she didn't have when he was home.

* * * * *

In early February 1931 orders were cut directing Lieutenant (jg) Jarrell to report to the U.S. Naval Academy "for duty in attendance upon a post-graduate course of instruction in mechanical engineering." Oglala was soon to sail from the Canal Zone for the Pacific, so the orders were for Jarrell to detach from Oglala prior to her sailing west, and report aboard U.S.S. Langley (CV-1) for transport to Pensacola, Florida. Langley, America's first aircraft carrier, was positioned at Cristobal, Canal Zone, at the Atlantic side of the canal. Once in Pensacola, he would then proceed to Annapolis, Maryland, and the Academy.

Jarrell left Oglala on 20 March and reported aboard Langley 24 March. Langley made a stop in Guantanamo Bay, Cuba, in April 1931 and then proceeded to Pensacola, Florida. Lt. (jg) Jarrell detached Langley 8 May and took some well deserved leave with Ann, who had booked passage on a commercial steam ship to rejoin Albert in Pensacola. The two of them made their way to his home in LaGrange, Georgia, and then caught a train north to Annapolis, Maryland, where they set up house near the Academy.

On June 25, 1931, Lieutenant (jg) Jarrell reported to the Superintendant, U.S. Naval Academy Post Graduate School, and began a one-year study in naval engineering.

* * * * *

On 19 May, 1932, Lt. (jg) Jarrell received orders stating that upon completion of studies at the Naval Academy he was to report by 4 June to the Commandant, Fourth Naval District, "...for temporary duty under instruction at the Fuel Oil Testing Plant, Navy Yard, Philadelphia, Pa." This instruction in fuel oil testing would be short, being completed 25 June.

Fuel oil was, and still is, a critical element in the operation of steam-powered ships, but it might be a common belief that it is simply a matter of loading fuel oil (bunkering) and burning it. However, fuel oil was a much more complicated proposition and a complete knowledge of fuel oil and how to test it was mandatory for a ship's engineer. The Fuel Oil Testing Plant provided classes in this and myriad other subjects related to the mechanical operation of ships.

Fuel oil for ship's boilers is almost always very heavy (viscous) and with various degrees of contamination. The viscosity can be a result of the source of the crude oil or the stage of the refinery process it is taken from. Some crude oil taken from offshore Trinidad, for example, is like paraffin as it comes out of the ground and must be heated to get it to flow in the pipelines. When this is processed and sold for ship's fuel oil, it has to be heated to a specified temperature in order to be useful aboard ship. Much of the crude oil in North America is lighter and does not require the same level of heating, but is used more for the making of higher valued products such as gasoline, kerosene, and diesel fuel.

The class Jarrell was taking dealt with the heating requirements, the filtration requirements, and the processes necessary to deal with various contaminants in the fuel – water, sulfur, minerals, bacteria, etc. Fuel oils may contain poisonous or explosive volatile substances which the ship's personnel must be aware of, and deal with, in order to maintain a safe environment.

*　　*　　*　　*　　*

After a short personal leave, Jarrell was to report to the Professor of Naval Science and Tactics, University of California, Berkeley for additional post-graduate instruction in Naval Engineering. He reported for duty on 13 July, 1932, and spent the next eleven months attending the post graduate school at Berkeley. He and Ann resided in a small second story apartment in Vallejo during his studies at UC Berkeley. Ann was adapting to the life of a Navy wife, following my dad around the world as his assignments permitted.

It was in Vallejo that my parents acquired their first pet, a dachshund they named Snitz. My dad took to Snitz and began a fun training regimen. He taught her to fall over on her side when he asked, "Would you rather be a Marine or a dead dog?" He also taught her to salute with her right paw when he would say any sentence with the word "salute" emphasized. She also learned to salute while sitting on her haunches, but it took some time because her left paw would automatically rise at the same time. Snitz solved this problem herself by placing her left paw on a chair or someone's leg when she raised her right paw to salute.

*　　*　　*　　*　　*

Following completion of the graduate school studies at Berkeley, Lt. (jg) Jarrell received new instructions to report to U.S.S. Buchanan, (DD-131), for duty as engineer officer. Buchanan was berthed at San Diego, California, and he reported for duty on 31 May, 1933. He would serve three years aboard Buchanan in two different capacities.

Buchanan was a Wickes-class destroyer, with a length of 314 feet and displacing 1,260 tons. Wickes-class destroyers were four-stackers, like Pruitt, but were an earlier design.

U.S.S Buchanan (DD-131)
(Official U. S. Navy Photograph)

As Engineer Officer, Lt. (jg) Jarrell's responsibilities lay with all things mechanical and electrical: propulsion, deck guns, water, sewerage, ventilation, etc. Jarrell served as engineer officer until 25 April, 1935, when he received orders to assume the duties of Executive Officer aboard Buchanan. As the Executive Officer, or XO, Lieutenant (jg) Jarrell was responsible for running the day-to-day operations of the ship, freeing the Commanding Officer to deal with strategies and relationships with other commanders and organizations. The XO is considered, in most cases, to be the second in command of the ship.

Ann and Al rented a small house in San Diego that had a fenced yard for Snitz. Being attached to a destroyer meant that Jarrell would be at sea a great deal of the time. Most often, when he was at sea, Ann would drive with Snitz to Eureka to visit her parents.

The Navy Department, Bureau of Navigation, issued orders dated 4 September, 1935, advising Lieutenant (jg) Albert E. Jarrell that, "The President of the United States, having appointed you a Lieutenant in the Navy, from the 30th day of June 1935, I have the pleasure to transmit herewith your commission, dated 4 September 1935." The Executive Officer of U.S.S. Buchanan was now a full Lieutenant! Jarrell would perform XO duties for fourteen months aboard Buchanan.

During Jarrell's tenure aboard Buchanan she was attached to Division 5, Destroyers, Battle Force, operating along the West Coast. After a summer cruise to Alaska with ROTC cadets aboard in 1934, she returned to San Diego and became part of Rotating Reserve Destroyer Squadron 20. In December 1934 she resumed normal operations with the Battle Force. In April 1935 Buchanan sailed for Hawaii to take part in Fleet Problem XVI, a series of war games north of Hawaii. Later in the year she worked with the Naval Research Laboratory testing various camouflage schemes. In the latter half of 1935 she resumed normal ship operations on the West Coast, patrolling and maintaining her operational efficiency.

*   *   *   *   *

Orders issued by the Navy on 9 June, 1936, detached Lt. Jarrell from the complement of Buchanan and ordered him to report to the Naval Inspector of Machinery, New York Shipbuilding Corporation, Camden, New Jersey. Buchanan was docked at Mare Island, California, when the orders were received, and he detached on 15 June, 1936, took some vacation time with Ann, and reported for duty at the Philadelphia Navy Yard on 6 July, 1936. On the trip east to the new billet they and Snitz visited Dad's relatives in Georgia and Mom's in Upstate New York.

The new assignment was to be an assistant Naval Inspector of Machinery. In this capacity Jarrell would verify that the shipyard was conforming to all Navy standards and specifications in the building of ships, and that any variances were properly investigated and approved. Jarrell would hold this assignment for sixteen months.

My parents took up residence in Woodbury, New Jersey. During the summer they and Snitz would drive to the beach at Atlantic City on an almost weekly basis. In November 1937 their first child, Joan, was born.

*   *   *   *   *

The Navy instructed Lt. Jarrell in November 1937 to report for duty in connection with the fitting out of U.S.S. Nashville (CL-43), which was completing her build at the New York Shipbuilding Corporation. On 15 December, 1937, Jarrell began the final commissioning of Nashville. His orders also stated that upon commissioning of Nashville he was to report to the ship's commander for duty as the Assistant Engineer Officer.

U.S.S. Nashville was a Brooklyn-class light cruiser with a length of 600 feet and displacing 10,000 tons.

U.S.S. Nashville (CL-43)
(Official U. S. Navy Photograph)

U.S.S. Nashville was commissioned 6 June, 1938, and at that time Lt. Jarrell began his duties as Assistant Engineer Officer. In July Nashville began her shakedown cruise in the Caribbean. As with any new ship, a shakedown cruise keeps the Engineering crew very busy investigating and identifying potential mechanical and electrical problems. He would continue in the capacity of an engineer officer for another 15 months until September 1939.

Following shakedown, Nashville sailed for Europe and then south to Brazil and back up to the East Coast of the United States.

In June of 1939 Nashville sailed west, through the Panama Canal, to California. While Nashville was in Long Beach, California, Lt. Jarrell received the orders he had been preparing for since graduating from the Naval Academy: Command of his own ship.

CHAPTER 9
U.S.S. STURTEVANT

On 9 September, 1939, The Chief of the Bureau of Navigation, Rear Admiral Chester W. Nimitz, issued orders to Lieutenant Jarrell to detach from U.S.S. Nashville in Long Beach, California, and proceed to San Diego where he was to report to the Commandant, Eleventh Naval District, "for duty in connection with the fitting out of the U.S.S Sturtevant and in command of that vessel when commissioned."

Sturtevant was a Clemson-class destroyer like Lt. Jarrell's earlier billets, Sumner and Pruitt. Sturtevant had been commissioned September 1920 but had undergone decommissioning twice, once in 1931 and again in 1935.

Jarrell detached from Nashville on September 12 and reported for duty at the U.S. Destroyer Base, San Diego, California, on September 13, 1939. On 26 September the fitting out of U.S.S. Sturtevant (DD-240) was complete and Lieutenant Jarrell assumed "duty as Commanding Officer of U.S.S Sturtevant in compliance with basic orders." Jarrell would spend fifteen months commanding the U.S.S. Sturtevant.

During Lieutenant Jarrell's earlier billet on U.S.S. Nashville as Engineering Officer, his organizational abilities had been instrumental in winning a coveted award as described in this commendation letter that Jarrell received October 1940, after assuming command of U.S.S. Sturtevant:

UNITED STATES FLEET
CRUISERS, BATTLE FORCE, CRUISER DIVISION EIGHT
U. S. S. NASHVILLE

Pearl Harbor, T.H.,
October 22, 1940

From: Commanding Officer.
To: Lieutenant Albert E. Jarrell, U.S.Navy,
             Commanding U.S.S. STURTEVANT.

Subject: Commendation for Engineering Efficiency,
             Fiscal Year 1939-1940

1.   The Chief of Naval Operations has awarded the NASHVILLE the red "E" for standing second in the engineering competition in Cruisers, Battle Force, for the Fiscal Year 1939-1940.

2.   The commanding officer believes that your attention to duty, knowledge and successful application of sound engineering principles has contributed, largely, to this coveted award and to the efficiency of the engineering plant of this vessel during the past year. The commanding officer congratulates and commends you most heartily, for this achievement.

3.   A copy of this letter will be forwarded to the Bureau of Navigation for inclusion in your official record.

(Signed) R. S. Wentworth.

U.S.S. Sturtevant (DD-240)
(Official U. S. Navy Photograph)

Sturtevant operated in the Pacific from the time of recommissioning, 26 September, 1939, until June 1940 when she would transition through the Panama Canal to the Atlantic and operate out of Norfolk, Virginia, escorting convoys and conducting Neutrality Patrols. The war in Europe required extra vigilance at home.

On the way to the Canal Zone, Jarrell was ordered by the Commander, Special Service Squadron (ComSpeRon) to patrol in the Costa Rican waters and make observations of activities there. ComSpeRon was tasked with patrolling Caribbean waters in what was known as "gunboat diplomacy," a strategy in which a display of naval power might help to achieve U. S. foreign policy objectives. Information related to activities taking place in

Caribbean countries was of vital interest to ComSpeRon, and to our national interests. Lieutenant Jarrell, the consummate observer, diligently performed the assigned task.

Here is his report:

RESTRICTED   U.S.S Sturtevant (240)
                                               Enroute Balboa C.Z.
                                                    5 July, 1940

From: Commanding Officer.
To: Commander Special Service Squadron.

Subject: Visit to Costa Rican Waters – Report of.

Reference: (a) ComSpeRon dispatch 282115 of June,
                   1940.

1.   In compliance with reference (a), Sturtevant patrolled areas 2, 3, and 4 during the period 1-6 July, 1940; a stop was made at Puntarenas on 3 July.

2.   At Puntarenas Mr. William E. Brown, an American citizen, came aboard with a letter from the American Minister. Mr. Brown is the port pilot, and cooperates with the legation in performing consular duties, since there is no regular consular agent at Puntarenas. The letter from the Minister contained a cordial invitation to the Commanding Officer and officers to attend a Fourth of July celebration at the legation, but the invitation could not be accepted, due to the lack of time, and the Minister was informed by letter and telephone.

Two German merchantmen have been anchored at Puntarenas since the outbreak of war; they are the EISNACH and the WESER. The Italian steamer FELLA has been anchored there since Italy entered the war. Mr. Brown stated that these ships radio transmitters have been removed, but they are believed to have other sets on board. All cargo of these three ships has been discharged.

Mr. Brown stated that on about 12 June a group of men from the German ships conveyed four or five boxes marked "earthen ware" to the SCOTIA, under charter to the Grace Line, and attempted to send them to San Francisco, where they would be called for. Captain McKenzie of the SCOTIA refused to accept the boxes unless they were opened and taken through customs, which the Germans refused to do; the boxes were taken back to the German ships.

Generally, the crews of the German and Italian ships are kept on board, but a few men are allowed on shore occasionally. The Germans and Italians do not fraternize with each other or with the Costa Ricans. The Germans have run out of funds, and subsist by means of voluntary contributions from German residents of Costa Rica. Apparently, the Italians still have funds.

The Costa Ricans distrust both the Germans and the Italians very much and a feeling of apprehension exists. The natives report to the police every move made by them. For instance, when the Germans ordered two steers instead of one, as is customary, the steer dealer immediately informed the police. The engineer of the local power plant, one of the engineers of the railroad, and the port pilot have been fired recently; all of these are of German extraction.

A man of German extraction named Paul Hirschel, who has been in Chile with the Guggenheim interests, is engineer of the Pacific Refrigerating Company. He is not believed to be naturalized. He will not associate with anyone except Nazis. He killed his wife in a drunken rage, according to Mr. Brown.

An official call was made on the governor of the Province of Puntarenas, Mr. Juan Rafael Sotomayor; present were the port Captain, the first and second officers of the local police force, the Port Medical Officer, and several others; the Port Medical Officer is Dr. Rafael A. Nunez, a graduate of the University of Virginia. The meeting was very cordial. The Costa Ricans are strongly pro-American. Dr. Nunez stated that several German sailors are being treated by him, and that they insist that they will sail about 15 July; he also stated that he lost a wager to a German sailor when Paris fell within two weeks after the drive started.

The American Minister, Mr. William H. Hornibrook, expressed through Mr. Brown his desire that a destroyer be stationed at Puntarenas, if one is available.

3.   Mr. Brown, during his visit to STURTEVANT, mentioned a new settlement in the Gulf of Dulce, established by the United Fruit Company. He also said there was a new navigational light in that area. In order to investigate, STURTEVANT went into the Gulf of Dulce on 4 July. The ship lay to about three miles southwest of the entrance to Golfito, and Ensign Herbert A. Cassidy was sent ashore (See H.O. Chart No. 1037). The settlement is located near the northern end of Golfito, and at present has

a population of about 2,000, only a few of which are Americans; the majority are Costa Ricans. The manager is a Mr. Moore, who is an American citizen. He has spent 25 years in Honduras with United Fruit prior to his present venture with the same company. He has been at Golfito since the project started, one year ago. The houses are small wooden structures, resembling those in the Canal Zone except that they are smaller. The settlement has a well-stocked commissary and a fine restaurant. There is a small machine shop located near the pier; this shop is to be enlarged within the near future to a capacity sufficient to service the settlement, but not sufficient to overhaul ships. A narrow gauge railroad runs from the settlement to a 50,000 acre banana plantation, 20 kilometers inland. The settlement was planned for the purpose of assisting the development of the plantation. Mr. Moore stated that he has unlimited funds available for the development. At present, United Fruit ships stand in close to the settlement at anchor; freight is handled by barges. There is only a very small pier at the settlement now, but it is to be enlarged soon, and will be capable of handling ships of 35 feet draft. Soundings still are being taken. The maximum range of tide that has been noted is 11 feet. At times, there is a strong current in the channel; Ensign Cassidy estimated 2 knots during his transit on a flood tide. Two fuel tanks are being built, and will be completed in two months; one will have a capacity of 50,000 barrels of bunker oil, and the other 5,000 barrels of diesel oil. At present, water is taken from a small stream, but it will soon be piped from the hills, 3 kilometers distant. No facilities have been planned for supplying ships with boiler feed water. There are three railroad cranes in the settlement, of about 10 tons capacity each.

Two black buoys are located on the port side (north) of the entrance channel; ships entering should leave them close to port. Beyond these two black buoys are two red buoys, which ships on entering should leave close to starboard. The four buoys are about 800 yards apart, and the red buoys are at a sharp angle to the right of the line of the black buoys. The two black buoys will be in range with the large fuel tank when it is completed. A pilot and a small tug are available. Ships have gone about one mile southeast into Golfito, but some have touched bottom.

There is an airplane field near the settlement. It is about 1,000 yards long and 200 yards wide, and runs approximately northwest-southeast, or approximately perpendicular to the channel entrance. The valley in which the field is located turns sharply near the northwest end of the field, and planes land from the southwestward. Clearing of the field is still in progress. The field has a hard surface, resembling clay. The field is used to ferry workers to inland towns for spending holidays. Three company planes were seen. Recently some commercial planes have used the field.

The construction of a navigational light is now completed. Although the manager stated that the location and characteristics have been reported to the Hydrographic Office, they are reported here for the information of Commander Special Service Squadron. A copy of the company's report is available in STURTEVANT.

The location is given as follows:

Latitude   8° - 38' - 30"
Longitude: 83° - 12' - 50"

The above location, however, is not correct. STURTEVANT checked the location several times and the light actually is located one mile east of the position given above. The light is flashing white; period five seconds, with two seconds luminous and 3 seconds eclipse; are of visibility from 251°, through north to 154°, through 8-1/2 points of the compass (This is obviously incorrect, and probably should be from 154° to 251°), range of visibility 30 miles. The framework is open steel tower painted yellow. Height of center of lantern above mean high water is 640 feet; height of structure from base to vane is 40 feet; the light was placed in service on 5 June, 1940; the illuminating apparatus consists of a 375 millimeter lantern with cut lens, automatic flasher, sun valve, with a 1 cubic foot gas burner of 550 candle power. There is no fog signal. The light is unattended, but a caretaker is in the immediate vicinity.

Another light is to be erected across the channel from the present light in about two months. Its exact location and characteristics are not yet known.

A. E. Jarrell

During the mid-1940 passage of the Panama Canal from the Pacific to the Atlantic, Lieutenant Jarrell was called upon to perform the duties of Judge Advocate of Court of Inquiry. His performance impressed his superiors, as evidenced by this letter of commendation:

OFFICE OF
COMMANDANT FIFTEENTH NAVAL DISTRICT
BALBOA, CANAL ZONE

6 February, 1940.

From: Captain F. L. Riefkohl, U. S. Navy,
(President Court of Inquiry Convened by
Order of Commander Special Service
Squadron)

To: Commander Special Service Squadron.
(Convening Authority)

SUBJECT: Lieutenant Albert E. Jarrell, U. S. Navy,
(Judge Advocate of Court of Inquiry) –
Performance of duty as Judge Advocate.

1. As President of the Court of Inquiry, and in behalf of the members of the Court, I desire to bring to your attention the excellent manner in which Lieutenant Albert E. Jarrell, U. S. Navy, performed his duties as Judge Advocate of the Court of Inquiry.

2. The members of the court were most favorably impressed by the manner in which Lieutenant Jarrell conducted the inquiry, and prepared the record of proceedings. It was quite apparent that he had a thorough understanding of his duties as Judge Advocate, and he devoted considerable time and effort to insure their being properly executed.

(Signed) F. L. RIEFKOHL

On September 3, 1940, the Navy Department, Bureau of Navigation, advised Lieutenant Jarrell that "The President of the United States, by and with the advice and consent of the Senate, having appointed you A Lieutenant Commander in the Navy, from the 1st day of September 1939, I have the pleasure to transmit herewith your commission, dated September 3, 1940." Signed: C.W. Nimitz, Chief of Bureau.

U.S.S. Sturtevant, now based out of Norfolk, Virginia, since July 1940, and under the command of newly promoted Lieutenant Commander Albert Jarrell, would undergo another overhaul just one year after being re-commissioned, and before performing her duties escorting convoys and patrolling along the western Atlantic. Mom and Joan had joined Dad in Norfolk and set up a home while he was assigned to Sturtevant.

On September 18, 1940, Dad wrote his friend and Annapolis classmate, Lt. Comdr. Ira E. Hobbs, a letter saying he was "enclosing a check for fifty rocks to pay off the wager we made when we both were confirmed bachelors." Apparently, Dad was the first to marry. He continued, commenting that "I hope that you are enjoying your duties with the fleet. I don't like being away from the big show for so long, but being skipper, of even an old can that breaks down all the time, has its compensations. We are undergoing our first overhaul since re-commissioning a year ago."

CHAPTER 10
BRAZIL – BEFORE WWII

In November of 1940, Lieutenant Commander Jarrell received orders to travel to Rio de Janeiro, Brazil, to be the Engineer Member of the U. S. Naval Mission to Brazil. This would be a two-year assignment, from February 1941 to February 1943. His family would be accompanying him to Brazil. He and Ann, who was now pregnant with their second child, made plans to meet in Key West, Florida, where they would have passage aboard a Navy ship.

Mom and Joan flew in a DC3 aircraft from Georgia to Key West. During the flight something didn't quite set well with the not-yet-born child and, upon landing in Key West, Mom was rushed to the hospital where she gave birth to Lewis Albert. Mom and Dad had planned on some vacation time in Key West, but the newborn boy garnered much of their attention.

The Jarrell family would travel to Brazil aboard the troop transport ship Argentina. Upon arrival in Brazil on February 8, a series of formal meetings took place to introduce LCDR Jarrell and Anna to the various Brazilian officials and their wives. Any time an officer is assigned Embassy duty there are always concurrent social and official events and luncheons that must be attended. Ann will become quite used to these over the years.

Joan had just turned three when they arrived and remembers living in Brazil. She later wrote some of her remembrances in an essay for her family, and the following is an excerpt recounting that time:

> The first thing I can remember is living in Brazil. We had a large, two-story house with a large and beautiful garden about a block from the beach in Rio de Janeiro. I think Lewis and I shared a room.
>
> My dad used to take walks on the sidewalk by the beach, and one of my best treats was when he would take me along. There he would be, striding along, and I would have to run to keep up with him. I was three when we went to Brazil. Lewis had just been born. I don't remember much about him at that time, except that he didn't know much English when we returned to the United States.
>
> Snitz, the dachshund who was a member of the family even before I was, went to Brazil with us. The next door neighbor had a monkey who came into our garden. One day Snitz killed the monkey. I guess there was a big incident over that. Daddy maintained that the monkey had no business being in our yard – and he was right!
>
> When we were in Brazil, we acquired Butch, a "semi-dachshund." Butch was a black and yellow dog, and he loved to travel. He used to go to the end of the street and catch the bus into town. There, he'd make his usual rounds, then, at the end of the day, he'd catch the bus back home. The bus driver got to know him and would always let him off at his stop. Butch also liked to chase cars, which was his eventual downfall.

I remember Daddy taking us up to the Christ [Christ the Redeemer atop Mt. Corcovado], which overlooked Rio de Janeiro. It was a scary drive up, and boring being in the car, but the view from the top was magnificent. Mother and Daddy tried to locate our home from the top; I couldn't see it though.

Daddy was very strict about not disturbing his sleep or his six o'clock evening news hour. We had to be super-quiet. He used to listen to an old upright radio in a dark room. We also had to be very quiet on weekends when Daddy would sleep in. He would bellow at us if we did something wrong. He did have his sleep interrupted one time, and not by us, when he caught a burglar in his bedroom. Daddy was a light sleeper, and awoke to find a thief at the dresser. He had a pistol in the drawer of his bedside table, and scared the burglar away. The person left in such a hurry that he didn't take the ladder he had used to climb to the second story balcony outside Daddy and Mother's bedroom. That was another big event in our stay in Brazil.

Lieutenant Commander Jarrell kept a hand-written daily account of his time in Brazil. He was there when word came that Japan had attacked Pearl Harbor. Here are some of his comments from that "Day of Infamy" until the end of December, and may give a perspective of how people reacted at the Embassy upon hearing the news.

War Notes

7 December, 1941 (Sunday)

About 1800 local time Harry Covington told me that
Hawaii had been attacked by the Japanese. First radio
reports indicated heavy U.S. losses. Attack was made
before the Japs declared war. I am delighted that we are at
war with the Japs, because a war at the present time will
prevent a much more serious war later. I feel thankful to
Hitler for only one thing; he brought Japan into the war
against us.

(Monday) 8 December, 1941

Went to the office with a copy of my old request that had
asked that I not be sent to Brazil, but be retained on sea
duty indefinitely. I planned to request sea duty, but Capt.
Eldredge said he did not wish to forward requests at the
present time. Several Americans, and also Mario Penna,
criticized the U.S. Army and Navy at Hawaii. I told them
they didn't know what they were talking about; they didn't.

(Tuesday) 9 December, 1941

Williams and I held meeting in arsenal to determine a stock
of material for Brazil under Lease-Lend Act. Present
besides Williams and myself: Santos Rosa, Santos Rocha,
Rego Monteiro, Mario Penna, Murillo Silva. We have been
trying for months to get the Brazilian Navy to submit a list
of material, but without result.

10 December, 1941 (Wed)

We decided on a list of war material for the Brazilian Navy.
The Minister of Marinha [Navy] didn't like the idea of
procuring the material that might be used by any nation

other than Brazil. We got the list in however. The Minister submitted, in general, a list of complicated material that would require several years for the Brazilian Navy to install, and would insure the inactivity of the fleet for the duration of the war.

11 December, 1941 (Thurs)

Criticism of armed forces in Hawaii began to diminish, but still heard same, all from Americans. I offered to wager anyone that, If Hawaii was attacked from forces afloat, then the bulk of our forces were not there. I do not believe that Hull [Secretary of State Cordell Hull] was deceived by the Japanese peace talks, but do believe that he forced action before the Japs were fully ready.

In a talk with Mario Penna, Dorwal Reis, Murillo Silva, and Rego Monteiro, I agreed that the Brazilian public was solidly behind the U.S. but that Brazil would be more secure politically if a few of the high ranking Nazi lovers in the Army were removed. I mentioned specifically Dutra, Gois Monteiro, and Cavalcanti.

12 December, 1941 (Fri)

Brazilians appear to be recovering from the shock of the losses at Hawaii, and are disgusted at Japanese treachery. The weak attacks against Luzon indicate that our submarines are taking a heavy toll of Jap forces before they arrive in Philippine waters.

13 December, 1941 (Sat)

Roosevelt is as popular in Brazil as Vargas [President of Brazil]. It appears that Jap plans have failed. I don't believe they have any chance at all. Even if Hull had not rushed them, they would be doomed to failure.

14 December, 1941 (Sun)

The beginning of the second week of the war finds Japs losing heavily at sea. They got off to an active start, but certainly not successful.

I went to the races with Ann, Joan, and Jim Callery; saw more Britishers and fewer Germans than usual.

Had a talk with several Americans at "Sugar" Woolman's new house; not as much criticism of Hawaii now, and none of it vindictive, or even strong.

15 December, 1941 (Monday)

At lunch at Arsenal Brazilians talked very little about the war. They are not interested in preparing their fleet, but are pro-American.

Sec. Knox [Secretary of the Navy] made statement that Navy was off guard at Hawaii. I don't know what he meant.

Went to races in afternoon. Talked to Jim Callery & Herb Horn in evening.

22 December, 1941 (Mon)

Visited AMIC [Naval Arsenal in Rio de Janeiro]. Papers report heavy landing of Japs in Philippines.

23 December, 1941 (Tues)

Churchill in Washington. Don't like joint statement Roosevelt-Churchill. Apparently Philippines will not be reinforced.

24 December, 1941 (Wed)

Adm. King's statement lacked confidence; no aggressiveness. Don't like the idea of even considering declaring Manila "an open city." Why should we even insinuate that the Japs fight a civilized war; that they would respect an open city? Why should we weaken our own position when we are ready to bomb Jap cities? Roosevelt says: "Our powerful stimulant, in this war, is our faith in the dignity and fraternity of men." I, like everybody else, am sick of words. I want to see orders to murder.

25 December, 1941 (Thurs)

Joan and Lewis had a nice Xmas. I wonder if the fleet shakeups are worth anything. Nimitz in the Pacific, Ingersall in the Atlantic, King overall. I'm inclined to believe that neither the Army, the Navy, nor Washington was ready for war. Especially Washington. Hong Kong and Wake Island fell to the Japs. Why didn't we defend Wake adequately, or else remove the garrison?

26 December, 1941 (Friday)

Churchill addressed the Congress. His speech was stronger than any that Roosevelt or Hull have made. "What kind of people do the Japs think we are, anyway?" Hull does not like the Free-French occupation of Miquelon & St. Pierre. Hull is an appeaser. We need to use a strong arm with

Vichy. I visited AMIC; am suspicious of several Brazilian naval officers being Nazis.

27 December, 1941 (Sat)

Japs bombed Manila for over three hours, after defenses had been removed or destroyed. Are creating havoc, outraging women. This is no surprise to me.

28 December, 1941 (Sun)

Brazilian newspapers are disgusted with Jap method of warfare. Stinson promised Quezon half as soon as possible. The Philippines will not be easy for the Japs, but I want to see reinforcements sent as soon as possible.

29 December, 1941 (Monday)

Rio newspaper "Meio Dia" has reverted to its old policy of favoring the Axis. Lourival Fontes, Director of Press and Propaganda, no doubt has been bribed. Philippines are doing very well; so are Dutch East Indies which are helping out exceptionally well. Japs made some gains in Malaya. Milo & I had conference with Admiral Teixeira. He says he will inaugurate a coastal patrol on 2 Jan, 1942.

30 December, 1941 (Tuesday)

Troops in Philippines appear to be digging in to stave off Jap attacks. I can't understand Jap air superiority; we must have diverted some planes from Philippines to Malaya. Papers say Tokio [Tokyo] fears attacks from Aleutian Islands. We must be preparing something.

31 December, 1941 (Wednesday)

Papers report air reinforcements arriving for defense of Philippines. However, afternoon papers report fall of Manila imminent. If we lose Philippines, war will be long one. Why don't we defend them properly, by using the fleet? For what reasons have we developed night carrier operations & fueling at sea? Have we no troops ready?

Through 1942 Jarrell continued writing his thoughts on the war in his journal. Interspersed with war comments were other things he found interesting, such as a Brazilian woman who gave birth to triplets and named them America, Getulio [Vargas, President of Brazil], and Roosevelt.

Lt. Cmdr. Jarrell was an avid reader of newspapers and publications, and his analytical mind never skimmed over subliminal messages. While reading *Time Magazine* in early September 1942 he noted that the magazine was using disparaging rhetoric when referring to the Navy that Jarrell so loved. His letter to *Time Magazine* was the first he had ever written to a publication, but over the course of his life there would be many hundreds more:

Rio de Janeiro, Brazil
13 September, 1942

United States Naval Mission to Brazil

The Editors,
Time Magazine,
Time and Life Building,
Rockefeller Center,
New York, N.Y.

Gentlemen:

This is the first letter that I have ever written to any publisher in protest of anything.

Frankly, I have a bellyful of your use of the term "Battleship Admirals." On page 4, column 1, of your issue of September 7th appears the following: "The Navy air arm although no longer an outcast is still a stepchild to the Navy's battleship admirals."

TIME has used the expression "Battleship Admirals" many times. Yet TIME has never specifically named any "Battleship Admiral." The term, nevertheless, embodies, apparently, a large number of admirals who are stupid, determined to defend their pet whims, and who are a menace to the national effort. I request that TIME reflect carefully; if TIME cannot name a single admiral that it considers a "Battleship Admiral" then I further request that TIME discontinue the use of the expression.

Our naval air force was the best in the world ten years before this war started. It still is the best in the world. It was developed by old timers, largely, who never studied aviation at the Naval Academy. These air minded old timers did not spring out of the ground. They received the fundamental naval training. They received backing from the navy. As a result, the navy has developed the aerial torpedo, the airplane carrier, and the dive bomber, as well as the best coordination of effort between surface and air forces that the world has yet seen.

TIME is startled, and insists on startling our civilian public, with the feats of aviation. TIME may rest assured that the U.S. Navy is not startled. The navy is no more startled with the development of aviation than it was with the development of the ironclad warship or the submarine. I believe that battleships serve a useful purpose; also cruisers; also destroyers; also submarines; also aircraft. I believe that the navy must be a well balanced team. I am convinced that it will continue to be a well balanced team whether or not our publishers attempt to understand the navy. When was the naval air force ever an outcast? Air instruction is mandatory for all officers. In peace time, an examination in theoretical aviation is necessary for line officers before they can be promoted. Officers designated for aviation duty receive 50% extra pay over base pay. What do you mean by outcast?

In peacetime neither TIME nor any other magazine, excepting a very few published largely in the interests of the armed services, made much of an effort to keep up with progress in naval or military subjects. Now TIME is so shocked with aviation progress that it insists that the whole reading public be shocked. Aviation is being kept in the background by the scurvy "Battleship Admirals," damn them, who, for some inexplicable reason, hate the sight of a plane, in spite of the fact that they developed it, and know how to use it.

As long as I am writing, I will mention a few other items in connection with the same issue I am discussing, the issue of September 7th. Page 15, "Battleship News," regarding the Iowa, I note that "a heavy bomb can only dent her deck, but a lucky hit down a funnel into the magazine might do [it] for her." If this statement is correct, then my 21 years in the navy have been wasted, for I certainly am not familiar with magazine funnels. "Would the Iowa spend the war ignominiously tied to a dock?" This question insinuates, while not stating as a fact, that our older battleships spend most of their time tied up to the docks. Does TIME know of any battleship, in any navy, that has spent most of its time tied up to docks, in peace or in war? I suggest that TIME study the reports of the evacuation of Dunkirk and learn something about the effectiveness of battleships versus planes. Why didn't the Germans invade England? – Because of the British fleet. Why didn't they take Malta, which is between Sicily and Axis controlled Africa? Why didn't they continue on to Cyprus and Asia Minor, after taking Crete?

I note that the Iowa will be "the only United nations battleship afloat able, without giving odds, to take on the powerful Nazi TIRPITZ - ." "- the Iowa is the only battleship of the United Nations which can attempt to fight her (TIRPITZ) singlehanded -." A note following this statement then refers to tonnage of various warships. A comparison of tonnage is not a comparison of warships.

Last, your picture of Colonel Carlos Brazil on page 22. The officer in the center looks like Colonel Vasco Secco.

> Yours very truly
> (signed)
> A.E. Jarrell
> Lieut. Comdr.
> U.S. Navy

Observant readers may note that Jarrell quoted *Time Magazine* as using the term United Nations (and United nations) in his 1942 letter. Although the UN did not come into existence until 1945, the name United Nations was coined by President Franklin D. Roosevelt in January 1942 and was used in a declaration by the Allied nations who united together to fight the Axis Powers.

In September 1942 my mom became a volunteer with the Brazilian Red Cross. Volunteer work at various duty stations and residences would become a regular part of her life. She especially was drawn to assist in the Navy Relief Society, which helped personnel and their families overcome hardships in their day-to-day lives.

Life in the Naval Mission entailed considerable travel and working with the Brazilian navy to assist in helping them improve their capabilities. Jarrell made trips to Sao Paulo and the Brazilian port of Recife. In Sao Paulo he visited various industries to see if they were capable of performing work that might be beneficial to the United States Navy in the future. In Recife he met with Brazilian Navy officials and the U.S. Commander South Atlantic Force to "confer in regard to material upkeep of Brazilian Naval Units."

In 1942 the Brazilian government broke ties with Germany and impounded the Axis ships that happened to be in Brazilian ports. The United States was interested in purchasing ships for use as transports, and purchased two of the impounded ships with an eye on purchasing more. Lieutenant Commander Jarrell was sent to inspect the ships and report on the condition of their refurbishment.

SS Conte Grande was an Italian liner that was laid up in Santos, Brazil, a seaport of Sao Paulo. It had been renamed by the U.S. Navy the U.S.S. Monticello (AP-61). Jarrell reported that there had been very light sabotage to her by the departing crew and that the guns that had been installed were not sufficient to defend her on the open ocean.

TS (Turbine Ship) Wyndhuk was a German cargo liner also located in Santos. It was renamed the U.S.S. Lejeune (AP-74). Jarrell reported that the ship had been heavily sabotaged by the departing German crew and that the temporary engines and equipment being installed for the trip to the United States probably would not be sufficient to get her there. He recommended that she be towed and accompanied by a destroyer for protection.

Included in LCDR Jarrell's report was a recommendation that any further ship purchases not be refurbished in Brazil, but be towed under destroyer escort to the United States for refurbishment there. This would get them into service faster and less expensively than the way the first two ships were done.

While serving in Brazil, LCDR Jarrell received a promotion to full Commander on December 16, 1942.

Working so closely with his Brazilian counterparts, his personality and motivations began to be seen. His drive and convictions were captured in a watercolor painting created by a close Brazilian friend. It depicts him as a world traveler, explorer, Navy man, and, of course, his ever-present cigars.

Vasco da Gama was a fifteenth-sixteenth century Portuguese naval explorer who is credited with making the first voyage from the Atlantic Ocean to the Indian Ocean, thereby opening an unopposed route to India. The ensuing spice trade boosted Portugal's economy and afforded expansion of their empire. Vasco da Gama was a leader, explorer, risk-taker, innovator, and was driven to success. Apparently, Jarrell's artist friend saw similar attributes in him.

Albert Edmondson Jarrell – Twentieth Century Vasco da Gama

At the end of Jarrell's tour of duty in Rio de Janeiro the family returned to the States. Because of the war, civilian passengers were not permitted on the ships available for transport. Arrangements were made to travel by plane, but the airlines didn't want any dogs. My dad was adamant that the dogs were returning, too, and finally managed to arrange for shipment of the dogs by air to Miami, but not on the same flight as the family.

The Jarrell family had flown directly to Atlanta and then made their way to LaGrange where Mom and the kids would wait while Dad began his new assignment and then sea duty. Dad took the train from LaGrange to Miami where he collected the dogs at the airport kennel and put them on a train to LaGrange. He then traveled to Philadelphia to his new assignment.

*   *   *   *   *

Following his two-year duty in the Naval Mission – Engineering, in Rio de Janeiro, Brazil, Jarrell was ordered March 10, 1943, to report "to the Navy Yard, Philadelphia, Pa, for temporary duty, in connection with Brazilian Destroyer Program." This was a short follow-up assignment to work with the Brazilians and the Navy Yard in the procurement and delivery of destroyers to the Brazilian Navy.

The Engineering aspect of Jarrell's assignment to the Naval Mission had kept him in touch with various Brazilian agencies that required knowledge and advice on matters pertaining to ship design and procurement. The Unites States was a leader in this sort of enterprise and Jarrell played a significant role interfacing with the Brazilian Navy. Jarrell was the perfect candidate for the Navy Yard assignment.

This work was completed March 20 and Jarrell was ordered to "proceed to Miami, Fla., and report to the Commanding Officer, Submarine Chaser Training Center, for temporary duty as Prospective Escort Division Commander."

*   *   *   *   *

CDR Jarrell reported for duty in Miami on March 26, 1943. Although his orders implied that he would be assigned as a Division Commander to the Gulf Sea Frontier, a cooperative effort between the United States of America and the Republic of Cuba in Naval matters, his expertise was needed elsewhere.

In April 1943 Jarrell reported aboard U.S.S. Hamul (AD-20) as a Staff Officer and Engineering Officer. Hamul was originally a cargo ship, launched in 1940, but was converted to a Destroyer Tender in January 1943. In April, after CDR Jarrell reported aboard, Hamul became the flagship of the Destroyer – Destroyer Escort Shakedown Task Group in Bermudian waters.

U.S.S. Hamul (AD-20)
(Official U. S. Navy Photograph)

In the ten months that Jarrell was assigned to this duty, ending February 1944, he accomplished much, as evidenced by his Commander's commendation:

UNITED STATES ATLANTIC FLEET
FLEET OPERATIONAL TRAINING COMMAND
Naval Operating Base
Norfolk, Virginia

RESTRICTED

5 February 1944

From: The Commander, Fleet Operational Training
Command, U.S Atlantic Fleet.

To: Commander A.E. Jarrell, USN

Subject: Commendation.

1.   Upon your detachment from duty with the
Commander DD-DE Shakedown Group, I desire to express
by this letter of commendation my appreciation for
excellence in the performance of your duties with that
command from April 1943.

2.   You were the first regular Naval officer to join the
staff of the Commander, Destroyer-Destroyer Escort
Shakedown Group, in the early days of its organization.
Much had to be accomplished in order to execute the
directives under which that organization was set up. You
were assigned duty as the Material officer, one of the
principal staff officers of that command. In view of the
relatively new status of the destroyer escort, the material
problems arising from the operation of such type vessel
during shakedown were completely unexplored.

3.   It has on numerous occasions been evident to the
Commander, Fleet Operational Training Command, that
you attacked your assignment with broad vision, excellent
judgment, splendid initiative, intelligence tempered by
experience, and thorough going force. It has been
commented that your abilities in general naval
administration and in all phases of organization for battle
are of the highest order and are unsurpassed by any
experienced officer of relative precedence.

4.   Worthy of particular comment is the part you played in the development of the excellent organization publications for destroyer escorts, including the Destroyer Escort Organization Book, Type Damage Control Books, and the Type Engineering Casualty Control Books.

5.   You have contributed materially to the efficiency of the Destroyer-Destroyer Escort Shakedown Group by your performance of duty and this letter of commendation is an expression of regard for work well done in connection with a program of the highest magnitude and importance.

6.   A copy of this letter should be included in the report of fitness currently to be filed by you.

(Signed) D. B. Beary

Having returned to the United States from Brazil, Mom and the two children took up residence in a rented house on Gordon Street in LaGrange, Georgia, while Dad was on sea duty. Because of the uncertainty of the war, the family would be in LaGrange for almost three years, and would not make another move until the war was over. Mom had plenty of help in LaGrange, as this was my dad's home of record and there were many relatives. In October 1943 their third child, Henry Edgar, was born. Many years later my mom told me that they had planned on only having two children, but that my arrival was a pleasant and welcome surprise.

The war made many retail products hard to get and many things were rationed, such as gasoline and milk. Items that contained metals needed for the war effort were also in short supply. Households would receive ration tickets for the controlled items, and when the tickets were gone there would be no more until the next month. Because I was a new-born, Mom received extra ration tickets for gasoline and milk, and other items needed for an infant's care.

Joan remembers living in LaGrange, and tells her story of living there and about the house in which our dad grew up:

> After we had been in Brazil for about two years, Daddy was called to the war in the Pacific. We went home to Georgia, where Daddy's relatives lived, and we rented a home in LaGrange. It was a nice little house on Gordon Street. Beste, my mother's mother, came to live with us there. Beste took good care of us with the help of a big black lady who was our nursemaid. Daddy would show up from time-to-time. I guess he stayed long enough, because my youngest brother, Henry, was born there.
>
> Our house was kind of neat in that it backed up to some undeveloped land – our forest. Every summer we would all traipse back there to pick wild blackberries. The only trouble with blackberry bushes is that they bite. One time when we went out to pick, Beste got into some poison oak. She broke out in great itchy sores, and we soon followed suit. I guess we all got into the same stuff. In the winter we went to the forest and cut down our Christmas tree, which we brought back on my wagon. That was great fun.
>
> My brothers and I arrived three years apart from each other, so I was starting school when Henry was born. Henry had something wrong with him, and he had to go to a hospital in Atlanta for about a month after he was born. I was just short of six years old when Henry was born, and had really been looking forward to his joining the family. I was told that he would be very small, and anticipated that

he would be about the size of my doll-baby. When he finally got home, I was sorely disappointed. Henry was way too big, and Mother wouldn't let me play with him at all.

All of the folks we met in LaGrange seemed to speak in a foreign language when we first arrived from Brazil. They all had a deep southern accent, and I, for one, didn't have a clue what was being said when we first arrived. Not only did they talk funny, but they used words I had never heard before, like "yonder," and "y'all." Eventually I began to learn how to speak "southern" also, and I soon forgot Portuguese.

The best part of living in LaGrange was Grandmother Jarrell, or "Grandmommy" to us. She lived in a wonderful, big house on the other side of town. Her house had large, high-ceilinged rooms, feather beds, and chamberpots for us to use at night so that we wouldn't have to go out in the dark and scary hall to make our way to the one bathroom. She lived in the house with her sister, Anna Mell, who was Aunt Mell to us (except for Lewis, who thought she was Aunt Milk, and called her Aunt Lete in Portuguese when we first got back from Brazil).

Next door to Grandmommy and Aunt Mell lived the King family, and my best friend was Winard King, their oldest child, who was two years older than me. He and I had great and wonderful adventures.

I would go to the Sunday matinee often with my cousin Billy who was just a year older than me. Billy and I were good friends, too. In fact, he and I and Winard would sit under Grandmommy's house, which was raised about three feet above the ground, and tell ghost stories.

Billy's dad, Uncle Bill, owned the LaGrange Hardware Company store, and we used to go in there to get money for the movies. It was a large, barn-like store with ladders which rolled on wheels along the sides of the building so that the items which were stored up high could be retrieved. It really wasn't much of a fun store, just a lot of tools and things. But Uncle Bill was nice, and so was Billy's mom, Aunt Betty.

We lived in LaGrange for about two years; I was about five when we arrived, and almost eight when we left. During my younger days there, Winard and Billy and I would explore the countryside. Grandmommy had a parcel of land behind her house which used to belong to her, but which she had sold. It was her orchard in times gone by, and we could get wild pears and pomegranates when they were in season. We would continue on back through the weeds and brush to the railroad line and walk down to the old cotton mills. Back in that area is where the "colored" folks lived. They had lovely dirt roads that felt wonderful on our bare summertime feet. We'd hang around there until a mother would come out of her house and chase us off. Grandmommy didn't like us to visit there because she said it wasn't safe. I expect the people who weren't safe were the black folks, when we were in their territory. I suppose the Ku Klux Klan was as active in that area as in any other part of the South, and those people would have been blamed had anything happened to us, whether it was their fault or not.

Aunt Mell was much stricter than Grandmommy. She always seemed to have a dour expression on her face. She had been a painter in her younger days, and had painted beautiful ladies in flowing diaphanous robes kneeling by pools or washing their beautiful, long hair. I was totally entranced, and wanted one of those paintings badly. On cold or stormy days we would sit in the front parlor and I would gaze upon Aunt Mell's paintings.

Grandmommy's house was a child's joy. The front porch extended all across the front of the house and had a swing on it so that we could sit and swing and watch the street. Lots of wide stairs led up to the porch, and a double front door opened into a wide hall which extended to the back of the house. But you couldn't see all the way back because there was a mirrored divider separating the front entry area from the back of the hall. On the right side as you went in was Aunt Corinne's room which Mother and Daddy used when we all stayed there. Aunt Corinne had died from some strange thing that we didn't talk about because it upset Grandmommy.

To the left of the entry was the parlor. There was a fireplace, a piano, a sofa and several chairs, a desk of sorts and some lamps that didn't give much light. The room was very crowded, and you had to always be quiet and decorous there. It was okay to play Chinese checkers with Grandmommy there, but there wasn't much more you could do.

Behind the parlor was the bedroom used by Grandmommy and Aunt Mell. It had the other half of the fireplace that was in the parlor, and a large feather bed that both Grandmommy and Aunt Mell slept in. Behind her room was the dining room. This room was always light. There was a passageway from the formal dining room to the kitchen. This part of the house had been added on after the house was built. The kitchen originally was separate from the house. The kitchen was wonderful! Grandmommy had two stoves, one of which was an old wood-burning stove, and the other was a gas stove. In the middle of the room was a third small pot-bellied stove used for heat.

On the other side of the house, behind Aunt Corinne's room, was the room Lewis and I stayed in when we came to visit. Even with the chamberpot under the bed, you would still have to get out of bed and reach on your tiptoes in the dark for the pull chain to the light hanging from the ceiling. Then, in the morning, you would have to empty the chamberpot into the toilet at the rear of the hallway and wash it out – yuk. So, occasionally, when we were feeling exceptionally brave, we would make the long and scary trip to the bathroom at night.

The "rental" was behind our bedroom. It consisted of a large room, a bathroom, and a kitchenette. The lady who rented from Grandmommy would sometimes invite me in for a visit. She would provide tea and cookies and stories. It was fun, and it was interesting to see the part of the house which was "off limits."

As I mentioned before, the one bathroom available to all of us in the house was at the rear of the hall. It often didn't work too well, and the toilet was in trouble much of the time it seemed. A back porch extended across the back of the house behind the bathroom from the area of the passageway to the kitchen across to the rental bathroom.

And that was Grandmommy's house. It stood on a large piece of land, and had several large trees. One was on either side of a wide sandy front entrance walk. We would be asked to use the leaf rake on the front walk to make the pretty designs on the sand, as well as get the leaves off the walk. Grandmommy's house was a wonderful place.

CHAPTER 11
THE SOUTH PACIFIC - WWII

In April 1944 Commander Jarrell's wish to enter the hostilities was granted when he received orders to take command of Destroyer Division 42. DesDiv 42 had been commanded by his friend and classmate, Captain Harold O. "Swede" Larson, and had seen plenty of action in the Pacific. As Division Commander, Jarrell's flagship would be the U.S.S. Fletcher (DD-445), the first of the Fletcher-class destroyers. The Fletcher-class destroyers were considered the most successful design up to World War II. They were fast, long-ranged, and well armed. The Division consisted of four ships: Fletcher (DD-445), Jenkins (DD-447), La Vallette (DD-448), and Radford (DD-446).

Fletcher was based out of Long Beach, California, but the War found her in the South Pacific. During the eight months Jarrell was Division Commander, the ships remained primarily in the vicinity north of New Guinea, with excursions to New Caledonia and Leyte. DesDiv 42 got as far north as Taiwan for action there. In April 1944 Jarrell took command of Fletcher and the Division at Purvis Bay, Solomon Islands, some twenty miles north of Guadalcanal.

U. S. S. Fletcher (DD-445)
(Official U. S. Navy Photograph)

Jarrell kept notes of the action in which he was involved. Once censorship was eased, he would summarize the action and send reports home to Ann.

Censorship regulations have been relaxed. We can now write about operations in which we have taken part provided we wait thirty days after releases to the press have been made.

I left San Francisco, as you know, on 12 March; arrived Pearl Harbor 13th, where I expected to attend CIC (Combat Information Center) School for ten days to two weeks, but Commander, Destroyer Pacific told me to get to my division. I arrived at Purvis Bay, Florida Islands on 27 March, via destroyer, but Swede didn't get in until 1 April. In the meantime, I went out for a few days operations in another destroyer. I relieved Swede as soon as he arrived, and shortly afterward left with three of my ships for Milne Bay, eastern New Guinea, where we fueled. We then steamed to the Cape Sudest area, where I based for the Aitape – Humboldt Bay – Tanahmerah Bay operations, commonly called the Hollandia Operations. We hit the three areas simultaneously.

The Battle of Hollandia (Code name Operation Reckless) in April 1944 encompassed invasions at three locations: Aitape, Humboldt Bay, and Tanahmerah Bay. Aitape is a small town on the north coast, about one hundred miles east of the present border between Indonesian Papua and Papua New Guinea. Humboldt Bay, now known as Yos Sudarso Bay, is about one hundred twenty miles west of Aitape, and Tanahmerah Bay is thirty miles west of Humboldt Bay. In Humboldt Bay was the town of Hollandia, now called Jayapura. All three locations were fortified Japanese garrisons, and were essential to the Japanese for their expansion in the war.

I had command of an escort for Aitape forces and a destroyer gunfire support unit for the landings. My destroyers bombarded Tumleo, Seleo, and Ali islands off Aitape prior to the landings. We had no trouble. When the troops landed there were no live Japs left. Some troops were surf bathing an hour after they landed. Three or four Japs managed to swim to Angel Island, from Seleo, and these were picked off from shoal water by a surface craft. We hung around all day to furnish call fire if requested, and it was requested once for a spot on New Guinea proper, then escorted a large number of miscellaneous empty ships back to Sudest. Later I ran a fast convoy to Humboldt Bay (Hollandia), and returned the empties to

Sudest. Shortly after, I was released and, after escorting LSTs [Landing Ship, Tank] to the Russell Islands, was ordered to Noumea, New Caledonia, where I stayed one week. It is a punk place. I did not like it. However, I suppose it was good for the crew. It is the only settled place that I have visited since Pearl. I saw Halsey and Carney there.

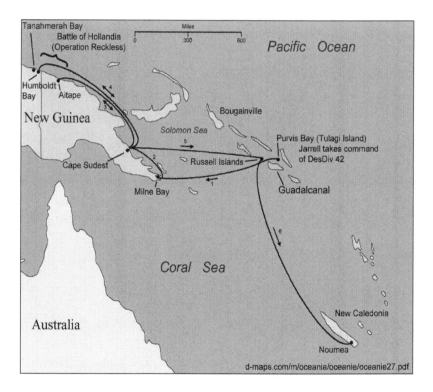

Jarrell's First Operations with Destroyer Division 42

May-June action for Fletcher and DesDiv 42 included anti-submarine operations south of Truk Island, and escort duty for convoys to Noumea, New Caledonia, several hundred miles off the east coast of Australia. Basing out of Noumea, Fletcher saw night action with the Japanese force northwest of Biak on 8-9 June, 1944. Noumea, in World War II, was an important Allied base for Army and Navy forces and, with the massive transport of men and materiel, the Japanese submariners were well aware of the potential for rich targets along the supply routes.

My fourth ship had joined at Sudest. From Noumea I was ordered to take my division to the Treasury Islands, south of Bougainville, where I arrived late in May. En route one of my ships went 300 miles out of its way and rescued a downed aviator. An air-surface search had failed to locate him for two days. He was found 50 miles from where he was reported downed. The ship got a "well done" from Halsey.

I was at Treasury only a short time when I was ordered to take part in a submarine hunter-killer operation between Green Island and Truk. My part was simple; only to screen the carrier. DE's [Destroyer Escorts] did the sinking; England [U.S.S. England (DE-635)] alone got six. Once we thought the Japs were going to hit us with destroyers from Nomoi. We were set, but they didn't show up. I completed these operations early in June. I was recommended for a commendation ribbon for "materially assisting in sinking two, and possibly three, Jap subs." I don't suppose I will get the ribbon, and don't think I rate it.

During June 1944 the Japanese were attempting to reinforce their hold at Biak, a somewhat large island in the Cenderawasih Bay toward the northwest coast of New Guinea. Fletcher and DesDiv 42 patrolled the area in order to prevent the Japanese reinforcing their Biak Island stronghold. In the book, *World War II At Sea – An Encyclopedia Vol. 1*, Edited by Spencer

C. Tucker, (Copyright 2012 by ABC-CLIO, LLC, isbn 978-1-59884-457-3), one of CDR Jarrell's actions is described. U. S. troops had invaded Biak with the intent of defeating the Japanese. It was slow going. The Japanese thought that if they could continue resupplying their garrison on Biak and reinforce the Jap troops there, the Americans might be forced off the island. Six Japanese destroyers -- three towing troop barges -- and two cruisers were observed approaching the area, and the British Commander of Task Force 74/75, Admiral Crutchley, formed his ships into a battle formation to engage the Japanese. The Japanese saw this action, abandoned the troop barges, and turned to run. Commander Jarrell observed the enemy's action and, contrary to Crutchley's order, gave chase with Destroyer Division 42. Admiral Crutchley released the other two Destroyer Divisions to follow DesDiv 42 and they engaged the enemy ships from a distance of 8 miles. Hits on one Japanese destroyer were seen but the ship was not disabled.

> *After our previous operations I went to Manus for fuel, and reported to Kinkaid [Admiral Thomas C. Kinkaid, Commander Allied Naval Forces] for duty; was directed to get to Hollandia expeditiously and we got there one day before they were ready to use us.*
>
> *On the night of 8-9 June we chased five Jap destroyers for a little over three hours. The Japs were trying to reinforce Biak when we intercepted them. We closed from about 23,000 yards to 14,000 yards with Fletcher firing her two bow guns. The Japs spread out and kept us under heavy fire, and I think, fired about 56 torpedoes at us, all to no effect. We damaged the rear Jap. We were directed to retire at 0230, as the Task Force Commander didn't want us to be far into Jap territory at daylight. The TFC [Task Force Commander] did not give orders to chase, when contact was made, and I started out*

with my division, informing him. He apparently thought this was correct, since Kinkaid later made some nice remarks about me.

After our chase of the Japs on the night of 8-9 June, the Japs never again tried to reinforce Biak. We returned to Hollandia for logistics but, believe it or not, we had to go 400 miles to Manus to get fuel and provisions. It was several days before some of the ammunition was available. Yet I am sure that everyone at home thinks that we have absolutely everything that we need. It has been months, right now, since we have had any fresh vegetables. However, we are much better off than the Army.

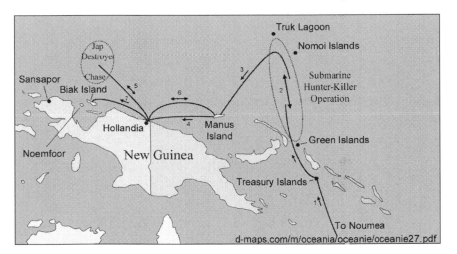

Anti-Submarine Operations and Chase of Jap Destroyers

Dad knew that Ann, and all the families at home, would be in a constant state of worry about their loved ones. To try to alleviate her concerns he always downplayed the danger, while still reporting the events that were transpiring. His comments such as, "We had no trouble," probably meant that there was action but that he was fine. Naval ships in constant battle are always in the line of fire, but mentioning it will just cause worry back home.

> *From Manus I returned to Hollandia and reported to Barbey [Rear Admiral Daniel E. Barbey, Commander, VII Amphibious Force] for duty, and in a few days I took a reinforcement echelon to Biak. Biak was hot at that time, so I was given two additional destroyers. We ran the first big freighters (Liberty Ships) to Biak. We had no trouble. We then brought the empties back to Hollandia and, about the end of June, we took Noemfoor.*

Following the action at Biak Island, Destroyer Division 42 moved west in July-August to support the U.S. invasions of Noemfoor, an island just west of Biak, then Sansapor, on the western coast of New Guinea, and in September, Morotai, an island some 550 miles northwest of Biak. These were all enemy strongholds and U.S. troops had to clear them. In addition to providing shore bombardment to clear the enemy forces, Destroyer Division 42 provided escort patrols for the ships arriving with reserves and materiel.

> *At Noemfoor I had a heavy bombardment schedule, to be accomplished quickly from a position 1,000 yards off the coast. There wasn't much room. The amphibious people said it was the heaviest bombardment that had yet been conducted by Barbey's forces. My area included the Kamiri airdrome. We had no trouble. One of my ships found an unexploded Jap shell on its fantail. We hung around all day and then ran assorted ships back to Hollandia. A week later I was back at Noemfoor with a reinforcement echelon. I was the senior naval officer present and found it necessary to go ashore and clear up some points with the*

army commanding general. I was glad of this chance afterwards, because I saw at first hand the results of our bombardment. I rode the full length of Kamiri airdrome. It was completely devastated. The general was full of praises for the naval gunfire. The army had come ashore and simply walked onto the airfield. Forty-six Jap planes, by official count, were battered to pieces. We had smelled a bad odor while miles off and I asked about it. I was informed that it was not caused by poor army sanitation, but by many bits of Jap bodies that the army had not been able to scrape up. After two days at Noemfoor, furnishing various kinds of support for the army, including anti-aircraft gunfire, we escorted our empty ships back to our base. In all of these runs we had various tangles with Jap aircraft, occasionally being up all night. These trips required anywhere from about six days to two weeks. We were never bothered by subs although we had a few phony contacts and killed a whale or two.

On July 4, 1944, Jarrell wrote Ann and gave an update on his status:

My Darling,

We got back into port this Independence Day, and celebrated it by taking on fuel and ammunition. I may be getting out again shortly, so wanted to get this letter off to my old sweetie. I got two letters from you when I got in, which pleased me very much.

I had had a little touch of grippe [influenza] for about four days when we pasted the Japs this time, but the action cured it. We really cracked the place. The Japs tried to put up some kind of a show, but they were literally smothered. They never had a chance.

Don't think for a minute that my Division is winning all the laurels out here. It is good, one of the best, but our Navy uses team work, without individual stars. I'm keeping my fingers crossed, not that I think I need to. No ship of my Division, and not any ship escorted by it, has yet suffered a scratch since I got out here.

I imagine Henry [Al's brother] would rather have had a destroyer than his new job, in spite of the promotion that went with it. However, he probably has one of the most interesting jobs of the war. He probably will some day be Ambassador or High Commissioner to China.

All my love, darling,

Your devoted,

Al

Jarrell's brother, Henry Thompson Jarrell, had followed him into Annapolis and graduated in the class of 1927, two years after Albert. While stationed in China in 1933-1935, Henry had the opportunity to attend the Chinese Language School and learn to read and write Chinese. Albert had warned him against it, arguing that he would be forever stuck in Chinese assignments and embassy duty. Albert was right. Although Henry served in many billets, he always seemed to revert back to the Chinese arena.

In July we took Cape Sansapor. Jap opposition was so weak that our bombardment was cancelled, although we had some rather delicate ship handling to do in order to get to bombardment positions right off the beaches, in case gunfire support was needed. We escorted empty ships back to the base, and then ran a reinforcement echelon to Cape Sansapor, and empties back to Hollandia.

We usually did our rehearsing at Wakde, where we had a perimeter, but scrapping was always going on. On one occasion shells from land fell near my ships.

Wakde was an island roughly half way between Biak and Hollandia and two miles off the north coast of New Guinea. Although it was only about two square miles in size, it was an important Japanese holding and was taken by the U.S. in a three-day battle in mid-May 1944.

Staff of Commander, Destroyer Division 42, Aboard Fletcher, 1944. Commander Jarrell Top Center

In mid-September 1944 the Battle of Morotai took place. Although U.S. forces secured the island in about two weeks, Japanese holdouts continued to fight until the end of the war in 1945. Morotai was an essential staging area for the battles that would take place in the Philippine Islands.

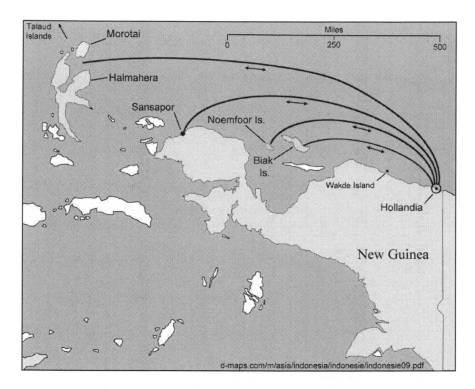

Operations to Biak, Noemfoor, Sansapor, and Morotai from Hollandia

In September we took Morotai. I really studied this area, and knew it before I ever saw it better than I ever knew Hill Street [Jarrell's home]. We had our most difficult bombardment problem here. I had only two destroyers in my bombardment unit. There wasn't room for any more.

There were too many shoal spots and small islands off shore. We had to get to a place 600 yards from the landing beaches and the troops went in behind our fire. It was a sight to see the jungle disintegrate as our shells hit. We fired 1200 rounds of five inch in 15 minutes. Later some call fire was delivered in designated spots.

After our bombardment there, I hung around for a day or so, patrolling either between Morotai and Halmahera or Morotai and the Talaud Islands [150 miles NW of Morotai, now known as Kepulauan Talaud]. During the bombardment two of our friendly cruisers came very close to shooting up my unit, but due to the layout of the area, I had expected this danger and took action to stop the dangerous firing. I escorted an echelon back to Hollandia, then took another convoy to Morotai, where I remained several days. At Morotai Jap planes heckled us nightly. On one occasion they bombed and strafed one of our hospital ships, the Bountiful, which was well and properly lighted, and could be seen for many miles.

Hollandia had become a significant base of operations with ships and troops passing through continuously. To support all the logistics of the war effort, there was a sizeable shore contingent. It was not all work and no play, and the officers and men arranged for leisure activity for when there were a few moments to relax. Sports were always a welcome diversion, and it was not uncommon to see baseball and football games being played – sandlot rules. The officers commandeered an abandoned group of native huts that was built on sticks over the shallow waters off Hollandia and turned it into an officers club. One of Jarrell's shipmates, who was gifted at art, sketched an image of the O-Club and gave it to him.

Officer's Club – Hollandia – October 1944

Sixteen months after leaving his previous post in Brazil, Commander Jarrell received notification through the Bureau of Naval Personnel that the Government of Brazil had bestowed upon him, "Decoration and Diploma of National Order of the Southern Cross (Official)."

The National Order of the Southern Cross is an award given by decree of the President of the Republic, and is the highest award given to foreigners. The award is given "As a token of gratitude and recognition for those who have rendered significant service to the Brazilian nation."

Decoration of the National Order of the Southern Cross
Brazil

The memorandum, dated 18 July, 1944, came at a time when Jarrell was focusing on his role in the war in the Pacific. At about the same time, he received official notice of his being recommended for a commendation for his actions while chasing submarines in June. He wrote home to Ann about these things in a letter dated 21 September, 1944:

My Old Sweetie,

I got a letter from BuPers [Bureau of Naval Personnel] saying that Brazil had sent a medal and diploma, and asking where I wished them sent. I have answered, telling them to send them to you. I certainly don't want them out here.

I received a copy of a letter addressed to Commander-in-Chief, U.S. Pacific Fleet by one of my former Task Group Commanders, recommending that he

(Nimitz) give me a letter of commendation for "contributing immeasurably" to the destruction of two, and possible three, Jap subs. This letter came as a distinct surprise. I don't think that Nimitz will give me the letter. Frankly, I don't think that I deserve it. You can tell Bill [Al's older brother] that other people got all the Jap prayer mats, chopsticks, and other junk that came up from the subs. I still have no souvenirs and probably won't get any. All this happened some time ago. Tell my mother not to try to figure out where I am, and not to ask me.

Your devoted,

Al

Destroyer Division 42 sailed for Manus Island, arriving in early October 1944, to make preparations for the invasion of Leyte. The Division provided screening and escort for the transports during and after the initial invasion of Leyte on 20 October, 1944. It was involved in the initial assault of Leyte, and remained to the next evening when they escorted a convoy out of the area. DesDiv 42 missed the action of the Battle of Leyte Gulf, one of the fiercest battles in naval history, but did engage some Japanese airplanes on the way out. They returned to New Guinea to provide protection for more ships sailing for the Leyte Gulf with reinforcements.

After taking an echelon back to Hollandia, I had very little time to get ready for the Leyte operation. Fletcher needed a little work done on her, and I just made it to Manus in time to take part in the rehearsals for Leyte by my task group. I was screen commander for one of the task groups. My group trained at Manus.

In early November, Fletcher operated for two days with another Division ship in San Pedro Bay, the small bay between Leyte and Samar. In a letter to Ann, Jarrell commented that "I am so far from the forward areas now that I doubt I could get back for over a month. I can't help but feel a little gouty about it, but convoys must be escorted."

My task group had the northern landing, nearest Tacloban. I had a gunfire support unit, stationed in San Pedro Bay near the coast of Samar. San Pedro Bay is at the northern end of the Leyte Gulf. We entered Leyte Gulf at night. The area had been heavily mined, but was pretty well swept and I recall that only one destroyer hit any mines, but that one hit two and was also bombed, but didn't sink. There were so many mines that it was difficult to take care of them all after the sweepers cut them loose. My duties were to knock out any Jap installations found on Samar, and to prevent Jap movements between Samar and Leyte. On Samar, the Japs had beaten it to the hills, and they did not attempt any overwater movements. Their planes came in fairly frequently and I kept my unit at general quarters all day, and at modified general quarters all night. I do not believe that any Jap planes got across from the Samar side. We had a lot of shipping at Leyte and our forces suffered some damage. The plan called for me to leave at dark on "A" Day, escorting a large number of empty LST's. I didn't get away until after dark on "A" plus one.

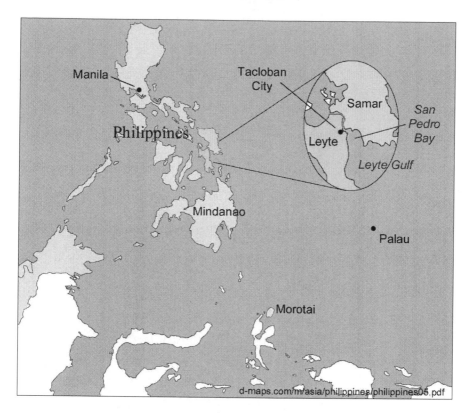

Leyte, Philippine Islands

Leyte was a busy place and we took some punishment. I left the second day after our landings, escorting a convoy of empties back toward Hollandia. Just in case something turned up, I fueled my destroyers en route, from a couple of freighters that were with us. This turned out well, since I got orders to take two of my destroyers to Palau, before I ever reached Hollandia. I was at Palau only about three hours, long enough to fuel, before we left escorting a large group of transports to Guam. At Guam we picked up a division of Army troops, with orders to take them to Noumea. En route I put in at Enewetok for an hour or so, to fuel, arrange for towing planes for practice firing, and to send some messages. Before we got to Noumea we were ordered to turn back and go to Manus.

* * * * *

On 17 November, 1944, CDR Jarrell turned command of Destroyer Division 42 over to his replacement and made his way to Ulithi, Caroline Islands, a major staging and repair area for the Navy during the war. Ulithi is approximately 800 miles due north of New Guinea and the same distance east of the Philippine Island of Mindanao. Here, Jarrell assumed command of Destroyer Squadron 55 on 21 November.

Jarrell was awarded the Legion of Merit with Combat "V" for exceptionally meritorious service as Commander Destroyer Division 42 in the Southwest Pacific Area in support of the Aitape-Humboldt Bay, Biak, Noemfoor, Cape Sansapor, Morotai, and Leyte operations.

Legion of Merit with Combat "V"

On 28 November, 1944, Jarrell wrote Ann about his leaving as Commander, Destroyer Division 42 and taking command of Destroyer Squadron 55. Included in his letter was a note that he was sending along his promotion letter, and asked that she file it with his papers. The promotion letter was not found in his records, but in an article he wrote for the *U. S. Naval Institute Proceedings* in 1960 he mentions that he received his promotion to Captain in "late 1944." ("Lessons Learned from the Hump." *U. S. Naval Institute Proceedings,* Aug. 1960, pp. 79-86.) It is clear that he received his promotion to Captain shortly before taking command of Destroyer Squadron 55.

In his letter to Ann he also talked about reading that three unions were on strike in America at a time when the entire country was galvanized to fight wars in Europe and the Pacific. He told Ann, "In the press news I note that we had three strikes going at the same time. To me, American strikers during war are more disgusting than the Japs."

Command of a Destroyer Squadron is a significant step up in responsibility over a Division. DesDiv 42 had consisted of 4 ships. Destroyer Squadron 55 consisted of two Destroyer Divisions totaling nine ships. DesDiv 109: Porterfield (DD-682), Callaghan (DD-792), Cassin Young (DD-793), Irwin (DD-794), and Preston (DD-795). DesDiv 110: Laws (DD-558), Longshaw (DD-559), Morrison (DD-560), and Prichett (DD-561). All nine ships were Fletcher-class destroyers.

It is interesting to note that at the time Jarrell assumed command of DesRon 55, the oldest ship of the nine was thirteen months old, and the youngest a mere eight months. Within six months, three ships will have been lost and only one, USS Cassin Young, remains today as a museum in Boston, Massachusetts.

DesRon 55 was assigned to the Third Fleet's Task Force 38. TF38 was a major element, with carriers, surface ships and submarines.

Flagship for Captain Jarrell, Commander Destroyer Squadron 55, was U.S.S. Porterfield. On 22 November Porterfield joined up with the other ships of the Squadron and headed for the waters to the east of Luzon, Philippine Islands, where they encountered enemy plane attacks. This tapered off as the Squadron steamed more to the east. Most of December was spent cruising between Ulithi and the Luzon area, with mid-December strikes on Luzon to soften the target for the Mindoro Operation. Mindoro is an island directly south of Luzon and would be a strategic airbase and staging area for the U. S. in the upcoming battle for Luzon. The weather was bad and the seas were high, so little action was seen for the remainder of December. January found the squadron involved in operations in the South China Sea.

At Manus my relief showed up, the day of our
arrival on 15 November. I turned over command on the

seventeenth, spent one night in a Quonset hut, and left on the eighteenth for Ulithi, where I arrived on the twenty first. I took command almost at once because the task force to which Destroyer Squadron 55 was assigned was leaving before daylight the next morning. We went off the east coast of Luzon and made very successful strikes. The Japs came out in considerable force; planes only. We returned to base after a rather short period at sea, and after a few days in port we made the December strikes on Luzon and Formosa [Taiwan]. Jap air power was decreasing, but we suffered considerable storm damage with three destroyers sinking, none of them mine. Late in December, 1944, we sortied again, and were out four weeks, supporting the Lingayen operation with strikes on Luzon, Formosa, the Ryukyus, French Indo-China, and the China coast. These were very successful operations. However, I have never encountered so much bad weather for such long periods of time. It was almost always bad.

When we returned to Ulithi, Halsey and McCain and their respective staffs departed for a rest, and to plan for the future, and Spruance and Mitscher took over. I was dog-tired when I got in, but certainly was delighted to take part in the operations. My ships have been doing very well. The force and the fleet have been having good success.

Under Admiral Chester Nimitz, Commander-in-Chief Pacific Fleet, the command of the naval forces in the Pacific would periodically rotate between Admiral William F. Halsey, Jr., and Admiral Raymond A. Spruance. One Admiral would be with the fleet directing activities, while the other would be at fleet headquarters planning and organizing. Under Halsey the fleet was designated the Third Fleet, and under Spruance it was designated the Fifth Fleet. Within each Fleet was an aircraft carrier Task Force. Under Halsey it was TF 38 commanded by Admiral John S. McCain, Sr, and under Spruance it was TF 58 commanded by Admiral Marc Mitscher.

Part of Nimitz's concept in changing the fleet designations from Third to Fifth and back, and the Task Forces from TF 38 to TF 58, was to add confusion to the enemy. The Third and Fifth Fleets comprised over 500 ships, and Captain Jarrell's DesRon 55 had played a significant role.

With the departure at Ulithi of the Third Fleet commanders in January 1945, designation was changed from Third Fleet to Fifth Fleet., and Task Force 38 became Task Force 58.

By February 25 the Task Force had returned to the Tokyo operating area. Weather was so bad that strikes were called off and the order was given to steam to Nagoya, Japan, for strikes on the 26th. Many Japanese picket boats were encountered on the way. Early on the 27th Porterfield engaged a picket boat, with a battle that resulted in the first combat casualty of Captain Jarrell's command of DesRon 55.

> *Our last operations took us to Tokyo. Task Force 58 went to a point near Tokyo Bay, and made air strikes on the Tokyo area on 16 and 17 February, 1945. The Japs did not touch us during the operations. A few days later, at Iwo Jima, we provided support for the initial beach landings. On two different nights, the Japs tried to get in with aircraft for about three hours each night, but they were not successful.*
>
> *We ran into quite a few Jap picket boats and sank all of them. I can no longer say, however, that the Japs have never laid a hand on my outfit. Nothing serious to the*

ship, but one of our fine young officers was killed, and a few men injured. I have written a letter to the youngster's mother. We destroyed the Jap ship.

On February 27, 1945, Captain Jarrell transferred his command off of Porterfield so that Porterfield could return to Ulithi for repairs. In early March Task Force 58, including DesRon 55, retired to Ulithi. DesRon 55 was detached from duty with Task Force 58 and assigned to an Amphibious Group for the upcoming operations at Okinawa.

Under new orders, the Amphibious Group, with DesRon 55, left Ulithi for Okinawa on March 21, 1945. Captain Jarrell had returned to Porterfield as his Flag Ship.

CHAPTER 12
THE OKINAWA CAMPAIGN

Records of the Okinawa operations by DesRon 55 were kept by Captain Jarrell, but were lost when his ship was hit and sunk by a kamikaze aircraft. All the letters from his wife, Ann, also were lost. While his memory was fresh, the account of the battle was written after the war as an article for publication. Jarrell submitted the article to The Saturday Evening Post on 20 October, 1947, but it was rejected with an explanation that America is weary of war stories. In 1965 he submitted the article to the United States Naval Institute for publication but they, too, chose not to publish it. Following is Captain Albert Jarrell's story of his actions, and Destroyer Squadron 55, during the Okinawa Campaign.

THE OKINAWA CAMPAIGN

Early in March, 1945 I was ordered to report, with my squadron, to the Commander Gunfire and Covering Force, for duty in connection with the forthcoming Okinawa campaign. These orders were received shortly after the return of Task Force 58 to Ulithi, following the first strikes on the Japanese Empire by this force, in support of the Iwo Jima campaign. During these strikes on Japan, my flagship, U.S.S. PORTERFIELD, had been damaged by enemy action and several other ships of the squadron had suffered derangements to their sonar equipment caused by heavy seas. After about ten days at Ulithi, and even though all destroyers present had to take their turn on radar picket stations, which duty slowed repair work, all ships were ready to sortie with the main body.

Destroyer Squadron 55 had been operating with the Fast Carrier Task Forces, Task Forces 38 and 58, since I assumed command in November, 1944. I enjoyed this type of duty, but was pleased with the thought of returning to the amphibious forces; I had served as a destroyer division commander in several amphibious operations in the southwest Pacific. Desron 55 consisted of nine destroyers, PORTERFIELD, CALLAGHAN, CASSIN YOUNG, IRWIN, PRESTON, LAWS, MORRISON, PRICHETT, and LONGSHAW; the first five constituted Desdiv 109 and the last four Desdiv 110. Vice Admiral J. B. Oldendorf had been designated Commander Gunfire and Covering Force but was injured at Ulithi before departure for Okinawa and was relieved by Rear Admiral M. L. Deyo.

Our groups arrived off the southern end of Okinawa the night of 24-25 March. The minesweepers already had been at work one day, principally in the waters of the Kerama Retto, a group of small islands lying about twenty miles west of the southern tip of Okinawa. At daylight the chief staff officer of Commander Underwater Demolition Teams boarded PORTERFIELD for rendering assistance during the day's operations and, with three destroyers and six gunboats, we proceeded to the Kerama Retto. Reconnaissance of all beaches was completed, under cover of continuous gunfire from our ships, without much opposition from the Japs. One of the gunboats suffered one casualty. We had expected considerable opposition from suicide boats, since we knew that several hundred had been stationed in the islands. However, not one single suicider came out, and it was several days before I knew the reason; during the previous night all suicide boat crews had been called to Okinawa for a conference to determine the best tactics to employ against our expected attack. We arrived earlier than expect, and the crews were caught flat-footed on Okinawa, with their unmanned boats in the Kerama Retto. The following day our assault forces captured over three hundred of these boats. Some weeks later I inspected some of them; all that I saw were equipped with engines of United States manufacture.

All operations for the capture of Okinawa were under the Commander Fifth Fleet, Admiral R. A. Spruance. Rear Admiral W. H. P. Blandy was in command of all local operations until the arrival of Vice Admiral R. K. Turner, with the Joint Expeditionary Force, on 1 April. During the night of 25-26 March I was ordered, with three destroyers and six gunboats, to keep the Kerama Retto under constant bombardment, with particular attention being given to the landing beaches. The islands were bombarded from all directions except the east, where sweeping had not been completed. There was no opposition from shore, and very little from the air. At daylight several planes attacked, but were driven off and, in other areas, some were shot down; our assault troops encountered little resistance in establishing beachheads; within one day enemy resistance was crushed to such an extent that we were using the Kerama Retto as a logistics base; a few days later it was also a seaplane base.

Shortly after daylight on 26 March we moved to a position north of Point Zampa Misaki and, with other units, bombarded west-central Okinawa until sunset the following day. We retired, with all units not required for night bombardment, to the westward of Okinawa during the night of 27-28 March. During the first few days of the operation there was little Jap air activity during broad daylight. Light attacks would occur usually at dawn or sunset, with individual hecklers annoying us throughout the night. At 0300 on the 28th, one of these hecklers damaged PORTERFIELD. The retirement group was returning toward Okinawa to resume day bombardment, with the battleships and cruisers in the center of the formation and destroyers in a circular screen, when a single enemy plane was picked up on the radar screen. This plane managed to reach the destroyer screen and, whether by accident or intent, then flew at very low altitude over the circle of screening destroyers; firing on this plane almost certainly would have damaged some of our own ships. The plane narrowly missed several destroyers and then struck PORTERFIELD's air search radar antenna, knocking it clear of the ship; PORTERFIELD was without the services of this radar until she retired for repairs on 22 April. Until she retired, PORTERFIELD usually operated with at least one other ship, which ship would advise her of approaching enemy aircraft.

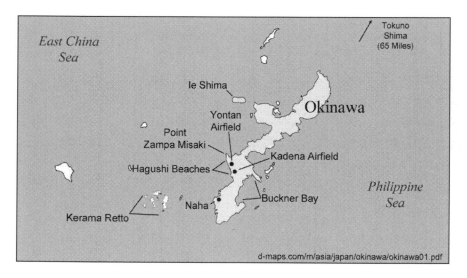

Actions at Okinawa

On the 28th and 29th close support was given to the underwater demolition teams while reconnoitering and clearing the Hagushi beaches on south-western Okinawa. These beaches were about six miles long and had been designated for the main landings; we were a little behind schedule due to the fact that the adjacent waters had been heavily mined. It was essential that this reconnaissance and demolition work be completed without further delay. The minesweeper SKYLARK, operating a few hundred yards from PORTERFIELD, struck two mines almost simultaneously and went down within five minutes. The work was completed, however, without the loss of any swimmers. In my opinion, there was no duty more hazardous than that performed by the underwater demolition teams. The personnel comprising these teams must be splendid swimmers and divers, capable of remaining in the water for hours; they must have excellent memories, and must remain cool when enemy sharpshooters have them under fire; they must know how to use underwater demolition charges. In any amphibious operation, when the work of these men has been completed, we know the exact layout of the landing beaches; we know where we can employ each type of landing craft; we know that all obstacles that can be cleared have been cleared, and we know the exact location of all remaining obstacles. To support the underwater demolition teams, it is necessary to move ships of comparatively light draft, such as gunboats and destroyers, as close in as practicable, and furnish constant gunfire covering all areas near the swimmers. It is very difficult to determine the exact location of enemy gunfire, especially small arms fire against the swimmers, and it is therefore necessary to cover thoroughly all adjacent terrain for a distance inland. The swimmers are carried in small craft to within a few hundred yards of the beaches, where they then take to the water. These small craft furnish support with small arms at very close range. Battleships and cruisers cover the area a considerable distance inland from the beaches. Gunboats and destroyers cover the area closer to the beaches. It is necessary to fire almost flat trajectories, with the shells passing only a few feet over the swimmers. I have seen prematures burst, apparently directly over swimmers, but without affecting in the least the calm performance of these men.

About 30 March PORTERFIELD and several other ships went to the Kerama Retto for ammunition and fuel. As previously mentioned, this logistics base had been established on 27 March; already we had lost two ammunition ships to enemy aircraft. Although the base was very vulnerable, it was essential that a large stock of fuel and ammunition be maintained in the immediate area of operations. In general, the fire support ships were able to carry out their bombardment schedule for several days and nights before finding it necessary to replenish fuel and ammunition. Later on, replenishments of food became necessary, as well as the obtaining of emergency repairs from tenders. Kerama Retto grew into a very large floating base.

We returned to our previous operating area, north of Zampa Misaki, where we were still operating on L-Day, April 1st. Our principal mission, along with other ships operating in the same area, was to sever, by continuous bombardment, communication between northern and southern Okinawa. Our landings began at 0830 and our covering support, both from planes and ships, was extremely heavy. During much of the day I was unable to see the island in the vicinity of the Hagushi beaches because of smoke, dust, and fires. Resistance to the landings was weak and our troops quickly captured Yontan and Kadena airfields and crossed the island, cutting it in half. Strong resistance soon developed in the southern quarter of Okinawa, however. It had been expected that much resistance would be encountered in the north, but this area was cleared in about three weeks.

In amphibious operations, excellent coordination between ships, troops, and planes is essential. We worked with the marines, in west-central Okinawa, the northern area of combat ashore, for several days. On one occasion a detachment of marines was

ambushed in a hilly area, and was in imminent danger of
extinction. We were informed by voice radio exactly where the
marines were located and, by grid coordinates, exactly where the
Japs were threatening. Within a very few minutes after we turned
our fire on the Jap-held grids the situation was reversed; a critical
situation for our forces, with the aid of voice radio, had been
turned into a rout for the Japs.

We maintained almost a continuous conversation with the
spotters and planes assigned to work with us. This was necessary
to insure that all radios were functioning, to keep informed of the
actual location of our troops, and to know the voice of our own
spotters and observers. The Japs were smart; although we changed
frequencies fairly often, the enemy sometimes was able to come in
on an operating circuit. Once a voice speaking perfect English
directed me to furnish heavy gunfire on a certain area into which
we knew, from our spotter, that our troops had just advanced. We
asked the voice to authenticate itself and it shut up like a clam. Our
own spotter, whose voice we recognized, quickly authenticated
himself, stated that our troops had not retired, and that no order had
been given for gunfire. On another occasion I overheard
instructions being given to one of my ships to retire and report to a
certain unit commander, which commander was at that time a
considerable distance away. This Jap didn't get away with his
trickery either. In fact, insofar as I know, no Jap ever was
successful at Okinawa in deceiving anyone with "phony"
instructions over the voice radio.

Working with plane observers was just as effective as
working with ground spotters. Planes were especially adept at
spotting and reporting enemy troop movements, locations of
hidden gun emplacements, blockhouses, caves, and isolated groups
of troops. The number of valuable reports from planes, that I
personally was interested in, was almost countless. No only would

the planes report the location of targets, but they would spot our gunfire until we were hitting.

Some Jap trickery was successful. One of our ships steamed through what was apparently floating driftwood, and was seriously damaged by a mine attached to the driftwood. A group of women swimming out from shore, ostensibly to be rescued, pushed a mine against a destroyer. Several suicide boats, darting out suddenly from hiding, were successful. Many kamikazes, flying low over land where they could not be picked up by radar, and then suddenly coming from nowhere, succeeded in causing us considerable damage; I saw one battleship, one cruiser, and about half a dozen other ships damaged by these tactics. The Jap midget submarines were not successful. During the first two or three weeks of the campaign, we contacted many of these subs; we maintained, at all times, an anti-submarine screen for all ships not equipped with sonar apparatus. Insofar as I know, not one of these subs ever made a successful attack at Okinawa, although they were difficult to locate, due to their small size, and it was almost impossible to determine when one definitely had been sunk; on being sunk, they left little evidence. After about 15 April we made almost no underwater contacts, clearly indicating that this menace had been eliminated; we continued, of course, to take full precautions against this form of attack.

On 3 April, PRICHETT, which had been detailed to operate on a radar picket station, received a bomb hit on her fantail and suffered severe material damage. She was fortunate in having no personnel casualties. The ship withdrew to Ulithi for repairs, returning to Okinawa in May.

The first heavy, well organized Jap air attack on our ships at Okinawa occurred on 6 April; an estimated 400-600 enemy planes participated. Task Force 58, operating in support of the Okinawa invasion, destroyed 248 of these planes. Our picket stations were hit hard but the ships on these stations, with their combat air patrols, destroyed many more enemy aircraft. Only a few kamikazes reached our fire support ships, which had been formed into an anti-aircraft defensive disposition. Late in the afternoon about a dozen suiciders broke through, reached our fire support ships, and scored several hits. Just ahead of PORTERFIELD, the destroyer NEWCOMB was hit by three suiciders, and a fourth was shot down so close aboard [near the side of the vessel] that it also caused considerable damage. Captain Roland Smoot, whose flagship was NEWCOMB, later told me that only one gun still was in action against this fourth kamikaze, and that this gun destroyed the plane a fraction of a second before it would have crashed into the bridge. The destroyer LEUTZE received a kamikaze hit aft. Although we could see many men in the water, mostly from NEWCOMB, we could not commence rescue operations for several minutes, due to the necessity of clearing the air of enemy planes. A ship dead in the water is a "sitting duck."

We picked up about twenty men that had been knocked overboard from NEWCOMB, and other ships recovered more. I was ordered to take command of rescue and salvage operations, and was assigned five destroyers, one tug, and one small minesweeper. However, I was directed to release three of the destroyers as soon as practicable, since the threat of a Jap surface attack from Kyushu waters was imminent, and the services of every available combatant ship were needed in the retirement group. These three destroyers were released about 2100, after all survivors picked up by them had been transferred to other ships, after the services of their medical staffs had been utilized, and after their stocks of plasma had been transferred to other units of the rescue-salvage group.

NEWCOMB was the most heavily damaged ship that I ever have seen. All of her superstructure above her engineering spaces was gone, and one could see directly into her firerooms and enginerooms. Sitting low in the water and having only about a foot of freeboard aft, she resembled a floating, well scooped, half of a watermelon. Her bridge superstructure was fairly intact, and I was delighted when voice radio communications were established and I could talk with Captain Smoot. We placed a portable radio set in PORTERFIELD's radio center, and another in her combat information center; from the latter location we could talk to NEWCOMB, but not receive, and from radio center we could receive but not transmit; no doubt the heavy damage to NEWCOMB had brought about this unusual condition.

NEWCOMB and LEUTZE were taken in tow by the tug and minesweeper, and we proceeded toward Kerama Retto, about thirty miles to the southwest. Before daylight, LEUTZE was able to proceed under her own power. We were fortunate in having a flat sea, but I did not like the bright moonlight. All ships of the group were instructed not to take any enemy aircraft under fire unless attacked; I did not wish to draw attack on us, since any sudden movement of the water, such as would have been created by a bomb near NEWCOMB, almost certainly would have caused that ship to plunge. We were not attacked, although several enemy planes approached to within a few thousand yards, and on two or three occasions I thought that we had been spotted and was on the verge of opening fire when the planes withdrew.

The personnel left aboard NEWCOMB were in need of food and hot coffee, but we did not furnish these items until after dawn, when the movements of men aboard the ship could be better controlled. An accumulation of men on one side of the ship could have caused a dangerous list; in fact, NEWCOMB was so low in the water and so wide open that I did not wish to risk the wash, from a small launch going alongside, causing more flooding. Shortly after daylight, NEWCOMB and LEUTZE were delivered to repair crews at Kerama Retto. It was determined that repairs to NEWCOMB would be uneconomical; repairs to LEUTZE were effective.

The wounded were transferred to transports equipped for handling large numbers of casualties. During our slow trip to Kerama Retto I had visited the wardroom on several occasions to see how these wounded men were fairing. I was impressed greatly by their cheerfulness. Many were badly injured, but wanted cigarettes and coffee. Plasma and drugs were used in large quantities. Two men were severely burned over more than half of their bodies, and had no control over their arms and legs which were continually moving in jerks, but they calmly puffed away at cigarettes held by hospital corpsmen while being treated by other medical personnel. Within a few hours all were resting quietly and, at the time they were transferred, I was told by the medical officer that all probably would recover. I never heard a complaint from any of these wounded.

I can only speculate as to why the Japs did not make a heavy, concentrated air attack on Okinawa earlier than 6 April. I suspect that they deliberately waited for a heavy concentration of auxiliary ships after L-Day; that after this concentration they planned to weaken, by successive heavy air attacks, our Gunfire and Covering Force, then make an all-out attack on our auxiliaries, forcing our weakened Gunfire and Covering Force to restricted maneuvers in order to protect these auxiliaries. This all-out attack probably would have been a joint air-surface attack, the surface force being composed of the formidable battleship, YAMATO, the cruiser YAHAGI, and about fifteen destroyers. The Jap surface force actually had concentrated in Kyushu waters prior to the heavy air attack of 6 April, but was wrecked a few days later by planes of Task Force 58; YAMATO, YAHAGI, and four destroyers were sunk, and only three destroyers escaped undamaged. If this Jap surface force could have reached Okinawa and attacked jointly with heavy air forces, after our forces had been further weakened by air attacks prior to the main attack, the enemy would have had a chance for local success, thus delaying the end of the war. All of our battleships at Okinawa were old and slow, and several had been damaged severely and had withdrawn for repairs. Several of our cruisers had been hit, and many destroyers and smaller ships had been sunk or damaged. Frankly, I didn't believe that the YAMATO force could upset our operations, but this force was a definite threat and the news of its destruction was most gratefully received.

We continued for several days to operate off west-central Okinawa, furnishing fire support for our forces ashore. On 9 April, PORTERFIELD received orders to cease fire support at daylight on the 10th and proceed to the eastern side of Okinawa to furnish anti-aircraft support to our minesweepers which were operating in those waters. In order to arrive east of Okinawa at the time designated, it was necessary for PORTERFIELD to take the route around the northern end of Okinawa. Neither the captain of the ship, Commander Don Wulzen, nor I liked the idea of taking this route, unaccompanied and without air-search radar, but it was necessary. We had already rounded Okinawa and were heading south, at maximum speed, with visibility reduced to about two miles due to haze, when a single Jap plane attacked; he was set afire, and disappeared into the haze, still burning; one of our patrol planes reported that he splashed. Our fire on this plane had just ceased when a kamikaze came out of the haze from north, with definite intent of suiciding. PORTERFIELD's 5 inch guns were still trained to port and, before they could be brought to bear on the plane, the forward port 40 millimeter mount already was firing on the Jap. One of the 40 millimeter shells hit 5 inch gun No. 2, causing a few casualties, and placing the gun out of commission. The Jap was splashed very close aboard to port, his bomb exploding and causing such a thud that I, in the combat information center, thought that we had been hit. This near-miss, I believe, unbalanced PORTERFIELD's port main reduction gear.

After a day or two supporting the minesweepers, we returned to the waters west of Okinawa. On the 12th another heavy Jap air attack was launched. Although the fast carrier and escort carrier planes shot down 151 enemy aircraft and our pickets accounted for many more, a few managed to penetrate to Okinawa. Again, the Gunfire and Covering Force was formed into an anti-aircraft disposition. At about 1700 around fifteen kamikazes attacked this force, simultaneously, from various directions and at different altitudes. It was a well-coordinated attack. Just ahead of PORTERFIELD, a destroyer was hit forward of her bridge; a battleship and cruiser also were damaged.

When observing gunfire from behind, or almost behind our own guns, one can follow with the naked eye the flight of the projectiles. I saw three of PORTERFIELD's 40 millimeters hit three Jap kamikazes. I suspect that the enemy planes were armored. One kamikaze, after being hit forward of the cockpit, turned ninety degrees to the left and appeared to be on the verge of splashing. He regained control, however, and dived for the old battleship TENNESSEE but was splashed about twenty yards short of his mark.

During kamikaze attacks, the gunfire of our ships always caused me more concern than the kamikazes themselves. Many smart suiciders deliberately avoided attacking ships of the screen. If they successfully penetrated the screen they would then head for the battleships and cruisers, in the center, at low altitude, thus placing themselves between the screen and the main body. The heavy ships, on firing at the attacking planes, sometimes hit friendly ships. I have been straddled by our own ships' fire on several occasions; the first time, which happened when operating with the fast carriers, I was about to broadcast a warning over the TBS [Talk Between Ships, a radio link system from ship-to-ship] when I caught myself just in time to avoid this stupidity. A ship must defend herself against suiciders, and if she happens to hit another friendly ship it is just bad luck. No ship in which I have served has suffered any damage of consequence from friendly gunfire, but I have seen many fragments from our ships' shells fall aboard. When a plane attacks your ship, you always feel that your ship has the ability to knock it down. When your own ships fire on you, unintentionally but necessarily, there just isn't anything that you can do except try to get out of the line of fire.

During the air attacks of 12 April CASSIN YOUNG, on a picket station with other ships, suffered a kamikaze hit when the station was attacked by about sixty enemy aircraft. The ship was badly damaged, suffering the loss of her forward fireroom, all radars, and about 65 personnel casualties; excellent work by the damage control parties saved the forward engineroom; she was sent to Ulithi for repairs. This ship, after shooting down a kamikaze early in the Okinawa campaign, had recovered the body of the pilot before the wreckage sank; in the pilot's clothing was a Japanese code book which proved to be of considerable value.

For the next two days we continued to furnish fire support to our forces ashore. On the fifteenth I was designated to command the destroyer-gunboat unit which assisted in covering the reconnaissance of the southern beaches of Ie Shima by our underwater demolition teams. My designation for this duty was made only a few minutes before the operation began, and was caused by defects in the radio equipment in the flagship of the officer originally scheduled to command this unit.

The reconnaissance was successful. No swimmers were lost and none of our ships suffered any casualties. Our troops landed on the following day, under cover of heavy gunfire from supporting ships. During these landings the enemy launched another heavy air attack, both against our forces at Okinawa and against the supporting fast carrier task force. Task force 58 destroyed 210 enemy aircraft and had to cancel ground support in order to defend itself. Ships on our picket stations, together with their combat air patrols, accounted for many more but suffered severe damage themselves. Only a few kamikazes reached our forces at Okinawa; two were shot down by our ships supporting the Ie Shima landings, one of these being credited jointly to PORTERFIELD and another destroyer, and the other to the flagship of the amphibious group commander.

Ie Shima lies about two miles off the northwest coast of Okinawa. It is a small island, about the size of Iwo Jima, but its defenses were not comparable to those of Iwo. The Jap defenders fought desperately, but were subdued after a few days of intensive action. Ernie Pyle, great reporter and friend of the "little man," was killed on Ie Shima on 18 April.

While en route to join the retirement group shortly after sunset on the 17th, PORTERFIELD developed a heavy knock in her port main reduction gear. It was necessary to lock the port shaft, leaving only the starboard main propulsion unit in use. The ship carried out her bombardment missions until the 19th, when she was given permission to anchor near the Hagushi beaches for the purpose of lifting her gear casings for a careful examination. The gear and pinions were badly scored, calling for major repair facilities, which were not available at that time at Okinawa. It was clear that PORTERFIELD would have to retire to Guam or Ulithi, if not to Pearl Harbor, for repairs and therefore on 22 April I moved with my staff to U.S.S. CALLAGHAN, my relief flagship, named for Rear Admiral Daniel J. Callaghan who was killed aboard the cruiser SAN FRANCISCO during the battle of Guadalcanal.

So great was the need for escort ships, due to the heavy damages suffered by destroyer types at Okinawa, that PORTERFIELD was retained in the combat area until about the 24th, at which time a convoy of empties departed for Guam, with PORTERFIELD acting as one of the escorts. On arrival at Guam it was found that a convoy was ready to depart for Okinawa, and PORTERFIELD's services again were utilized as an escort. The ship finally commenced repairs at Ulithi about the middle of May.

I think that it was about the time that I hoisted my pennant in CALLAGHAN that the night retirement group was abolished. ["Hoisting my pennant" is a reference to establishing command in a location. Flags and pennants are never flown on ships in any combat area.] Due to damages sustained by fire support ships, almost all of these ships available were required for night bombardment until about the middle of May, after which time about three-fourths were required. CALLAGHAN, at this stage of the Okinawa campaign, was a fire support ship; later, she became a picket ship.

Night fire support naturally is more complicated than day fire support. During daylight the firing ship frequently has the support of plane observers; shore spotters are more accurate; piloting is easier. At night, piloting is done principally by radar. At Okinawa, night fire was interrupted, by Jap snoopers, far more frequently than day firing. Fire support, by destroyers, is furnished by the main battery, the five inch guns. These guns also are the ships' major anti-aircraft weapon, although the forties and twenties are very effective at close ranges.

We had excellent early warning of approaching enemy aircraft, furnished by the picket stations which ringed Okinawa. These stations were manned by destroyer types and LCS's [Landing Craft, Support]. We plotted the tracks of approaching enemy planes, in CIC (combat information center), from picket reports until we could pick up the planes on our own radar, after which the plotting was done from our own ranges and bearings. We would continue our fire support until it appeared, from our plot, that an enemy plane definitely had us spotted, was within 15,000 yards range, and was approaching to attack, at which time we would cease fire support, train our guns on the plane, and prepare to repel the air attack. Usually, when we ceased bombardment, the plane had difficulty in pressing his attack since, at night, the Japs were guided principally by our gun flashes.

Many enemy pilots remained in the area as long as their gasoline supply would permit. They hoped to interfere with our fire support or cause us, by continuing our required bombardment, to present an easy target to the attacker. On many occasions we shifted our guns between shore and plane several times within a few minutes. Our forces ashore received every support possible. On only one occasion was I concerned seriously with the problem of rendering effective fire support and at the same time protecting ourselves from enemy air attack. On this occasion a detachment of our troops, with which we were working, was being counterattacked at night by a strong Jap force. The need for our gunfire on groups of the Japs was urgent; the need for our star shell illumination behind the enemy lines was even more urgent. During this brief period of time several Jap snoopers were heckling us. One got into a position directly overhead where we lost him on our radar, and we never picked him up again until he plunged into the water a few feet astern of CALLAGHAN, causing no damage.

Enemy aircraft usually met with little success at night. One kamikaze, unable to locate a combatant target, expended his life on our hospital ship COMFORT. Our hospital ships always were brilliantly illuminated at night in order to make their identity unmistakable. The successful attack on COMFORT recalled to my mind another successful attack on one of our hospital ships, BOUNTIFUL, which was strafed at Morotai while brilliantly illuminated and easily identifiable.

The fast carrier task force was attacked in strength by suiciders on 29 April, but the forces at Okinawa were not heavily attacked again until 4 May. Sporadic daylight raids in small numbers and the ever-present night hecklers had caused our damages to mount, however, but the enemy himself had suffered severe plane losses. The heavy suicide attack of 4 May fully was the equal of the attacks of the 6th, 12th, and 16th of April. An estimated 400 to 600 enemy planes participated. Planes from Task Force 58 shot down 98 Japs over Okinawa. Ships on our picket stations with their combat air patrols almost eliminated the remaining attackers, but we suffered heavy losses; about 12 ships were sunk or damaged. MORRISON, on a picket station, was hit by four kamikazes while the station was under attack by some sixty planes, and sank with heavy loss of life. This was the first ship of my squadron to be sunk. MORRISON, jointly with STOCKTON, another destroyer, had sunk the large Japanese submarine I-8 off Okinawa on 30 March; they forced the sub to the surface with depth charges, then sank it with gunfire, and picked up several Jap prisoners as proof of the sinking.

The last heavy enemy air raid on Okinawa occurred on 11 May. It was not the equal of previous raids and very few kamikazes reached the ships at Okinawa. Enemy aircraft, however, appeared in the area more frequently, singly or in groups of small numbers. It was clear that the heavy tolls exacted on the Japs by our forces had caused the enemy to change his tactics. He no longer could risk the loss of hundreds of planes in single raids, even though these raids caused heavy damages to our ships.

This change of tactics on the part of the Japs made effective fire support more difficult. So long as raids were heavy and clearly indicated, we could form our ships to meet them with maximum effectiveness; fire support lapsed only during the time of the raids. When the raids became frequent, even though light, we often had to shift our guns from shore to plane; we could not afford the necessary time from bombardment to concentrate our ships. Although daylight heckling annoyed us, night raids interfered far more with our duties. One night in May, CALLAGHAN's CIC crew recorded over eighty raids, while the following night over sixty were listed. Personnel became strained, but I can recall only one case of suicide and one case of combat fatigue in my squadron.

During bombardment, except when heavy fire was required, only two 5-inch guns were manned; usually these two guns alternated in providing fire support. I had little difficulty in sleeping, even with No. 2 gun firing almost directly above my quarters. Crews and guns were rotated every four hours. On the approach of enemy aircraft, the ship went to general quarters, manning all battle stations.

It became evident in April that the campaign would be prolonged and that some diversion was essential. We showed movies for the off-watch crews in a compartment below decks during the afternoons, and for the officers in the wardroom in the evenings. Movies did not interfere with our bombardment schedule, but the programs frequently were interrupted by enemy aircraft and the necessity of going to general quarters. Except for letters from home, movies were the greatest morale booster; ice cream ranked third.

As our forces ashore advanced south, much fire support had to be furnished from ships in very restricted waters. When the waters were so restricted that maneuvering was impossible, we anchored and were furnished a smoke screen from smoke boats. On certain nights scores of ships were required to anchor in the same vicinity, requiring a very large area to be covered with smoke. Particularly skillful suicide pilots, knowing that the concentration of ships was covered by the smoke, sometimes flew in circles at very low altitude within the smoke screen, hoping to crash into a ship. Concentrations of cargo ships and transports, off the Hagushi beaches and in Buckner Bay, were particularly susceptible to this form of attack which, however, was never successful. Some of the suiciders strafed as they flew. One man on the fantail of CALLAGHAN was killed by strafing. Once a kamikaze got inside a smoke screen, he was safe from our gunfire for we could not risk firing into our own ships.

On 18 May LONGSHAW was sunk about one mile west of Naha, the capital of Okinawa. The ship had been furnishing fire support to our troops in that area. She was sunk by an enemy mobile shore battery. I did not know about this sinking until later, since I was in CALLAGHAN at Kerama Retto when it occurred.

There was considerable fog in May and the kamikazes took advantage of it. They would fly from the empire to northern Okinawa, then fly low overland to southern Okinawa, where the majority of our ships were located. We always knew, from picket reports, that enemy planes had reached Okinawa, but we seldom contacted them until they darted out from shore to attack. One of these foggy days, with visibility about 2000 yards, CALLAGHAN was furnishing fire support in very restricted waters near the southern end of Buckner Bay. We knew that enemy planes were in the area. CALLAGHAN was under way but unable to maneuver freely. The ship was at general quarters, with guns trained toward land, the direction of greatest danger of attack. Suddenly two Betties (medium bomber-torpedo planes) stood out from land and headed for CALLAGHAN. They came in strafing and intending to suicide. CALLAGHAN's forties and twenties riddled both of these planes, causing them to deviate slightly from a straight course. One passed over the forecastle, burning, and splashing just short of the range of visibility. The other apparently was going to score a hit when it suddenly swerved upward a few feet and passed over CALLAGHAN amidships, causing no damage except severing the radio antennae. This plane must have lost control just before it would have crashed. It appeared to be disintegrating as it passed overhead. It splashed close aboard CALLAGHAN.

The fuselage and some of the wing structure of this plane held together, and did not sink all at once. We soon saw two Japs, their bodies in the water, apparently hanging on to the wreckage. We approached the plane and saw that one Jap was holding on to the wreckage desperately with one hand, and with the other hand was holding an apparently unconscious Jap above water. Not trusting Japs, which is natural, but desiring anything that might be of intelligence value, a few machine gun shots were fired in the water near the men before picking them up.

The unconscious Jap was a lieutenant, junior grade, and probably had been the plane's pilot. He was badly injured and, although our medical officer performed an operation immediately and worked tirelessly to save him, died about ten hours later. The other Jap was not injured. He was an enlisted man. He spoke some English, and talked a great deal. He kept asking, "Why don't you kill me?" When asked, "Why did you try so desperately to be saved if you want to die?" he shut up. Insofar as I know, this was the only would-be suicider ever captured alive and in a healthy condition.

This uninjured Jap, named Hitaka, quickly was nicknamed "Joe." He was given cigarettes, candy, and coffee. I never personally talked to "Joe" or had anything at all to do with him. I didn't want him to think that he was important enough to attract my attention. As Hitaka was brought aboard, I stood on deck near him, smoking a cigar and trying to show no interest. I wanted to give him the impression that the shooting down of his plane was nothing more than a trifling incident in our humdrum lives. I can't explain why I did this, but at the time it gave me some amusement. I learned during the war that most Americans are far more sympathetic toward persons in distress, including enemies, than I ever before had realized. This is both a good and bad characteristic.

Hitaka was kept under guard until we could turn him in to the interrogation unit. He had nothing of value on his clothing. The officer's clothing was loaded down with papers, pictures, and trinkets. A few items were of some intelligence value. There was one photograph showing him with an old couple, probably his parents, and another showing him with a young Japanese woman who may have been his wife. I remember that, at the time, I had a feeling that I would like to return these pictures to the officer's family after the war, with a note concerning his death. This feeling soon disappeared. The kamikazes were tough.

PRICHETT and CASSIN YOUNG, after completing repairs, returned to duty at Okinawa in May. On 28 May Fleet Admiral Halsey relieved Admiral Spruance as fleet commander, the Fifth Fleet thus changing its name to Third Fleet. On the same date, Vice Admiral McCain relieved Vice Admiral Mitscher as commander of the fast carrier task forces, TF58 becoming TF38. Admiral Spruance's flagship, NEW MEXICO, had received a kamikaze hit at Okinawa, and the admiral had been forced to shift his flag.

Commencing early in June fire support from battleships and cruisers generally was not required, due to the fact that our troops had moved so far south that destroyers were able to handle the requirements; areas requiring bombardments had become restricted; destroyers could enter shallower and more confined waters than the heavier ships. We could no longer fire star shells from the south, due to the fact that, after releasing their flares, the empty shells would fall into our own lines. Star shells now had to be fired from behind our troops, from the northward.

On 18 June, just three days before the end of organized resistance, Lieutenant General Simon Bolivar Buckner, U.S.A., Commanding General of the Tenth Army and the Ryukyus Forces, was killed. Major General Roy S. Geiger, U.S.M.C., assumed command of the ground forces until he was relieved by General Joseph W. Stillwell, U.S.A., on 23 June.

The declaration of the end of organized resistance on 21 June did not mean that all enemy resistance on Okinawa had ceased. Isolated enemy pockets had to be mopped up. It did mean, however, that no more fire support from our ships was required. I was glad of this, because CALLAGHAN, PRESTON, LAWS, and IRWIN, the only ships of my squadron that had gone through the campaign unsunk and undamaged, all had fired more rounds than their guns supposedly were able to stand. LAWS, in fact, had fired almost double the number of rounds allowed before regunning [replacing the barrel] becomes necessary. It had not, however, been practicable to release the ships for regunning.

Even though organized resistance had ended, there still was great demand for destroyer services. The Japs continued with their sporadic air raids, and some pickets were required. However, some time was available for upkeep. CALLAGHAN moored alongside the destroyer tender HAMUL, commanded by my classmate, Captain Carleton Hoffner. The ship's computer had been damaged in a recent typhoon, and her guns had excessive lost motion. Engineering work was required, but only one main engine could be disabled at a time, since kamikaze attacks on ships in the Kerama Retto occurred frequently, and all ships had to be able to get underway at any time. CALLAGHAN's upkeep period lasted about two weeks, and her code name, "Sitting Bull," was said by many to be very appropriate. Her material condition was improved, but some lost motion in her computer could not be removed.

Following the upkeep period I was assigned to command a picket unit, and was stationed about forty miles southwest of Kerama Retto. The unit consisted of three destroyers and three, sometimes four, LCS's. We were required to report flights of enemy aircraft from Formosa [Taiwan] toward Okinawa and, when possible, to intercept the aircraft. A tour on picket station lasted about four days, after which we would return to Kerama Retto for fuel and relaxation. Small liberty parties were now permitted ashore on one of the islands for a few hours in the afternoon.

The first few tours of picket duty were uneventful. During daylight, and when there were no enemy planes in the area, we fired gunnery practices to keep ourselves in shape. I was agreeably surprised to find that my own ships, in spite of many rounds fired, still had good salvo patterns. Occasionally, I had a new destroyer, not in my squadron, attached to my unit, and I checked the dispersion of the guns of my ships with that of the new destroyers. My ships had more dispersion, but not a great deal more. Since the main threat was from the air, I felt that this dispersion was an advantage.

During one rest period in July, while anchored off the Hagushi beaches, I made a tour in a Jeep of southern Okinawa. The entire area was a desert. The city of Naha, normally containing a population of 60,000, was a mass of rubble. Not a building was left intact. In fact, during this trip I did not see a single structure, not even a hut, that had not been damaged.

I previously had visited occupied areas in other combat zones of the central and southwest Pacific. Conditions always were about the same, except that rain caused a foot of mud and drouth [dry weather] a foot of dust. I don't think I would make a good soldier, after having become accustomed to fresh water showers, hot food, and an absence of dirt and vermin. During war, ships in combat areas usually are fairly free of contagious diseases. Late in the Okinawa campaign, however, IRWIN had a serious outbreak of influenza.

Early on 28 July I was ordered to proceed with CALLAGHAN, CASSIN YOUNG, PRICHETT, and three LCS's to the same picket station previously occupied. We arrived on station during the forenoon and relieved the unit that had been patrolling this station. Incidentally, this was the last picket station manned in the Okinawa area, all of the others having been abolished.

I had received several decorations to be awarded to some of CALLAGHAN's officers and men and, the weather being good, personnel off watch were assembled on the forecastle during a quiet period of the afternoon for the presentation ceremony. The presentation of awards always was one of my most pleasant duties. I always talked for a few minutes to the men assembled, before presenting the awards, and I always stressed the point that awards to individuals not only reflected credit on the persons receiving the decorations, but also on their ship and their shipmates. Very rarely do men, officers almost never, earn special recognition without the aid of some or all of their shipmates. On this occasion I reviewed CALLAGHAN's performance at Okinawa; the ship had been able to serve throughout the campaign, without a break, because she had suffered no damage; she had suffered no damage because of the skill and eternal vigilance of her officers and men.

I informed the personnel assembled that CALLAGHAN was due, within the next few days, for and extended major overhaul in the United States, and that I hoped that everyone aboard would enjoy the well-earned rest that was forthcoming, and that I knew that each man would return refreshed and ready to play his usual effective part against the enemy. CALLAGHAN, along with five other ships of my squadron, had served continuously in the central Pacific for eighteen months. It was the Navy Department's policy to order ships home after this period of time. LONGSHAW would have been eligible for orders home, had she survived. MORRISON, had she not sunk, and IRWIN would not have been eligible since these two ships had received major battle damage repairs in the States, following the action on 24 October, 1944, in which the light carrier PRINCETON was sunk.

Early in the evening of the 28th I received a despatch from the commander of the light forces at Okinawa advising that Comdesdiv 110, Captain Walter Price, would relieve me and LAWS would relieve CALLAGHAN, and that CALLAGHAN would return to Okinawa that same night for logistics before proceeding home for overhaul. This news was received with great pleasure by the crew.

About thirty minutes after midnight I was called by CIC and informed that we had a radar contact. I pulled on my slippers and went into CIC, just across the passageway from my quarters, to investigate. The contact was blurred, moving very slowly and erratically, and we thought that it might be a rain squall. It was picked up at a range of only nine miles. All ships were ordered to general quarters. The contact slowly closed on CALLAGHAN, zigzagging, and at about six miles range appeared distinctly on both the air and surface screens, indicating clearly that it was a plane, or several planes in close formation, flying at low altitude.

We were steaming on course north, speed eleven knots. The contact approached from the southwest, from Formosa. The moon had been up for an hour and a half, the night was clear, and I knew that we were well silhouetted in case we were sighted. I had stationed the LCS's on my starboard beam, as I wished to have freedom of gunfire for the destroyers in case of an attack from Formosa. The destroyers were in a wedge formation, CALLAGHAN leading, CASSIN YOUNG on the starboard quarter, and PRICHETT on the port quarter, insuring that at least two destroyers could fire simultaneously at any time.

At about 8000 yards I ordered all ships with a clear range to commence firing. I held my course and speed until the range had closed to 2000 yards, at which time I ordered a reversal of course to starboard, speed 25 knots. Torpedo planes usually launch their torpedoes at about 2000 yards from their target, and this range is fairly close to the range at which a kamikaze launches his final death dive. I wanted to give the enemy a good target, provide uninterrupted gunfire for our ships and, in case we were unable to shoot him down, attempt to defeat his attack by late maneuvers. As we turned, the enemy was thwarted temporarily, but did not splash. As we approached 180 degrees I ordered by TBS, "Keep turning," hoping to get the enemy silhouetted against the moon and permit the use of our forties and twenties. At 0042, as we were passing 220 degrees I felt a thud aft. I did not know whether it was a hit or near miss, so I inquired of the bridge and was informed that we had been hit aft by a kamikaze.

At 0045 a heavy explosion shook the ship. I knew that one of the after magazines had blown up. CALLAGHAN listed so rapidly to starboard that I thought she was going to capsize, but at about 15 degrees list she steadied. Over TBS I told Commander

"Red" Ailes, captain of CASSIN YOUNG and next senior officer of the unit, to take command. Strangely enough, CALLAGHAN's TBS continued to function for a brief period, but only in certain directions. CASSIN YOUNG could not hear me, but PRICHETT received the message and relayed it, and I heard CASSIN YOUNG acknowledge.

CALLAGHAN's captain, Commander Charlie Bertholf, called over the phone and told me that his ship was heavily damaged, with her stern submerged, and that he thought that we should start immediately to evacuate the wounded. Two of the LCS's were instructed, by blinker gun, to come alongside, one to starboard and the other to port. LCS's are equipped excellently for fire fighting.

CIC was by this time completely inoperative, so I directed the personnel to leave their stations, go outside to the weather deck, and report to the executive officer. I crossed to my room, put on my shoes, helmet, and life jacket, and secured my knife to my belt. I always slept, at Okinawa, with my clothes on, but anyone who went through this long campaign knows that it was impossible to obtain much rest while wearing full equipment. I always checked contact reports before taking time to put on any additional gear.

I left my quarters and took a last look around the wardroom country before going out on deck. I found Lee Jenkins Wallace, of Canton, Ohio, my steward's mate, sitting calmly in the pantry. He had not left his station when others nearby had been ordered to leave. Wallace's duties at general quarters required the furnishing of hot coffee and sandwiches during long periods at battle stations. These duties were important. Wallace thought that he might be able to assist me during this emergency and he was waiting for my personal orders. Two or three days later I asked Wallace why he had not gone on deck with the others, and he said, "I was waiting for you to tell me what to do. Besides, when my number is up, I can't do anything about it."

I dreaded going on deck. I did not know what to expect. However, when I got outside I found that the wounded already were being assembled on both sides, ready for transfer to the LCS's, which had not yet come alongside. There was no confusion whatever. I have never been more impressed in my life than I was the moment I stepped on deck, expecting anything, finding complete order.

The plane had hit over the after engine room, just forward of No. 3 five inch gun. The bomb, or bombs, carried by the plane had exploded and no doubt hot fragments had penetrated No. 3 magazine. The damage control parties arrived promptly at the scene of the crash and were fighting fires when the magazine exploded. These parties were wiped out by the explosion. All personnel in the after engine room, the magazine, and the handling rooms were killed.

I went up to the bridge to talk to Charlie. We agreed that the ship probably could be saved, provided that the area could be cleared of enemy planes, so that one of the destroyers could be free to attach mooring lines aft to CALLAGHAN's stern, until salvage tugs could arrive. We also agreed that it was best to get everyone off the ship except for two or three officers and about a dozen men, who would assist in salvage work.

The LCS's were now alongside, and by 0130 all living personnel, excepting the salvage crew, had been removed. Spread of damage appeared to be under control, due to the efforts of the LCS's. Fires were out, smoke was diminishing, and I could see the extent of damage, but could not get aft of the after fireroom area because of complete wreckage. The starboard side amidships and as far aft as I could see was blown out. The main deck was under water as far forward as the forward depth charge throwers, about one quarter of the ship's length. There was no superstructure from the after fireroom to No. 4 gun.

At about 0200 the ammunition in several of the machine gun magazines began going off, creating an immediately dangerous situation. CALLAGHAN could not take much additional damage and remain afloat. I released the LCS to starboard. The captain of the LCS to port asked to be released; it was a reasonable request; I was informed later that these minor explosions caused one casualty in his ship. I told Charlie, "Let's get the rest off," and personally told my chief staff officer to leave; he was the last of my staff aboard. We abandoned ship, and cast clear of CALLAGHAN.

Almost immediately after we cast off I noticed that some of our night fighters from Okinawa had arrived in the area. One of these fighters flew over us for a while, firing his machine guns. I never found out why he was firing.

I manned the voice radio and found out that Walter Price in LAWS had arrived. Walter wanted to start salvaging CALLAGHAN and asked that CALLAGHAN's damage control parties be sent back aboard; he did not yet realize the extent of CALLAGHAN's damage or personnel casualties. I told Walter that a few officers and men could go aboard, but first I wanted a report from him that the area was clear of enemy planes.

I went out on deck to observe the operations. A few survivors in the water were picked up. At 0220 CALLAGHAN suddenly stood on end. She steadied, her bow pointed straight upwards, with half her length out of the water, for about five seconds. She then sank rapidly. Before she disappeared, she was rent by an extremely sharp and violent explosion.

I went aboard PRICHETT, with all the other survivors in the LCS, shortly after CALLAGHAN sank. All ships searched the area for survivors until after daylight, after which PRICHETT and CASSIN YOUNG headed for the anchorage off Hagushi. Walter Price, with a completely fresh picket unit, continued the search until certain that no survivors were left in the water.

Aboard PRICHETT, commanded by Lieutenant Commander Charles Miller, I learned what had happened while I was without radio communications. After CALLAGHAN's magazine blew up, Ailes had directed PRICHETT to furnish close support to CALLAGHAN, while recovering survivors from the water. PRICHETT did a good job, both with her guns and her smoke. If CALLAGHAN had been hit by a second Kamikaze she would have sunk rapidly, with heavy loss of life. While covering CALLAGHAN, PRICHETT herself had been hit, at about 0130, by a suicider. The third LCS, the one that was not called alongside CALLAGHAN, had been directed to assist in covering CALLAGHAN while rescuing survivors. Both PRICHETT and this LCS recovered several survivors that had been blown overboard.

Ailes, with CASSIN YOUNG, had furnished more distant support, with excellent results. On contacting an approaching enemy plane CASSIN YOUNG had headed at full speed in the direction of the contact, to intercept with gunfire. Using these tactics, CASSIN YOUNG had shot down two enemy aircraft.

While en route to Hagushi, I inspected PRICHETT's damage. She had been hit on the port side, just abreast No. 3 five inch gun. Material damage was light, but several personnel casualties had been sustained. A 20 m.m. mount had been wrecked, and its crew wiped out. The Kamikaze had been under fire by PRICHETT and almost splashed clear of the ship. The starboard wing structure and a small part of the fuselage had struck the ship, the remainder of the plane falling clear, and its bomb exploding in the water and causing no damage except a dented hull.

The name plate data and wreckage indicated that the plane had been a flimsy Jap trainer, single engined, constructed largely of light wood. It had maneuvered radically and had been hard to hit. I feel sure the same type of plane hit CALLAGHAN.

At Hagushi all survivors were transferred to CRESCENT CITY, a transport equipped for handling casualties. Every survivor of a sinking, whether wounded or not, is required to take a physical examination. CALLAGHAN's complement had been approximately 22 officers and 305 men. She suffered 51 killed and about 100 wounded. Aboard a destroyer, everyone knows every person on board. Many of my personal friends were lost. The only officer killed, young and capable Lieutenant (jg) Gilbert Paine, was last seen as reported by several survivors, with his clothes on fire dragging an unconscious man clear of the wreckage.

The night after CALLAGHAN was sunk, CASSIN YOUNG was assigned anti-aircraft patrol duties east of Buckner Bay, and was hit, over the forward fireroom, by a kamikaze. I did not know of this until about daylight of the 30th, several hours after the action. I went aboard and found the damage to be heavy; the forward fireroom and all radars were out of commission, and there was much structural damage. There were about 65 killed or wounded. Lieutenant Commander Alfred Wallace, who had been aboard only a few days, was among those killed. He was slated to relieve Ailes of command, after a week of observation on board. "Red" thought that he had been attacked by two Kamikazes simultaneously, with one deliberately drawing the ship's gunfire while the other attacked, without being fired on.

I remained in PRICHETT two or three days before shifting to PRESTON. I interviewed all of my staff and was delighted to find that my chief staff officer, radar officer, chief signalman, chief yeoman, and steward's mate were in good condition and did not wish to leave. After a sinking, all survivors are entitled to thirty days leave in the States.

Shortly after hoisting my pennant in PRESTON, I had an attack of flu, which I think I contacted after going aboard IRWIN to check up on the epidemic of this disease which had broken out in that ship. I had been confined to my bunk for only a few hours when I received orders to take command of a unit of various types of auxiliaries and ride out an approaching typhoon. These orders broke my illness; within six hours after getting the unit clear of port I was well.

The convoy was hard to handle. One ship, with diesel engines, reported that her engines were continually tripping out at the slow convoy speed of six knots. Another ship reported that she could not maintain station, in the rough seas, at this speed, and requested a reduction of speed. The problem was solved by leaving the area assigned and keeping the wind about a point on the bow, thus reducing the heavy rolling. My escort consisted largely of small mine sweepers, and these ships also had their troubles. We skirted the left or safe semicircle of the typhoon until we were almost half way to the Philippines, and then, several days later, to the rear of the storm, returned to Okinawa. In riding out a storm, freedom of action to meet local conditions always is authorized, regardless of general orders received from higher authority.

This was the second typhoon that we had ridden out in the area of Okinawa. The Japs knew that we were more vulnerable during rough weather, largely because storms affected the operation of our radars, and on both occasions the enemy launched suicide attacks against our forces. The enemy planes could locate Okinawa, even during a typhoon, but they found it difficult to find our ships, due to very low visibility. However, during both of these typhoons, the enemy scored some hits.

The Japs no doubt guessed that our next step, following Okinawa, would be the invasion of the empire, and they desired to postpone as long as possible this invasion by hitting our forces at Okinawa. Had an invasion been necessary, Okinawa would have been one of our major bases.

I was impressed by the enemy's futile efforts. Recently, he had been using every type of plane available. He never attacked in large numbers. He appeared to be on his last legs, and I felt that an invasion of the empire would not be as difficult a task as the conquest of Okinawa. I hoped that Japan would either accept the invasion or quit before Russia entered the war.

I regretted Russia's entry, which had no effect on the outcome of our war with Japan. It merely complicated the post-war problems of the Far East. I believe that Japan deliberately waited for this new enemy before capitulating, with the hope that allied difficulties would, at some time in the future, improve Japan's position.

CASSIN YOUNG, after receiving emergency repairs, departed on one engine for the United States on 8 August; PRICHETT departed on 13 August. Of my squadron, only PRESTON, IRWIN, and LAWS remained at Okinawa.

Heckling by enemy aircraft, particularly at night, continued. On the night of 11 August, a cargo ship was hit, and the following night the old battleship PENNSYLVANIA received a torpedo aft. Commencing the 13th, I was assigned several destroyers and ordered to furnish night anti-aircraft protection to the ships anchored in Buckner Bay. We patrolled eastward, clear of shoal water.

Our own planes usually were in the area, and enemy planes came in so low that it was difficult to distinguish them from friendly planes until they were close aboard. During the night of the thirteenth a plane was picked up, a few feet above the water, close aboard and headed for Buckner Bay. Not knowing if he was friend or enemy, PRESTON tried to make him show his hand by firing a white phosphorous shell ahead of him. A friend would have turned away, but this plane continued on his course, and PRESTON opened up. He was not shot down, but may have become confused, and crashed into the mast of a floating drydock. These shots fired by PRESTON, Commander G. S. Patrick commanding, I believe were the last fired by our ships at Okinawa during the war.

Even though Japan capitulated on 15 August, (east longitude date), a few kamikazes visited Okinawa after this date. Two of these crashed harmlessly into a small outlying island, apparently mistaking it for a ship.

Following the end of recognized hostilities, I was assigned to "birddog" duties; a pair of destroyers was placed at 100 mile intervals, from Okinawa to Tokyo Bay, to act as guides and rescue ships for our planes flying to Tokyo. Few of our planes took the "bird-dog" route, most of them electing to fly over the Ryukyu Islands chain.

One of our planes, with only a pilot aboard, had a forced landing on Tokuno Shima, a garrisoned island which had not been occupied by our troops. With two destroyers I approached the island, prepared to encounter resistance, but found none. The airfield where the plane had landed was surrounded by thousands of Japs, filled with curiosity. They did not molest us while we sent a launch ashore to pick up the pilot.

IRWIN was the only ship of my squadron to be ordered to Japan. Once the war was over, I had a strong desire to return home, and I was glad that I had no part in surrender ceremonies or occupational duties. On 8 September PRESTON was ordered home, and arrived at San Pedro on the 24th. LAWS arrived a few days later.

The war was over. The country had changed. I could get no plane reservations and waited five days for a train reservation before going to Georgia on eighteen days leave. The regular navy was not popular; it just couldn't demobilize fast enough. Now look at the hole the country is in!

Author's note -

In writing this article, I have relied largely on memory. Copies of my war diaries and action reports have not been available. I have made no errors in my descriptions of events, but I may have erred in giving certain dates. For example, I am not positive whether PENNSYLVANIA was torpedoed on 12 or 13 August, or whether PRESTON fired her last rounds on the 13th or 14th. I believe that all dates given are correct.

The article is a narrative of my activities at Okinawa. Since I was a destroyer squadron commander at that time, and since I reported the operations of my squadron in my war diaries and action reports, it is natural that I remember the actions of my own ships far better than I remember the actions of other ships.

I recall some splendid performances by ships not under my command but, since I cannot recall all such performances, I have chosen to leave out full descriptions of actions in which my ships did not participate. I do not want to create the impression that Desron 55 outshone all the rest. It didn't; all ships gave a good account of themselves, many gaining lasting recognition by receiving the Presidential Unit Citation or the Navy Unit Commendation. Of the ships in my squadron, CASSIN YOUNG, PRICHETT, and MORRISON received the latter award for Okinawa duties.

The campaign was difficult. I believe that future historians may classify it as one of the hardest fought amphibious operations of all time. I kept a record of sinkings and damage to our ships at Okinawa, not counting the damages to ships attached to the fast carrier task forces, until CALLAGHAN was sunk. On that date, 29 July, I remember that 117 ships of destroyer types had been sunk or damaged, and that 9 battleships and 9 cruisers had been damaged; this total did not take into consideration duplications; many ships were damaged two or three times.

The opinions or assertions contained in this article are the private ones of the writer and are not to be construed as official or reflecting the views of the Navy Department or the naval services at large.

A. E. Jarrell
Captain, U.S. Navy

When the kamikaze hit Callaghan and Jarrell left his compartment, the only things he took with him were his helmet, life vest, and a knife that his brother had made for him out of a band saw blade from a Georgia saw mill. All his clothing, letters and personal possessions were lost. The knife, ultimately, was given to his son, Lewis.

A number of writings about the Battle of Okinawa refer to my dad as "Commodore." Although his rank at the time was

Captain, it was traditional to apply the title "Commodore" to an officer who was commanding multiple ships, especially during a time of war. Desron 55 consisted of nine ships, and the title of Commodore would distinguish my dad from the captains of the ships under his command.

During the battle of Okinawa, Captain Jarrell sent a number of letters home to Ann. Since censorship was still in effect, Jarrell could not mention that Callaghan had been sunk but that he was okay. The Japanese did not have a lot of damage assessment capability, especially with the only observer, perhaps, being the suicide pilot who had died, the U.S. did not want to take the chance that a letter home might be obtained by the enemy and valuable information gleaned from it. If the enemy did not know that Callaghan had been sunk, but discovered their accomplishment through a letter, they could use that information as propaganda and as a means to bolster their troop's morale. Jarrell, in his letter home, let Ann know that he was all right.

Tuesday, 31 July, 1945
Dearest Ann,

> *I am now in another one of my ships. Please note the date of this letter and, also, I want you to know that I am in fine shape and enjoying everything. This change in flagships will not affect my expected return to the United States fairly soon. I am going to have to expend some money when I get back for replacement of clothing and other equipment that I have lost. The navy will reimburse me sometime in the future for most of my losses, however, I regret especially the loss of your letters and pictures. I also lost Admiral Kinkaid's classified citation and the medal. The medal can be replaced easily, and I think that I shall*

*write the Admiral and ask if he will give me a duplicate
citation. The final citation will, of course, arrive later and
will be signed by the President or the Secretary of the
Navy.*

*I was informed a few days ago that I was
recommended last May for the Navy Cross for duties
performed in the early part of the Okinawa campaign.*

*In my last letter I brought you up to 25 May. For
quite a period after that my squadron enjoyed continued
success. We had a few minor difficulties, such as combat
fatigue cases and repairs to equipment, but nothing
important. One ship had an influenza epidemic that has
been cleared up. From 19 to 21 July I had to take a unit of
16 merchant ships and auxiliary ships and ride out a
typhoon. I can't say that it was pleasant, but we had no
troubles that we couldn't handle. The Japs tried hard with
their aircraft during this bad weather, when it was difficult
to maneuver.*

*Well, darling, I hope all of you are feeling fine. I am
in excellent shape except for my bay window. Give our fine
ones a kiss for me. My best to your mother.*

Your devoted,

Al

Callaghan sank about Fifty miles southwest of the southern
tip of Okinawa. There is disagreement on the date of Callaghan's
sinking. Most reports show the sinking to have occurred at 0235 on
either July 28 or July 29. Captain Jarrell's observation is that
Callaghan sank on July 29. Additionally, author Barry J. Foster's

book, *"The Last Destroyer: The Story of USS Callaghan,"* based upon the log books of Callaghan, gives the date of sinking as July 29. Mr. Foster's father was one of the survivors. Finally, a summary of the 2007 U.S.S. Callaghan (DD-792) Reunion (http://wgordon.web.wesleyan.edu/kamikaze/stories/callaghan/index.htm) shows the date of sinking to be July 29, 1945. U.S.S. Callaghan was the last destroyer to be sunk in World War II, and it happened on the day she was to return to the United States.

January 14, 1946, Commander Destroyers Pacific Fleet awarded Captain Jarrell the Navy Cross. The citation reads:

The President of the United States of America takes pleasure in presenting the Navy Cross to Captain Albert Edmondson Jarrell, United States Navy, for extraordinary heroism and distinguished service in the line of his profession as Commander of a Destroyer Squadron and of the screen of detached groups which served as Gunfire and Covering Force, in action against enemy Japanese forces on Okinawa, Ryukyu Islands, from March to May 1945. Alert to constant danger of enemy aerial attack and aggressively maintaining the officers and men of his command at the highest peak of efficiency during prolonged and hazardous naval operations, Captain Jarrell skillfully directed the ships of his command in bringing effective gunfire to bear upon hostile aggressors of this area. Instantly assuming command of rescue and salvage operations when two destroyers were severely damaged in the intense aerial attack of 6 April 1945, he contributed to the saving of many lives and to the safe return of both crippled vessels. His unfaltering decision, cool judgment and resolute fortitude in the face of continual peril reflect the highest credit upon Captain Jarrell and the United States Naval Service.

Navy Cross

CHAPTER 13
POST WAR

Upon arriving in San Pedro, California, Captain Jarrell's orders were to report to Commander, Training Command West Coast, in San Diego, where he would serve as Chief Staff Officer from October 1945 to March 1946. In this position he would perform duties similar to those of Executive Officer on a ship; he would ensure that the day-to-day operations of the unit proceeded smoothly, allowing the Commander to engage in planning for the future and to interrelate with other organizations, both military and civilian.

My dad had accrued leave time, and traveled to LaGrange, Georgia, to reunite with Mom and us three kids. After arrangements were made for our household goods to be shipped to San Diego, we all loaded into their car and drove the 2100 miles to our new home. Our family settled into a rented house on Lark Street, overlooking the San Diego airport.

Joan tells the story of living in San Diego:

> When the war was over, Daddy came back, and we moved to San Diego. The trip to San Diego from LaGrange took five days. We had to be ready to leave each day at eight in the morning, and we stopped at about four in the afternoon. Mother always had games and toys for us to play with, but it was BORING.

We only lived in San Diego about six months this time. Mother and Daddy rented a house on a hill on Lark Street. It was right next to a vacant area with lots of eucalyptus trees. The house was great because the bedrooms were downstairs. You entered on the street level to the living area, and the house was built down the hill. Even with that, it was on stilts in the back, and we could climb up under the house and slide down the dirt hill.

It was when we lived in San Diego this time that Henry decided to run away from home. He was only two years old, and was not allowed to go outside without being accompanied. One day he decided that he wanted to go for a walk, but could find no one to take him. So he got mad, and said he was going to run away. Mother didn't pay too much attention to the tantrums of a two-year-old child, since she had already lived through two other children in the "terrible twos." But later, she couldn't find him. She called me in, and asked if I had taken him out. Of course, I hadn't. So we all spread out to look for Henry. Mother eventually called the police, and Henry was found and returned to us.

Daddy had really strange food habits. Early in his life, he decided that he didn't like fresh meat. He was probably a natural vegetarian, but Georgia in the early 1900s did not allow for weird food habits such as vegetarianism. It was a chicken in the pot every Sunday for dinner after church. Daddy had a rough time as a child because his mother would not accept that eating meat made him sick. Eventually he decided that, whereas he couldn't abide fresh meat, he could tolerate cured, dried, and smoked meat. So all our dinners when he was home revolved around that type of food. Anyway, he realized that not everyone in the world was totally fond of his diet, and recognized that Mother was giving up some of her favorite foods to accommodate him. So one day he arrived home with a large box, looking proud as punch. He had managed to acquire Mother's favorite food for her: lobster – a live lobster. He gave the box to her and departed. Mother, it is true, was very fond of lobster, but the "cooked and served on a plate" variety. She didn't have the vaguest idea of what to do with the beast. After checking in her cookbook, she learned that one dropped a live lobster into boiling water to cook it. So she got the largest pot she had, filled it with water, and set it on the stove to boil. As it was coming to a boil, she opened the box with the lobster. Well, the beast got loose and there was Mother chasing it around the kitchen. She was at a distinct disadvantage since the lobster had large claws that it waved around, and she didn't know how to go about capturing it. About that time we were sent away from the kitchen, so I don't remember just what eventually happened.

*   *   *   *   *

On 18 March, 1946, Captain Jarrell received notice from President Truman's Secretary of State, James F. Byrnes, that he was to perform duties at the Embassy in Mexico City:

DEPARTMENT OF STATE
WASHINGTON

March 18, 1946

Captain Albert E. Jarrell
United States Navy
Navy Department

Sir:

Pursuant to a request from the Navy Department, you are hereby designated Naval Attaché and Naval Attaché for Air to the American Embassy at Mexico, D. F., Mexico.

You will perform, under the supervision of the Chief of Mission, such duties as may be assigned to you by the Navy Department.

Very truly yours,

(Signed) James F. Byrnes

Dad would serve two and a half years as Naval Attaché in Mexico City. He was authorized to have his family accompany him, so we packed our household goods for shipment and then drove by car the 1,900 miles from San Diego to Mexico City. We lived in a rented, two story home on Avenida Paseo de las Palmas.

A Naval Attaché would work within the American Embassy to provide expert consultation on matters dealing with naval operations and, in Captain Jarrell's case, matters pertaining to aviation. He worked closely with the Ambassador and with the staff of the embassy. Additionally, he was called upon to attend myriad functions of the Embassy as well as those of the host country, Mexico. Dignitaries arriving in Mexico City were met at the airport by Embassy staff and often by those holding high positions in the Embassy. Heads of State, such as presidents and world leaders, generated tremendous interest within the Embassy and Mexican government, and were met with great fanfare and ceremony. It was common for wives to participate in social functions, and Ann was kept very busy.

President Truman Visits Mexico - 1947. Jarrell in Foreground

Captain Jarrell had a communication line to Washington, D.C., and would provide information relating to Mexico's military readiness status as well as other observations that might be of interest to the United States. He would also be called upon to provide his expertise in advising the Mexican Navy on matters in which they might request help.

Joan remembers living in Mexico City:

> We left for Mexico City in April. Beste was there, too, but I'm not sure if she went with us, or arrived later to live with us. It took us five miserable days to drive down the center of Mexico to the capital over winding mountain roads. My folks rented two houses that I remember while we lived there, but I don't remember much about the first one.

> We lived most of the time we were in Mexico City in one-half of a duplex on the outskirts of town. There were lots of empty fields around our house, and the neighborhood church was just being built at the end of our street – Paseo de las Palmas. It was a large two-storied house that had four bedrooms upstairs and maids' quarters attached. I got my own bedroom, and my brothers had to share one. At least for part of the time, Beste had the third bedroom. Mother and Daddy hired two maids and a cook, but they always seemed to be fighting and arguing.

> Sometimes, on weekends when the maids were left in charge of us, they used to take us for "walks." The walks consisted of taking us out to undeveloped land at the end of the street where they would meet up with friends, especially boyfriends, and have a nice visit. We enjoyed going, but it was boring waiting for them to be finished visiting with their friends. We were admonished not to tell our parents that their friends just "happened" to come by when we were out on our walk.

At the opposite end of the street from our "walks," was the church building. We used to sneak down there because there were whole families camping out under tin and cardboard shelters. We'd play with the children, and manage to get fresh cooked tortillas from their mothers – right off the griddle, as it were. Mother would always get annoyed when she found we had been there, so we wouldn't tell her. Eventually she put a stop to it by forbidding us to go anywhere near that area.

I was enrolled in a truly bilingual school in Mexico City. The Mexico City School operated half a day in English and half a day in Spanish. We had to wear uniforms every day to school. They were kind of cute little sailor dresses, but I really got tired of wearing the same clothes day-in and day-out.

We had several outings while we lived in Mexico City. One of my favorites was the trip to Xochimilco, the famous floating gardens. We floated around the canals on flatboats, and passed musicians in other boats, and saw beautiful flowers, and I thoroughly enjoyed it. We also went out to the pyramids. I don't remember too much about that, except that I have a photo with Mario, Daddy's chauffer, and us kids at the pyramids.

Joan, Henry, Mario, and Lewis at Pyramids

The <u>best</u> trips were to Acapulco. It took the better part of a day to drive the winding road, and Lewis always got carsick, and got to ride in the front seat. But we stayed in a wonderful hotel, and ate out at the hotel restaurant for every meal. And we'd get to order off the menu! Breakfast was the best because there was a huge bowl of fruit on the table and we could have as much fruit as we wanted. Then we'd go to the beach. Mother would try to keep us out of the sun somewhat, but we invariably got burned to a crisp. One time when we went the jellyfish were in, and we got jellyfish stings in addition to the sunburn. The last day was always spent crying because of the sunburn, and the trip home was sheer torture.

We went to Veracruz once too. But it wasn't as nice as Acapulco. The water was not as clean and clear, and the beach was rather tacky. Another trip that we took was to Taxco, the silver city. Mother bought some silver pins and other jewelry. But I don't remember much about that either.

Acapulco 1948

Social functions in the Embassy were an on-going part of embassy life, but not all of it was entertaining dignitaries. Dad had a routine schedule of poker playing with a number of his embassy buddies and they met once a week to play poker, rotating the venues among the players. This became such a mainstay of life in

Mexico City that upon his departure in 1948 the other players gave him a large sterling silver serving tray with each player's name engraved on it. The inscription read:

To Captain A. E. Jarrell

In Memory of your Poker Friends

Jack Barron	W. H. Cowley
Alex H. Danon	Roy Kerr
Andy Anderson	Harold Ostrow
Roy B. Dean	Oscar Densiger

E. P. Budde

Mexico City   Sept. 10th, 1948

Mom became a player in the events held at our home, and the games expanded to roulette and bridge. As is common (required) in the social interaction of Navy officers, cocktail parties were the norm and card games were almost always played. Poker was such a common occurrence that my dad had a custom poker table built with foldable legs for easy storage.

*   *   *   *   *

Following the thirty months in Mexico City, Dad was reassigned to duty in Seattle, Washington, as District Intelligence Officer for the Thirteenth Naval District. His assignment would span eight months from October 1948 to June 1949. Our family made the long drive from Mexico City to LaGrange, Georgia, for a visit, and eventually to Seattle where we settled in to a home on Westview Drive. It was a two-story house with a basement, and a coal-fired furnace that had to be manually fed with a shovel, a task that Dad was not fond of.

Navy Intelligence dates back to 1882 when the Secretary of Navy ordered that "An 'Office of Intelligence' is hereby established in the Bureau of Navigation for the purpose of collecting and recording such naval information as may be useful to the Department in time of war, as well as in peace."

As District Intelligence Officer, Jarrell was responsible for gathering information regarding major criminal and security activities within the navy, as well as monitoring foreign maritime activities and reporting such to the intelligence analysts in Washington, D.C. This was the beginning of the Cold War and the United States had to know what activities foreign powers, especially the USSR, were engaged in. The District Intelligence Officer was charged with this task.

This was a time when Mao Tse-tung, with Stalin's backing, was leading the Communist takeover of China by defeating the Nationalist government of Chiang Kai-shek. The communist Mao forces were successful in instigating student unrest and protests, which ultimately helped to unseat Chiang Kai-shek. United States Army General George Marshall had worked to get Chiang Kai-shek to form a unified government including both the Communists and Nationalists, but this mission failed in January 1947. When the fighting between the Communists and Nationalists intensified, the U. S. was supporting the Nationalists with loans and weapons. The same month Marshall's mission failed, January 1947, Marshall became Secretary of State under Harry Truman and, much to Jarrell's befuddlement, later enacted an embargo on shipments to Chiang Kai-shek which coincided with Mao's offensive in China. In 1948-49 a massive maritime labor strike, concurrent with the embargo, was called on the West Coast which tied up shipping for six months. According to Jarrell, "Strikers placards in Seattle proclaimed 'We will load nothing for imperialist China.'" Imperialist China was the moniker Marshall had given Nationalist China.

The United States had supported Chiang and his Nationalist Chinese, who were good friends of liberty and enemies of communism. So the action by the labor unions seemed to Jarrell to be in support of communism, and the embargo by Marshall was a mystery. Jarrell said, "I went to Washington to make sure that the Office of Naval Intelligence understood the situation. I was told that 'somebody in Washington wants the Communists to win.' It took Mao six months to defeat Chiang: [then] the strike ended. John F. Kennedy, then a U. S. Representative, angrily blasted the administration in a speech titled, 'We gave China to the Reds.'"

Mao Tse-tung defeated Chiang Kai-shek's Nationalists, and China, the People's Republic of China (PRC), became a communist country in 1949. Chiang retreated to Taiwan with his army and government and proceeded to rid the island country of "counter-revolutionaries." It is significant to note that the Soviet Union was successful in helping Mao turn China into the communist People's Republic of China and only a year later China, in collusion with Stalin, was busy starting a war in Korea with the same goal.

The United States continued to recognize the Taipei government in Taiwan, the Republic of China (ROC), as being the sole legal government of China, but that changed during President Carter's administration when Beijing was recognized as the sole legal government of China. Taiwan continues to have US support and excellent relations, but is officially considered by the US to be a part of mainland China.

Three decades later, in an editorial printed in the *Arizona Republic* newspaper in September 1976 titled "The truth about Mao," the article's author asserts that Mao did, indeed, rule China through terror, but was a good tactician. Jarrell wrote, regarding the editorial, that he agreed with the statement about Mao ruling through terror saying "I once had a copy of a Stalin-Mao agreement which called for the liquidation of 100 million Chinese if necessary." Jarrell went on to say, "You give Mao credit for [being a tactician]. [T]he credit, or blame, should be given to our own government." Jarrell finished his letter with, "Mao was not a good military commander. We just made him look good."

During the events leading up to the toppling of Chiang Kai-shek's government, Jarrell's brother, Captain Henry Thompson Jarrell, USN, served as Chief of the Far-Eastern Branch, Office of Reports and Estimates, Central Intelligence Agency. His vast knowledge of China, having served there in a number of capacities including Assistant Naval Attaché, and translator and interpreter, gave him a distinct capability for analyzing and evaluating the events occurring in China. He subsequently was designated Naval Attache, American Embassy, Taipei, Taiwan, when Chiang moved his government there. His older brother's warning, that learning the Chinese language would keep him occupied in Chinese matters, rang true.

Joan remembers living in Seattle:

Returning to the United States was just as disagreeable educationally speaking as going to Mexico, as far as I was concerned. We arrived in Seattle at the end of the school year – the <u>Mexican</u> school year. I was reluctantly enrolled in the sixth grade in November, with no hope of a long vacation for eight more months.

We lived in a two-storied house on a hill, and I had a marvelous room. All of the houses that Mother and Daddy rented were furnished, and this was the best one yet, as far as I was concerned. My room was the largest, or nearly the largest, in the house. I had twin beds and a chaise lounge. I would spend hours in the latter reading books. While in Mexico, my reading ability had improved to the extent that I discovered the joy found in books. Often my father would catch me in the near dusk, curled up in a chair reading one of my favorites. I think he was pleased that I enjoyed reading so much, but I really got lectured when I came home from school with a referral to an optometrist for glasses. According to him, my poor eyesight was entirely my fault, for reading in poor light.

It was cold and rainy most of the time we lived in Seattle. We found a watery area down the hill from our house that filled and froze over during the winter. We used to walk out on the frozen ice pretending that we were ice skating. Fortunately the water wasn't deep because we usually broke through and ended up at home with soaking wet feet.

*   *   *   *   *

Following Dad's tour in Seattle, he was given a short assignment as Chief of Staff to Commander, Destroyers, Pacific Fleet. The family once again loaded up in the car and in June 1949 made the trek to Coronado, California, where we took up residence on "B" Avenue.

COMDESPAC, as the command was known, was responsible for the assignments and basing of the destroyers of the Pacific fleet, their maintenance, and the training of the crews. The Commander Destroyers Pacific reported to the Commander, United States Pacific Fleet, Admiral Arthur W. Radford. Jarrell's tenure would last from June to October, 1949.

Chief of staff can be a grueling job. Jarrell would be responsible for the operations of the commander's office and staff, would act as his right-hand-man and would be a trusted adviser. Any important meeting or events that the commander needed to attend, but couldn't, would be attended by Captain Jarrell.

Schooling was sometimes an interrupted affair for us kids. Arriving and departing at various times during the school year would probably be considered very disrupting, but it had become somewhat normal for us. It was all we knew, and we merely adapted and made new friends, or in the case of living in Coronado, re-connected with old friends.

Joan recounts her Coronado memories:

> We left Seattle and stayed briefly in Coronado during the early part of my seventh grade year. I was in pre-puberty at this time, and had gained some weight. I think I started getting chubby when we lived in Mexico. Anyway, the years of sarcastic comments from my father regarding my size were just beginning when I reached junior high school. Our father could zap us good with his rapier tongue. I remember such comments as, "Do you really think you need another helping?" or, "Do you know what you look like from the back?" when I was wearing a bathing suit to go to the beach. For a child who was shy and self-conscious already, Daddy's comments did not improve my self image.

I did not like junior high school in Coronado. There were a number of school bullies, and I took great care to keep out of their way. They delighted in picking on the "nerds" of that day. Being chubby, I was in the undesirable group. One day at school one of the most aggressive of the bullies got his come-uppance. It was the style at that time for the boys to wear their hair in duck tails with the sides all sleeked back to meet in the center of the back – just like a duck's tail. Another style that went hand-in-hand with the DA [Duck's Ass], was that of wearing the jeans just at the hipbone – the lower the pants, the more "cool" the boy was, at least according to the bully-boys. One day, at the end of the lunch hour, a kid slipped up behind the "coolest" of the cool guys, and yanked his jeans right down to his ankles in front of the entire lunch crowd. Fortunately he had underpants on, but he was, nevertheless, extremely embarrassed, and turned a bright red. It was felt by all that he had received his just due.

*   *   *   *   *

From his brief assignment with COMDESPAC Captain Jarrell was ordered to Panama City, Florida, where he took command of the Navy Mine Countermeasures Station. Panama City is located in the panhandle of Florida on the Gulf Coast, midway between Pensacola and Tallahassee. He would serve here from 15 November, 1949, until July 1950.

The Navy Mine Countermeasures Station was the home of a fleet of minesweepers as well as a research station for the detection and elimination of mines and other explosive devices that would be found in the seas. The station also provided comprehensive training and repair services for the minesweepers. A minesweeper would tow a cable attached to a paravane, a hydrofoil of sorts, which would keep the cable underwater at a set depth. Once the cable contacted a mine's anchor cable, it would cut through and the mine would float to the surface where it could be destroyed.

The long trip cross-country took us across the southern states on mostly two-lane roads. Every change of duty station seemed to be from one coast to another, entailing several days travel in the summer in a hot car. Air conditioning was not a feature in automobiles at that time, and even heaters were an extra cost option. When we arrived at our home it was a very nice house located on the Navy base. As the commander of the base, my dad was afforded housing on the Naval Station, but there being no school on-base, we kids had to commute to school in Panama City each day.

Minesweepers - Panama City 1949-1950

Joan's account of living in Florida:

I completed my seventh grade and part of my eighth grade in Panama City, Florida. My father was assigned as Base Commander to the navy base located five miles out of the town of Panama City. He received, as part of his remuneration, housing for the family on the base. Unfortunately for us children, we were the only family living on the base. We did have very nice quarters, though, and were close to a beach where we could swim in the Gulf waters, and also had a small pier where Mother would try to catch fish for dinner. I guess she must have caught one or two because I can remember being bored to tears when she took me fishing. I never caught anything.

We children were thrown back on ourselves for company on the navy base. Henry was only in the first grade, and Lewis and I would take great pains to leave him out of our adventures. We were forbidden to go to the working areas of the base, but would occasionally sneak down to the ships which were moored or docked near our home. One day we came upon a small boat which was three quarters filled with water. What a treasure! It was located on our side of a small inlet, and Lewis and I decided that we could paddle our way across the inlet to the other side just using our hands as oars. We did so, and found a dead stingray on the opposite beach. That scared us somewhat because the thing must have been alive at some time, and in the same waters we were traversing. We quickly paddled our way back, to arrive just barely before the entire boat sank in the ten-foot, or so, deep water. That was a narrow escape.

Daddy didn't figure too much in our lives as we were growing up. He was stationed at sea much of the time, and when he was home we seldom saw him except at dinner, and sometimes at breakfast. He was definitely the authoritarian parent of our family, and we felt his presence whether he was there in person or not. Mother would punish our failings with a hairbrush applied to our backside, but far more effective was the threat to "…tell your father how you behaved."

We still had Snitz living with us in Panama City. She was 15 at that time, and I was 12. It was unquestioned and accepted by all that Daddy loved Snitz much more than he loved us children. (I suppose in retrospect, that he really did love us, but he certainly didn't like us much. I never felt that he really liked me until I was fully grown and had children of my own.) Daddy didn't have much patience with children, and Snitz gave him unquestioning love, loyalty, and obedience. We didn't.

Snitz was quite ill as she grew older. She was white, and had large mammary tumors. It was obvious that she would not live much longer, but Daddy couldn't bring himself to have her put to sleep, even though she could hardly get around any more.

Mother and Daddy had the only air conditioned room in the house, and after Daddy got up and dressed on a weekend, we were permitted to go in the room and cool off, provided we did not touch anything. Snitz lived in that room also, so that she could have as much comfort as possible in her old age. It just so happened that I was in the bedroom and was looking at Snitz and had just finished patting her when she died. Mother told Daddy, who was very broken up, and they spent the rest of the day in the bedroom with Snitz. I asked to see Snitz again and was told that I could not. Mother later explained that Daddy was very upset and could not be disturbed. Snitz was buried on Daddy's old Hill Street homestead in LaGrange. Daddy took her up, and arranged for a stone to be set at her grave. I don't remember ever seeing her grave, though. I guess it was a pretty private place for Daddy.

CHAPTER 14
KOREAN WAR

North Korea and Chinese forces invaded South Korea on 25 June, 1950. The United States, with support from the United Nations, took action to stop the invasion and push the invaders out of South Korea. Although the defense of South Korea and the expulsion of the invaders was a UN action, Captain Jarrell noted that the Soviet Union, one of the permanent members of the UN Security Council, was actively supporting the North Korean efforts to take over South Korea in concert with the People's Republic of China. (In 1971 the communist PRC in mainland China would displace the democratic Republic of China (Taiwan) as the permanent member of the Security Council.) It was hard for Jarrell to comprehend how a permanent member of the UN Security Council and a future permanent member of the UN Security Council could collude to invade South Korea, while the defense of South Korea was undertaken by the United Nations. This fact was influential in forming Jarrell's belief, for the remainder of his life, that the last honorable war to be fought was World War II, and that the United Nations is inherently perniciously ineffectual and inimical.

The United States immediately began mobilizing for the war. Following WWII, the US had downsized its military readiness and it was a monumental effort to gear up for this effort. The Navy gave orders to Captain Jarrell to make his way to Yokosuka, Japan, where he would be given an assignment for duty in the war in Korea.

Our family, once again, loaded up the car in July 1950 and drove cross-country from Florida to Coronado, California. In West Texas we overnighted at a motel that had an attached café. The evening dinner was enjoyed, and Dad decided to smoke one of his favorite cigars. He picked up the matches on the table, took one out, and lit the stogie, commenting to Mom, "Remind me to buy some matches before we leave tomorrow." I observed this and asked, "Why don't you just take these?" Dad replied, "Because they are put there for our use, not for me to take. If I take these, then the next people to sit here won't have any." This was a lesson I remembered my entire life.

We took up residence in a rented house on 6th Street in Coronado. Dad only stayed long enough to see that we were all properly situated, and then made his way to Yokosuka, Japan, where he arrived on 25 August, 1950. He would remain away from home until August 1951, more than a year's time.

In Yokosuka, Captain Jarrell met with Admiral James H. Doyle, Commander Task Force 90. TF 90 was the Attack Force, responsible for the amphibious operations in Korea. At that meeting, Adm. Doyle told Jarrell to establish and then command Transportation Division 11, responsible for the Second and Third Echelon Movement Groups, which would transport the troops and equipment to the invasion beaches in Korea. What little staff he had available to create a ComTransDiv 11 (Commander Transportation Division 11) administrative office in Yokosuka was shared with Captain Louis D. "Dinty" Sharp, Jr., who would command Task Group 90.8, the Second Echelon Movement Group. Captain Jarrell would also have the additional responsibility of commanding Task Group 90.9, the Third Echelon Movement Group.

In preparation for loading the ships in his Task Group, on 31 August Captain Jarrell opened an office in the Bank of America building in Yokohama, some 30 miles north of Yokosuka. A Navy ship had been promised for his use as a command vessel, but it never did materialize. The ships available were all merchant ships contracted for use in the war effort. The immense task to mobilize for the war would mean that Jarrell would have to make-do with what was available.

Captain Jarrell's group was loaded at Yokohama. For the Inchon operation, his ships would be transporting the Army's X Corps troops and equipment. Fifteen merchant ships carried about 61 separate Army units and some one hundred thousand tons of cargo. None of the ships had stevedores to handle the loading, or even cargo nets, debarkation nets, signalmen, or radios. Jarrell arranged for about 140 Japanese stevedores and winch operators to be placed aboard each ship and they worked hard to get the loading done.

The Battle of Inchon, code named Operation Chromite, lasted from 15 September to 19 September, and Captain Jarrell and his merchantmen delivered their troops and materiel.

Captain Jarrell wrote home to tell Ann what was going on, and excerpts of his letters follow:

30 September, 1950

> *It usually takes four labor unions to load or unload a ship, so none of these ships were prepared to do anything. The Japanese are working hard for us and I don't know what we would do without them. Most of the ships didn't even have navigation charts. We installed some Army anti-aircraft artillery on the topside as gun batteries and held a few drills en route to Korea. The trip was fairly*

smooth except for the burning up of one ship's galley and a fight between two crew members, one of whom had his stomach sliced open.

Inchon is a lousy place. It has about a thirty foot range of tide, strong currents, many unmarked islands and shoals, and is the worst place I have been in except possibly Morotai.

On 29 September I was released and took my five officers and thirteen men to Kimpo airfield near Seoul. McArthur arrived just as I did. We flew from Kimpo to Ashiya, in northern Kyushu, Japan, got a bus to Fukuoka, then a train to Sasebo where I finally met my ship. We came aboard U.S.S. Henrico, my flagship, about midnight. I am certainly glad to be aboard a Navy ship after five weeks out here. The rest of my staff should arrive tomorrow, and maybe we can start operating as a transport squadron. I hope that I get no more jobs with merchant ships.

Returning to Japan, Jarrell finally got his flagship. U.S.S. Henrico was an attack transport that had been commissioned in November 1943 during World War II. Named for Henrico County, Virginia, she was 492 feet long and had a published speed of 18 knots (21 mph). Her cargo capacity was 4,500 tons. Henrico served in every major conflict from WWII to Viet Nam, and was sold for scrap in 1979.

U.S.S. Henrico (APA-45) TransDiv 11 Flagship
(Official U. S. Navy Photograph)

In early October Captain Jarrell and his transports picked up troops at Inchon and moved them around the Korean peninsula to North Korea for the planned invasion at Wonsan. His ships were standing off Wonsan, in North Korea, awaiting word to begin the assault of the beaches there. The waters had been heavily mined with Soviet-supplied mines, and the operation was delayed while minesweepers cleared the area. Two minesweepers were lost. During the delay, the defending North Korean troops retreated and the Wonsan landings were not necessary.

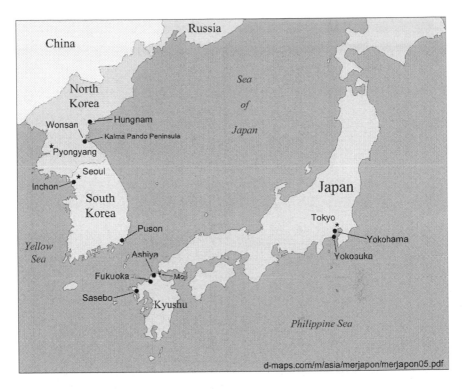

Key Ports Visited by Jarrell's TransDiv 11

Captain Jarrell continued the ship movements between Japan and Korea through the month of November 1950 deploying troops and providing supplies. Much of the loading activity was at Moji, at the northern tip of the Japanese island of Kyushu, where troops and materiel were being loaded onto ships.

Jarrell commented in a letter home that it may take ten or twenty years to beat Russia, but that he saw no alternative. Although Russia was the instigator in the war and provided materiel support, massive buildups of Chinese troops commenced in November to fight the land battles.

Jarrell updated Ann on his activities:

10 December, 1950

> *In early December I had command of a task element to withdraw our forces from Wonsan. It was done under some enemy pressure, but not much, although we had to expect the arrival of strong enemy forces. We set up our own defense perimeter, which we slowly shortened until we held only the small peninsula, Kalma Pando, which is about two miles long.*
>
> *As we loaded troops and equipment, our capability to protect ourselves was obviously diminished. The South Korean Marines had two ROK [Republic of Korea] battalions, who did a fine job with only three tanks for the last 60 hours. They suffered about fifteen casualties, only one of them serious. We had good naval gunfire cover, with one cruiser and three destroyers. We destroyed all captured enemy ammunition, guns, and materiel that we could not use, leaving nothing of military value to the enemy. On 7 December we completed our loading from the dock area and moved to Kalma Pando.*

The extraction of troops and equipment went fairly smoothly, considering the logistics of moving an army while under harassment from the enemy. The real challenge, however, would be the removal of a relatively small number of civilians who were government officials or United Nations personnel, or otherwise selected people. This task was to take a few hours but stretched out to nearly twenty four hours.

Captain Jarrell described what happened in his letter home:

> *The situation of the civilians is serious and pitiful. Wonsan has a population of about 75,000 but it was doubled due to people coming in from outlying villages, ahead of the Chinese, hoping to be evacuated. The Koreans like us, and hate to see us leave. Some communists came in with the friendly people.*
>
> *We were to remove about 800 designated civilians on December 8; city officials, UN personnel, missionaries, etc. They were told to be ready at 5:00 a.m., two hours before daylight, while the curfew was in effect, so as not to alarm the city. Boats were ready for them. However, the people of Wonsan were wide awake. They crowded toward the embarkation area. I had one Victory ship (SS Lane Victory) to put 800 screened [vetted] people in.*

Victory Ship

Barbed wire entanglements had been set up, backed by tanks, to keep the people back. They were a frantic, screaming, crying mass. They deliberately threw themselves into the barbed wire. Tanks and mortars were fired over their heads, but they didn't care. We had military government officials of our army, but one of our two battalions of ROKs was called in to assist.

Many of these people had burned their own homes, to keep the communists from using them. Many families were separated. It was impossible to avoid it. A mother and three small children were running frantically along the barrier; they had been passed through but wouldn't go to the boats. Through an interpreter I learned that the father was missing. He was one of the few calm ones, well back in the crowd. With a loudspeaker, he was located and joined his family. A small girl, about six, was being pushed into the barbed wire, her family screaming on the clear side. She was lifted over. A lot of men had to be knocked cold.

The master of Lane Victory had been told by the military governor to expect 800 people. I told him to be ready for 5,000. He said that in a pinch he could handle 2,500, but no more. He had hauled 1,800 out of Inchon and felt that he was experienced in these things. He got 7,009 by midnight, when we had to quit, instead of 800 in two hours. The last one aboard was a two year old boy left in the bottom of an LCM (Landing Craft Medium). No one would claim him. A merchant vessel, Trepanier, took him aboard and the first mate took him to his cabin.

The master of Lane Victory sent me urgent messages after 4,000 had gone aboard. "You tell that Commodore (meaning me) that he can't do this to me." I received a credible report that he was going crazy. Well, they arrived in the port of Pusan, Korea, yesterday [December 9], but I don't know what can be done with them there; 150,000 more could have been sent, with time and ships available. I radioed to have food and doctors ready.

A master of a Victory ship at Yokohama had once told me proudly that he could carry 200 passengers. He was wrong; the capacity is 7009. I know.

We also joined an LST (Landing Ship Tank), which is very crowded with 400 troops. We put aboard 900 prisoners of war under the guard of 650 ROK navy personnel, plus 500 civilians. The POWs were docile. They didn't want to go back to the communists.

If there is anyone that is opposed to mobilizing now to keep the war out of our country, and many such people exist, he should have seen the civilians at Wonsan. It was worse than handling the armed enemy. Sherman fought in a war between gentlemen [referring to General Sherman and the U. S. Civil War].

USS Marion County (LST-975)
(Official U. S. Navy Photograph)

After the Wonsan evacuation, Captain Jarrell's ships were busy with troop and equipment movements. He commented in a letter home that in mid-December he had completed his toughest operation yet; the redeployment of 22,000 ROK troops and their equipment, with only three Navy ships, three Victory ships, and one LST with which to do it.

Captain Jarrell had been watching the reports in the newspapers about the status of the war, and was not happy with what he read. The news media were not giving the public the complete truth. In a letter home to Ann he summarized some of his observations.

23 December, 1950

> *There are too many Monday morning quarterbacks in the press. My own map, which covers a whole side of my mess room [dining area], has been correctly marked. I have known that Chinese have swarmed across the Yalu River. They moved to the river without fear of being attacked from the air, then moved across at night. It was*

*perfect for them. We still don't attack them in Manchuria.
They have never had to protect their supply lines to the
border. But why it was assumed they would not attack us is
beyond my comprehension. It goes back to Washington. We
had the intelligence; it wasn't used. I have believed, ever
since the Chinese started moving across the border after
Inchon, that they were not coming into Korea to learn how
to play baseball. That is why I have been writing that we
should ask Stalin and Mao Tse-tung for a little straight
information before we make plans based on unjustified
assumptions. I heard an intelligence officer from
Washington say some time ago, with four admirals
listening, that he did not believe that the Chinese would
enter the war. I told him that I thought that we should base
our plans on the assumption that China would enter. The
officer from Washington had a decoration pinned on him.
He should have received a bouquet of onions.*

    *The Chinese ground troops are not supermen. The
Chinese leaders and Stalin are willing to let them get
killed, but a tough fight throws them into confusion. The
individuals don't want to get killed. There was nothing to
keep them out of Wonsan but two battalions of ROK
marines and four navy ships. When we moved to Kalma
Pando, the little peninsula two miles long and half a mile
wide, we used only one battalion. We could still be holding
it. The press talk about it being a Dunkerque [Dunkirk] is
just something to startle the public. We are redisposing our
forces to better positions against many enemy troops. The
enemy has had six of their divisions battered by one
division of marines. He doesn't like it when he gets close
enough for naval gunfire. He is close to our beachhead but
he won't take it until we leave with our troops and our*

equipment. I think that our troops will have a fairly satisfactory Christmas.

Within a month I think that the Chinese will realize that moving their supplies 300 miles while under attack is not the same as moving them unopposed into North Korea via Manchuria. The Chinese may offer to mediate soon. I don't think that we should bargain with them. They have plenty of human lives, but not too much equipment. Stalin is stingy, except with other people's lives.

Christmas Day, 1950

We arrive in Pusan in about two hours. We had a successful withdrawal for redeployment from Hungnam. I didn't have much to do, but it was a good job. Admiral Doyle certainly has had a series of tough jobs.

Captain Jarrell delivered his load from Hungnam to Pusan. In all, 193 shiploads of troops, civilians, vehicles, and materiel arrived in Pusan. The toll on the ships and men was starting to show. Task Force 11 had been operating in Korean waters or steaming to Japan for four months, but now Henrico headed to Yokosuka for a break. Jarrell explains in this excerpt of a letter to Ann.

29 December, 1950

We arrive in Yokosuka tonight, and I hope we can stay long enough for some upkeep, liberty, recreation, and inspections. Our lines in Korea should be fairly tough and stable, but the unexpected can happen. The Russians themselves might risk their own necks, but I have doubts about this happening within the next month or two.

We have been in Korea or Korean waters all this month, and it has been a month of very strenuous operations. I have seen members of our boat crews brought aboard unconscious from cold and fatigue or with no control over their movements and speech. Noble [U.S.S. Noble (APA-218)] had some casualties at Hungnam; Henrico had one wounded, caused by Army carelessness on Pink Beach. These two ships have done a fine job out here, as good as any I have ever seen. The whole fleet has been very busy.

Henrico shakes like a tuning fork and needs repairs. Noble has had four amphibious boats destroyed and two lost through sinking. I am hoping that these two ships receive the special recognition that they deserve.

Captain Jarrell was awarded a Gold Star in lieu of a Second Award of the Legion of Merit with Combat "V" for action from December 3 – 24, 1950. Rear Admiral James H. Doyle made the presentation.

Legion of Merit Ribbon with Combat "V" and Gold Star

In March 1951 Henrico sailed for Seattle, where long-needed repairs would be made. While in the Washington area, she participated in amphibious training exercises. On 3 August, 1951, Captain Jarrell received orders detaching him as Commander,

Transport Division 11, and ordering him to report to Commander, Destroyer Force, Atlantic Fleet to be Chief of Staff. Jarrell officially detached from Transport Division 11 on 10 August. Captain Jarrell was now out of the action in Korea.

Joan describes living in Coronado for the year our dad was away at war in Korea:

> This time we rented a house on Sixth Street. We each had our own bedroom, and Mother and Daddy's room was separated from ours by the community living areas at the front of the house. Mother took up den-mothering for Lewis' Cub Scout den. It was kind of fun when the den met at our house because there was always enough refreshments for a pudgy pre-teenaged girl.
>
> I graduated from junior high school in Coronado, but the event doesn't stand out in my memory. I think I was just relieved to be done with that part of my life, and looking forward timidly to turning, overnight, into a great success in high school.
>
> During the summer after my graduation, the Navy Relief Carnival took place in San Diego. I didn't attend, but both my brothers went. Lewis came home proudly with two baby chickens he had won for himself and for Henry. I was enthralled, and Lewis was proud as Punch of his magnificent gambling skills. After much pleading and persuasion on my part, Lewis finally agreed to return to the carnival the next day and win a chicken for me. I was so excited! And even more so, when Lewis arrived home with, not another chicken, but a baby duck for me. It was so cute, and so soft, and so sweet, that I gave it the sugary name of "Sweet Thing." I took Sweet Thing into my room with me for the first night it was home. We found a nice box which I

fixed up with blankets, and a clock (for the heartbeat), and a hot water bottle. Sweet Thing would have nothing to do with such accommodations. It wanted the real thing, and squawked loudly until I took it into bed with me. That was enough to settle the creature down. But I was afraid to fall asleep and roll over on the baby, which would certainly crush it. In the early hours of the morning, I finally put the animal in the box, covered my ears with my pillow, and got whatever sleep I could.

The next day I vowed that Sweet Thing would sleep in the bathtub with the chickens. That evening the chickens got tucked nicely into bed in the bathtub, and I introduced Sweet Thing to his new bed. NO WAY! This was not what Sweet Thing had in mind when he joined our family. But, like it or not, that's where he spent the night. During the daytime, my brothers and I would exercise our new pets in our patio. A large portion of the planting area in the patio was filled with geraniums as a ground cover. The chickens loved it, and hopped happily in and among the flowers. By this time Sweet Thing had decided that he was another chicken, and tried valiantly to follow. Of course, he fell flat on his little beak as his webbed feet caught on the large geranium leaves and flowers. We did enjoy our pets, though.

Shortly after all this took place, Daddy got his orders to move to Newport, Rhode Island, and we had to give up our fowls. I begged to take Sweet Thing, but my parents explained that it just wasn't possible. So the three of them were farmed out to someone who had a home in the country with some acreage, and who was happy to take them. To tell the truth, I was pretty relieved to have the night squawks of Sweet Thing, demanding to be released from the bathtub and to be taken to my warm bed, cease. He was one noisy duck. We heard later that Sweet Thing had grown into a mean drake that attacked anyone who came near him.

*   *   *   *   *

Our dad traveled from Washington State to Coronado to organize the move to Newport, Rhode Island. After packing up all our belongings, we piled into the car and made the 3,000 mile journey. We settled in to a nice home known as Sunnylea Manor, at the corner of Ochre Point and Leroy avenue, that had at one time been a stable for horses. It was actually a duplex of sorts, with an arched passageway between the two living spaces. Another Navy couple occupied the second home. The property had many pear and apple trees, which bore more fruit than our family could consume.

The new billet was located in Newport, Rhode Island, aboard U.S.S. Yosemite (AD-19), the ComDesLant (Commander Destroyers Atlantic) flagship. Jarrell reported for duty in his new assignment as Chief of Staff on 6 September, 1951, replacing Rear Admiral Ephraim R. McLean, Jr.

Chief of Staff for ComDesLant was much the same as his earlier billet in San Diego as Chief of Staff for Commander Destroyers Pacific. Captain Jarrell's job, then and now, was to ensure that the wishes of the Commander were carried out and that the performance of the destroyer fleet made the boss proud. Jarrell was good at that.

The ComDesLant flagship, U.S.S. Yosemite (AD-19), was a Dixie-class destroyer tender home-ported in Newport from 1946 to 1962. She would sail along the Eastern Seaboard and into the Caribbean performing duties both as the Flagship of ComDesLant and as a tender. Tenders are ships fully equipped to affect any repairs that would not require the destroyer to be in a dry dock. With a complete machine shop and foundry, and virtually any supplies and parts that might be needed, tenders can provide immediate support to the destroyers when needed.

U.S.S. Yosemite (AD-19) Flagship ComDesLant
(Official U. S. Navy Photograph)

Joan tells us about living in Newport, Rhode Island:

When Daddy returned from his tour of duty in the
Pacific, he was stationed at the naval base in Newport,
Rhode Island. We moved there in time for me to start my
freshman year of high school. I can remember my mother
taking me in to register me. It was the custom at that time
for all students to take Latin. We both wanted me to take
Spanish before I forgot all I had learned in my two years in
Mexico. There was much opposition to that request. It was
simply "not done" for a child to take <u>any</u> foreign language
except Latin before they were sophomores. Mother was
insistent, and I became the first student in the history of that
school (probably) to take a foreign language other than
Latin in the freshman year. I don't know what was the big
deal – I was top student in my Spanish class, thanks to my
years in Mexico.

Except for my Spanish class, my freshman year in
high school was a complete disaster. I barely managed to
survive. For starters, the people all spoke a foreign
language; my aunt was "ahnt;" r's were dropped in favor of
"ah's." I felt like a fish out of water.

I was really an odd-ball during my first year of high
school. Not only did I not speak the language, I dressed
funny. Actually, I was really proud of my clothes. I had no
idea that wearing a silk blouse with a cotton circle skirt in
mid-winter was not the height of fashion. The way this
strange manner of dressing came about was a result of my
father. When Daddy returned from the Orient, he brought
all of us presents. Mother and I really cleaned up with
beautiful hand-embroidered silk blouses. Daddy had even
picked out one that he meant especially for me! It had an
enormous letter "B" embroidered over the entire front.

When asked why he had chosen the letter "B," Daddy replied, "What 'B'?" So I attended school in Rhode Island wearing Chinese silk blouses and cotton circle skirts.

Our house was kind of neat. We lived in the ritzy, toney area of town with all the big mansions. We didn't live in a big mansion, though, but in one-half of a stable with horse stalls which had been converted to two living quarters. The two story section of the barn was converted to a living room downstairs, and Mother and Daddy's room upstairs. We children lived in converted stalls which stretched out behind the barn. There was lots of open land around, and during the summer we each were allowed to plant our own garden. I wanted to plant tomatoes. So Mother told me how to dig up the ground, and bought me tomato plants to put in my garden. They grew beautifully, and produced a marvelous crop – of yellow tomatoes. I felt I had really been cheated. When the nasty tomato worms arrived, I abandoned my garden.

Lewis was a real explorer at this time of his life. He and his sixth grade buddies would take off in the morning, and be gone all day. One day he came home with something totally unexpected – a tiny infant cat. Lewis explained, heatedly, that while he was in the woods, he came across a sack of newborn kittens which had been abandoned. Someone had taken the "easy" way out to dispose of unwanted livestock. Lewis was irate! Daddy, being a real sucker for animals, agreed that we could keep Lewis' kitten, if we could save it. First we tried feeding the baby with an eye dropper. That worked fairly well, but was tedious. Then I remembered that some of my old dolls were feed-and-wet baby dolls which came with doll bottles that were just the size for an infant cat who didn't even have its eyes open. We quickly put those into use, and Calico thrived! Lewis was thrilled, and the rest of us were pretty happy too.

* * * * *

In August 1952 Captain Jarrell received orders to detach from ComDesLant and report to the Naval Reserve Officers Training Corps Unit at Rice Institute (now Rice University) to be Professor of Naval Science. He was relieved in mid-September and traveled with the family to Washington, D.C., where he spent a week at the Pentagon, then on to LaGrange, Georgia, for family visits. The final leg of the journey was to Houston, Texas, where they arrived in early October.

We took up residence in a nice house on Milford Street, only three blocks from Edgar Allan Poe Elementary School where Lewis and I would be attending. Joan would be attending Lamar High School, which was some distance away, and would be car-pooling to school. Our house was less than a mile from Rice Institute, making it very convenient for our dad, Captain – now Professor – Jarrell.

After Jarrell's first semester of teaching, the midshipmen began their NROTC summer training program. They would spend 3 weeks in the aviation familiarization program in Texas and then three weeks learning about amphibious assault in Virginia. Ten Rice students, as well as another 30 from other schools, had just completed their aviation training and were en rout to Virginia when the aircraft developed a malfunction upon takeoff from Pensacola, Florida, after refueling. Tragically, the plane crashed, killing four crew members and thirty seven NROTC students, nine from Rice Institute. Five people survived the crash; two crewmembers and three students, one of whom was from Rice Institute. Captain Jarrell was devastated by the news of the crash. He immediately began organizing support for the families and contacted each family himself.

In November, as a birthday gift to Joan, Dad brought home a dachshund puppy. The deal was that Joan had to take full responsibility and clean up after it, feed it, and care for it. Secretly, the puppy was probably something Dad wanted, as he missed Snitz and was very fond of dachshunds. He controlled the name negotiations and the new puppy became Spiffy, because Dad said she had that kind of personality. And you could tell that he was quickly becoming attached to her.

On 1 October, 1953, Captain Jarrell received some good news: "Pursuant to the provisions of Officer Personnel Act of 1947, the President of the United States, by and with the advice and consent of the Senate, temporarily appoints you a Rear Admiral in the U. S. Navy to rank from the first day of October, 1953."

Our dad, Captain Jarrell, was now Admiral Jarrell. Our mom told us that Dad was especially proud of his promotion because he had never served in the Pentagon, which was thought to be a prerequisite for advancement to flag rank.

Admiral Jarrell left the NROTC billet 9 October, 1953, being relieved by Captain William Y. Allen, who would be the new Professor of Naval Science.

While performing his assigned duty at Rice Institute, Captain Jarrell had worked tirelessly to promote the positive image of the Naval ROTC Program, as well as the image of the United States Navy. Shortly after reporting to his next duty assignment as

Commander, Destroyer Flotilla ONE, Jarrell received a commendation letter acknowledging his efforts.

DEPARTMENT OF THE NAVY

OFFICE OF INFORMATION

WASHINGTON 25, D.C.

29 OCT 1953

From: Chief of Information

To: Rear Admiral A. E. Jarrell, U. S. Navy,
        Commander, Destroyer Flotilla ONE

Via: Commander, Cruiser Destroyer Force, Pacific Fleet

Subj: Performance of public information duties;
        commendation on

1.   Your personal interest in and development of a favorable public response to the U. S. Navy in the Houston, Texas, area during your tour of duty there as Professor of Naval Science, Rice Institute, September 1952 to September 1953, has come to the attention of this office through laudatory press comments and expressions of appreciation by local Houston civic groups.

2.   In view of the many benefits which can result from the goodwill acquired from the students of Rice Institute and of the citizens of the Houston area, you are to be

commended upon your successful attention to the important command responsibility of public relations.

(signed) Lewis A. Parks

Years later, in 1958, Jarrell commented to one of his Houston friends "I think that you know that I consider my year at Rice to be one of the highlights of my naval service. In my opinion, there is no better school in the nation."

Joan remembers the move to Houston:

> Our next move was to Houston, Texas, where Daddy was in charge of the Naval ROTC program at Rice Institute. He seemed to be pleased with the change, and I think he enjoyed teaching.
>
> It was about this time that Mother changed from being "Mommie" or "Mama" to Mother. I think the change began to take place at about the same time she began to lose any intelligence she might have been born with. Probably it started with: "Oh, Mooothher!," which was my usual reaction to most of her suggestions during that time in my life. Eventually, after having practiced with that phrase, I simply shortened it to Mother, and Mother she remained from then on. (Incidentally, she did regain her mental capacities at about the same time that I came of age.)
>
> We lived in a two-storied house within ten minutes drive of the college campus. Our house had a basement, the living area on the ground floor, and all the bedrooms upstairs. The most memorable feature to my mind was the large Magnolia tree that the neighbors had planted next to the property line. When the flowers bloomed on our side of

the tree, Mother would cut one and float it in a bowl of water. One flower placed in the living room or the dining room would fill the entire house with the most delicious fragrance.

I was a sophomore in high school in Houston. We lived some distance from the school I was to attend, and there was no school bus available for our area. Fortunately, our neighbors on the other side from the house with the Magnolia tree consisted of a family with a girl my age and a boy Lewis' age. Mother was one of five mothers in a car pool which drove us to the high school.

I started driver's education in the fall of my sophomore year. After I received my learning permit, Daddy would take me for instruction to the Rice Institute stadium parking lot. We would meander around the marked parking areas for an hour or so at a time. I found it to be dull driving, and begged him to let me drive on the streets. But he never did.

Calico, Lewis' cat, was just reaching puberty when we got to Houston. She came in heat shortly after we arrived, and must have stayed in heat for the next six months. We were not allowed to let her out, of course, and Daddy did not believe in "fixing" an animal that wasn't broken. So we suffered through months of yowling. Finally she got over it and was allowed normal cat privileges. Unfortunately, Calico would not always return home at bedtime to accompany Lewis to bed. On those occasions she would climb up in the neighbor's car and sit on the engine to keep warm. One morning the neighbor was late for work, and upon starting up his car, backed quickly out of his driveway and left. Lewis found Calico dead in the driveway and was completely distraught. Mother finally managed to calm him down, but I'm sure that experience made a lasting impression on him.

Daddy usually took us to the sports events at Rice Institute. I don't remember whether we went to football games, (they were never my favorite), but we always went to basketball games. I soon recognized the team members, and developed a school-girl's crush on one of the players who was also one of Daddy's NROTC students. I imagined all sorts of scenarios in which the young man would be overcome by my charm and beauty, and would not be able to live without me. At the end of summer, the NROTC group went to discharge their obligation to the Navy by going on a six-week training tour. Daddy got them off in good time, but soon received a phone call. The plane had crashed with all people on board. No one had survived. Daddy was responsible for seeing that all parents were notified, and that the press releases were appropriate.

CHAPTER 15
POST-WAR KOREA

Jarrell's new position would be Commander, Destroyer Flotilla ONE. He would hold this assignment for fourteen months, seven of which would be on deployment in Korea with the United Nations Command, Military Armistice Commission. In preparation, Admiral Jarrell had to get the family repositioned to Coronado, California, so they loaded up the car and made the drive in October 1953, settling into a house on "H" Street.

I remember asking my mom why we continue to make so many trips and live in so many different places. She answered, "When there is a place that has a problem, they send your daddy to fix it. Daddy is like a troubleshooter, and they know that he can fix the problem."

Joan gives her thoughts on returning to Coronado:

We moved back to Coronado after Daddy received his promotion to Rear Admiral. The parents rented a lovely sprawling house on H Street, and we lived there for Daddy's first tour of duty at sea. It fell to Mother to complete my education in driving a car so that I could apply for my license on my sixteenth birthday. She must have done a pretty good job, because I passed. (Despite the fact that my parallel parking left the car a good three feet from the curb.) The test drivers in Coronado were pretty tolerant of young drivers who were applying for their first license. We still had only one family car, but my parents, who retired for the night at 8:00 p.m., were pretty generous about letting me use the car in the evenings to visit friends, go to a movie, or some church function.

After a short time of living in Coronado on this tour of duty, my parents decided it was time that they buy a house. They surveyed the available houses, and finally decided on a four bedroom house on Adella Avenue. For the first time in their lives, my brothers each had his own room. I guess we each had our choice in descending-age order. I had a lovely back corner bedroom next to the parents' room. Lewis had the room in front of me, moving towards the living area. Both of our bedrooms had doors and windows that opened out into a narrow, but long patio. Henry had his own private suite, as it were, behind the one-car garage, with a bedroom and bath. His room may have originally been intended for a live-in servant, because it didn't match the décor of the rest of the house. All of the rest of the house was completely paneled in redwood. Each of the main bedrooms had built-in shelves, closets, and bed frames all done in redwood also. The parents bought the entire house with all the furniture intact. It stood on a narrow, but long lot, and was bordered on both sides by empty lots. Daddy spoke of buying the corner lot next to us to insure our privacy, but I guess he could never settle on a reasonable price with the owners. Fortunately for us, both lots stood empty for the entire time we lived there, so we had plenty of privacy.

Lewis was in junior high school when we moved to Adella Avenue. He was very much interested in reptiles, and Mother always hated to do his wash for fear of finding some lizard or snake. One time one of Lewis' snakes got away from him, and Mother told him that he couldn't leave his room until it was found. I was grateful that none of his "pets" ever found their way to my room. One of Lewis' favorite pastimes was skin diving, and he brought beautiful abalone home to Mother, knowing that she was extremely fond of shellfish. Mother didn't know how to cook a large variety things because of the many years she had spent cooking to accommodate Daddy's weird diet. Abalone was one of the things she didn't know how to cook. I do remember her pounding on it, but it never did soften up to her liking. I had no interest in trying it, so I didn't pay too much attention to what the eventual outcome was. But Lewis' abalone shells were lovely. He was taking shop at school during that time, and I badgered him into making me an abalone pendant to wear with one of my chains. He did a really nice job, and I wore the pendant for years after.

My junior and senior years of high school were my best years of all. I really enjoyed attending Coronado High School, population 357, and got to know most of the students there, at least by sight. I made many girlfriends, and we did lots of things together. I was active in two different churches, even though I was not a member of any church. (My parents decided early in our lives that they would not attach us to any special church denomination. The reason given to us was that they wanted us to be able to choose the religion of our preference without having a prior commitment made by them. I suspect that the real reason was that they were not churchgoers themselves, and they didn't want to start going just for their children.) It worked out well for me though, because I sang in the choir at the Presbyterian Church with my friend who was a member there, and I attended the youth group at the

Methodist Church with my friends who were members there. The Methodist young people were very active, and I had lots of fun participating in their activities.

Daddy loved to play tennis, and he bought a family membership to the beach and tennis club at the Hotel del Coronado. We were allowed to use the pool, the tennis courts, and the golf course, as well as the beach in front of the hotel. A big thrill was when we went to the pool when Daddy was playing tennis and, upon completion of his match, he would buy us a hamburger and French fries at a greatly inflated price. They seemed to taste so much better poolside. One of my best friends, Susie, liked to go to the hotel with me. We would play on the beach and in the ocean, and hope to be noticed by cute boys. If we were ever noticed, they never let on to us.

Another classmate was a friend of mine. Linda was tiny and cute, with short auburn curls. Her sister, Judy, was two years younger than us, and I liked them both. I spent a lot of time at their home in the evenings, especially after I got my driver's license and could use the car. The family had a television, and I had a standing invitation to visit and watch TV with them. I was enthralled by the "box," and tried to get my father to buy one for us. His standard reply was that he would buy one when color television was perfected. He never did think that it was perfected.

My senior year in high school was really fun. I finally felt some importance, and I enjoyed the year thoroughly. Graduation finally came, and the importance rapidly dwindled to nothingness again the next fall when I started college.

I had decided that I would major in elementary
education which was offered at all three of the colleges I
had considered. My counselor recommended a girls'
college in San Francisco, Mills College, and also
University of California at Santa Barbara. My parents
leaned toward Santa Barbara because it was state supported
and would cost less, and because it was co-educational. I
guess by now Daddy was beginning to worry that he would
never get rid of me, and he wanted to expose me to men in
the hopes that I would get married off.

I went along with my parents and applied to Santa
Barbara and sent in my application fee. Then I informed
them that I also wanted to apply to Mills. There was a fee
there too, and I was told that it was out of the question. I
could only attend one school, so there was no point in
paying an application fee to another school which would
just be lost. I didn't argue much about that, and, in due
course, was accepted at Santa Barbara.

Finally the high school graduation day arrived. We
were, all 97 of us, on stage in our caps and gowns, taking
part in the ceremony. Special awards were being
announced, and people were getting up to accept their
awards. The Spanish teacher was introduced to present the
Spanish award. I tried to think who might get that award.
As I was thinking about it, I heard my name spoken. I was
completely surprised and shocked. I knew that I was the
best student academically in the Spanish class because of
my prior experiences in Mexico, but that was all I had
going for me. Most of the other awards included
community service, school citizenship, and other altruistic
activities, of which I felt I had none. But, sure enough,
there was my name on the plaque. The teacher rambled on

and on, almost handing me the trophy, and then taking it back as he said more glowing things about me. I kept reaching for it so that I could escape back to my seat, only to find that he had taken it out of my reach again. Finally he finished, shook my hand, and released me from the spotlight. The rest of the ceremony passed in a blur, and before I knew it, I had graduated.

After getting the family settled into the new "H" Street home, the first stop Jarrell had to make on the way to his new billet was 24 October, 1953, when he reported to Commander, Cruiser-Destroyer Force, Pacific Fleet, in San Diego. This was a temporary duty assignment lasting several days to prepare him for the work that lay ahead.

On 4 November Jarrell detached from the temporary duty in San Diego and made his way to Long Beach, California, where he assumed command of Destroyer Flotilla ONE aboard his Flagship, U.S.S. Hamul, the same ship he had served on in 1943. Hamul set sail 13 November for Yokosuka, Japan, arriving 29 November. From Yokosuka Jarrell made his way to Korea, arriving 4 December, 1953.

The Military Armistice Commission was defined in the Armistice Agreement signed by both sides on 27 July, 1953, at 1000 hours local time. It specifies that "The Military Armistice Commission shall be composed of ten (10) senior officers, five (5) of whom shall be appointed by the Commander-in-Chief, United Nations Command, and five (5) of whom shall be appointed jointly by the Supreme Commander of the Korean People's Army and the Commander of the Chinese People's Volunteers."

The United Nations Command, Military Armistice Commission, Korea, was established shortly after the signing of the Armistice Agreement. Of the many UN organizations involved in the negotiations, Jarrell was only directly working within the Military Armistice Commission (MAC). This was an unsettled time and the various UN components were still trying to get organized.

Jarrell wrote home to Ann and gave her a flavor of what it was like.

Munsan-Ni, Korea
8 December, 1953

This place is about what I expected it to be. I occupy tent No. 22, about 50 feet from one occupied by Ambassador Dean [Arthur H. Dean], who is engaged in political talks. I am a member of a different group, the Military Armistice Commission, United Nations Command. Major General Julius K. Lacey USAF, who was in Panama City when we were there, is the senior member. Others are Major General M. C. Jitjanok Kritakara Royal Thai Army, General George E. R. Bastin of Great Britain, and Brigadier General Daley of our Army – five of us, with a supporting staff of about two hundred.

I have an oil heater, a wash pan and can of water, a cot with sleeping bag, some folding chairs, and a couple of makeshift shelves that I got from Bill Mendenhall.

I use my overcoat for a bathrobe, since the showers are about 50 yards away and the temperature has varied between 9 and 30 degrees. A one-holer "Chick Sale" [outhouse] is near the showers. The whole place is loaded with dust. Yesterday we had a little snow.

We came, in six hours, from fairly good weather to ice. We flew across Korea and I was fascinated with the rugged mountains and barren country. Seoul is a city that has been badly wrecked.

We flew in two helicopters yesterday [7 December] to Panmunjom, 18 miles away, for a "conference" with the Communists. It was about as I expected. We met in a shack with an oil heater, seated on opposite sides of a table. The meeting lasted over three hours. We had about four subjects to discuss and really had the Chinese and North Koreans over a barrel. They ignored, however, their violations of the Armistice terms and of course accused us of lying, using secret agents in their camps, and of being war-mongering monsters. It was so ridiculous that on one occasion I laughed and, believe it or not, they did too. I do not anticipate any success. They are going to be very ugly when the time comes to release our prisoners of war on 22 January. They have stopped explaining.[Explaining is the agreed-to term for the process of notifying the POWs of their release options -- repatriation or staying in the Western World.]

I met the members, Sweden and Swiss, of the Neutral Nations Supervisory Commission. They are reasonable people, but are blocked by the other members, the Poles and Czechs.

I am trying to get caught up, and I find the reading of past records to be very interesting. I hope to be out of here in about two months, but will enjoy it as long as it lasts.

The Neutral Nations Supervisory Commission (NNSC) was included in the Armistice Agreement, and provided for four countries, two picked by the UN Command and two by the Communists, to provide inspections and investigations to verify that certain terms of the Armistice were being abided. Sweden and Switzerland were selected by the UN Command, and Poland and Czechoslovakia by the North Koreans and Chinese. The primary role of the NNSC was to ensure that troop counts and armament levels did not increase above the numbers agreed to in the Armistice.

A subset of the NNSC was the Neutral Nations Inspection Teams (NNIT), whose task was to perform inspections in the demilitarized zone as well as in North Korea and South Korea to verify that the terms of the Armistice were not being violated. Although the Armistice clearly defined what the NNIT was, it did not specify how they would operate, which would became a serious issue for the South Koreans and the UN Military Armistice Commission.

Munsan-Ni, Korea
12 December, 1953

We haven't had a meeting with the communists since last Monday's, but will have to hold one next Monday, since the terms of the armistice do not permit a recess of longer than one week. Peiping [now Beijing] has been blasting almost continuously for the last two days, so we are expecting that our opponents have been instructed to accuse us of every violation they can think of.

15 December, 1953

We have had no more meetings with the cutthroats on the opposite side of the green table, so I have been able to finish reading all of the records of the Military Armistice Commission since the Armistice Agreement was signed on 27 July.

Ambassador Dean who has been having quite a time with the communists, trying to arrange for a peace conference, left for the States this morning. He walked out of a meeting last Saturday when the Reds called the United States a perfidious nation. Early this morning the Communists had the crust to send a letter to Dean here, asking for a meeting, but reiterating that the U.S. is a perfidious nation, so Dean shoved off. Kenneth Young, of the State Department, now is in charge of the political talks, but is not meeting unless an apology is presented.

On Christmas day, the five heads of the UN Military Armistice Commission fully expected the Communists to call a meeting, they knowing that Christmas is an important holiday. General Bastin (British) suggested that the five of them draw straws to see who would meet with them and represent the MAC. Jarrell "...volunteered to represent the UN side, and would have enjoyed doing so." However, the Communists fooled them and did not ask for a meeting.

Some of the leaders of the Military Armistice Commission were becoming very dissatisfied with the way the negotiation efforts were progressing. General Bastin, of Britain, was particularly fed up with his duty on the MAC. On 30 December, Jarrell sums up recent events.

Munsan-Ni, Korea
30 December, 1953

> *The Czechs, Poles, and Indians of the Neutral*
> *Nations Repatriation Commission have released a report*
> *that is very derogatory to the UN and especially to the U.S.*
> *The Swedish and Swiss members have written their own*
> *report, which disagrees with the communist "neutral"*
> *nations. I am enjoying picking the Communist report to*
> *pieces, but I doubt that we shall make any use of my report,*
> *as it pulls no punches and probably will be voted down by*
> *my contemporaries.*

The Military Armistice Commission (MAC) consisted of five senior United Nations commanders, three from the United States, one from Great Britain, and one from Thailand. Their communist counterparts were senior officers from North Korea and China. Once the Armistice was signed on 27 July stopping active hostilities, UNMAC and the Communists met on a somewhat regular basis to arrive at a final conclusion to the war – peace. The most significant stumbling block in a settlement at that time was the repatriation of Prisoners of War. Many Communist POWs did not want to go back to China and North Korea, and the Communists insisted that they be forced to return. This was a major issue.

In addition to the United Nations Military Armistice Commission (UNMAC), there were the Neutral Nations Supervisory Commission (NNSC) and its subset the Neutral

Nations Inspection Teams (NNIT), as well as the Neutral Nations Repatriation Commission (NNRC) which was only involved in the ultimate disposition of the POWs. UNMAC consisted of UN members who fought against the Communists, and represented freedom-loving countries. Sitting opposite the negotiating table was the Communist MAC team – the countries that invaded Korea. But the other three, NNSC, NNIT, and NNRC were made up of countries that had not taken part in the war. The "neutral" countries representing the Communists were, themselves, either Communist countries or Communist sympathizers, and would actively work to derail the peace talks in an effort to assist the Communists at the negotiating table. They did this, primarily, through written reports, which would be distributed to both sides of the MAC and often would contain lies. These reports would be repudiated by the UN members of the NNSC or NNIT, which would become another point of contention in the on-going negotiations at Panmunjom.

Admiral Jarrell was still the commander of Destroyer Flotilla ONE and was performing a remarkable balancing act in keeping up to date with the needs of the flotilla as well as the activities in Korea. Fortunately, the United States Navy has some remarkable personnel, and a lot of the flotilla responsibility was delegated to Jarrell's subordinates.

Munsan-Ni, Korea
14 January, 1954

Jim Cook, my operations officer, is coming up tomorrow. I want to keep up to date concerning my flotilla, but there will be no one else coming up for some time.

I am expecting a complete mess within a week – in Korea. It was a mistake to arrange for an armistice instead of winning the war. The Indians, under orders from Nehru, are favoring the Communists. Our prisoners, some 22,500, should be restored to civilian status midnight 22 January, but the Communists are threatening "grave consequences," etc., if this is done. In fact, they say that it will not be done.

Every member of the Military Armistice Commission and many other of our ranking officers have been invited by the Indians to a luncheon at Panmunjom this Saturday. I am the only one who has rejected the invitation. The Indians gave a party for the Communists last Tuesday and this party is supposed to be similar. I want no part of it. The Indians stink; there might be publicity which we could not prevent; and Panmunjom is no place for some 50 high ranking officers to be at one time.

17 January, 1954

Jim Cook went back to Yokosuka yesterday. He brought the record of an investigation into the collision of two destroyers and wanted my advice. Also, another destroyer went aground. He did say that I was being considered for command of the Blockade and Escort Force, in addition to my flotilla. Maybe I shall get back to the ships soon.

My mind is completely open regarding possible future events. Anything can happen. I sent word back by Cook concerning alertness, particularly next weekend. If I believed everything the Communists say, I would feel sure after every meeting that they plan open warfare. They certainly like to threaten, and I would like to reject abruptly every demand they make for interpretation of the armistice for their own benefit. Instead, we give a very carefully worded reply, just as if that had any effect. However, General Lacey tells me that his life here now is easier than before I arrived. The British member, who is an appeaser, had been very influential. I have given him, repeatedly, strong and straight talk in refusing to be influenced. He tried to "break me in properly."

24 January, 1954

There is no change in conditions here, so far as our Commission is concerned. We got back about 22,000 Chinese and Korean prisoners of war on 20-21 January, after much name calling and threatening by the Communists. At our meeting yesterday they were very tense, but did not use any nastier language than they have used before. Seoul had an air alert late yesterday. They (the Communists) are very angry and upset about the former prisoners. I really enjoy the actual meetings with the Communists. We have got the best of them at every session since I arrived.

2 February, 1954

General Bastin, the British major general, is over in Tokyo for a week, and his absence makes this place much more pleasant. His alternate, Brigadier Burrows of New Zealand, thinks just like I do. There is a lot of talk about what the Navy is going to do, with "peace" in Korea and the necessity of laying up 50 ships.

We got the 22,000 prisoners and freed them, but the Reds are still yelling like stuck pigs. I don't know whether they will start something or not; it depends on Moscow, and I think it's an even bet that they will order this war started again.

The 22,000 prisoners that Jarrell mentioned in his letter home were POWs in the hands of the United Nations, and for the most part were involuntarily forced into the war fighting against the UN forces. They were primarily freedom-loving Chinese who had fought against communism in China after WWII, and South Koreans captured by the communists and forced to fight against their homeland. When taken prisoner by the United Nations forces, they were placed into POW camps throughout South Korea. One major obstacle in the Armistice negotiations was what to do with these POWs. The communists insisted that they all be repatriated to China or North Korea, while the UN Command insisted that they be allowed to choose for themselves -- be repatriated or stay in the Western World. To sort all this out the Neutral Nations Repatriation Commission was formed to allow the prisoners to be advised of their options so they can make the decision of being repatriated, staying in South Korea, or going to Taiwan (where Chiang Kai-shek had set up his new government). By agreement, this process would start 24 September 1953 and the POWs would have 90 days to hear from both sides the explanations for or against repatriation. The prisoners were transferred to the Demilitarized Zone from the various POW camps, where they were held by the Custodian Force, India (CFI) for 90 days. The communists were adamant that all of the POWs be repatriated, but very few chose that option, which infuriated the communists. Any POW who wanted to be repatriated would be immediately processed for release. Any who did not want repatriation would be held for an additional 30 days past the 90 day period and then freed. When Jarrell said, "We got the 22,000 prisoners..." he was saying that the CFI had processed them and released them to the United Nations Command for transport to their homes or destinations. Very few -- a few hundred -- chose to go back to communism.

Constant turnover of key players and staff was another detriment to a smooth operation, although the UNMAC continued to perform. In late December General Lacey, the senior MAC member, took ill and went to Seoul for treatment. In early February Lacey traveled to Tokyo for a conference and again became ill.

Munsan-Ni, Korea
7 March, 1954

> *The Reds have asked for a meeting Tuesday and I shall be the spokesman for the U.N. side, since Lacey is still in the hospital in Tokyo. I don't know how Lacey is getting along. We called him by phone yesterday, but were informed that he was confined to his bed and should not walk to the telephone. I have doubts about his coming back.*

> *We have a new member, Major General Lin Sun Ha of the Republic of Korea Army. He replaces Brigadier General Daley, who leaves for the States tomorrow. We expect General Jitjanok, our Thai member, back today. He has been in Bangkok for about a month.*

> *There are so many members of our staff who have not attended a MAC meeting that I am going to have a rehearsal tomorrow so that they can get a general idea of*

the proceedings. It should help our Chinese and Korean translators too.

11 March, 1954

We had a long session with the Reds Tuesday. It was completely successful. All they could do was lie and squirm. I have received quite a few congratulations. I had a sore throat and slight cold, and had to use cough drops after each blast, but I don't think my sarcastic tone was affected. They called the meeting, which should have given them an advantage since they made the first statement; however, they never gained the offensive.

After the meeting, CBS asked me for a short television presentation of about two minutes. I complied, but had no time to plan a good statement, so had to read one. The TV probably already has been shown in the States. It was taken just outside the conference hut at Panmunjom.

Jarrell Giving Statement to CBS, 9 March 1954

In late March Admiral Jarrell traveled to Yokosuka, Japan, to look after his other responsibility, Destroyer Flotilla ONE. Admiral Lacey, who had been ill in Tokyo, had recovered and returned to Korea. Over the telephone Lacey advised Jarrell that the Military Armistice Commission had had a meeting 7 April, and that the U.N. took a beating. Admiral Lacey would be returning to Tokyo for a medical checkup, and Jarrell had received word that he was to relieve Lacey as the Senior Military Armistice Commission Member in the near future.

On 4 May Headquarters, United Nations Command, published the official document making Admiral Jarrell the Senior Member of M.A.C

4 MAY 1954

SUBJECT: Credentials

TO: Rear Admiral Albert E. Jarrell
             United States Navy

You hereby are accredited as the Senior United
Nations Command Member of the Military Armistice
Commission in Korea effective immediately, vice Major
General Julius K. Lacey, United States Air Force.

J. E. Hull
General, United States Army
Commander in Chief, United Nations Command

Munsan-Ni, Korea
9 May, 1954

*We are having quite a lot of correspondence now
with the Neutral Nations Supervisory Commission. The
Poles and Czechs are Reds, not neutral at all.*

*I have moved into Lacey's double sized tent, but
only because the Army would be embarrassed by having it
unoccupied. I have had to go to Seoul several times
recently. A number of meetings, but also attended the
Ethiopian Independence Day Celebration.*

*I was a "Guest of Honor" at the dinner
inaugurating the Princeton Society of Seoul, and am now*

an honorary member. President Syngman Rhee, Princeton class of 1910, was present.

14 May, 1954

We have made many changes to the M.A.C. The first being my relieving General Lacey as Senior Member. Brigadier General William J. Clinch replaced me as a M.A.C. member, and Brigadier General Hobart Hewett replaced our Thai member, Major General Jitjanok.

We still have quite a staff here, although I have made some heavy cuts, from about 460 to 220. In addition, we have a support group of about 800 officers and men.

The Reds called a meeting yesterday to blast us for propaganda purposes to try to support their position in Geneva. I let them have it in plain language, and demanded an accounting for 3405 UN prisoners and 54 foreigners they hold, as well as 2831 prominent Koreans. They were flustered, but nothing will come of it. I would like to present an ultimatum.

In early June 1954 Admiral Jarrell received orders to return to Destroyer Flotilla ONE and focus on that command. Prior to his departing Korea, Admiral Jarrell was awarded the Order of Military Merit Taiguk by Korean President Syngman Rhee.

SYNGMAN RHEE

PRESIDENT OF THE REPUBLIC OF KOREA

(Translation)   June 2, 1954

CITATION

In recognition and appreciation for his exceptionally
outstanding service, I take great pleasure in accordance
with the powers delegated to me by the Constitution of the
Republic of Korea, in awarding the

ORDER OF MILITARY MERIT TAIGUK

To

REAR ADMIRAL ALBERT E. JARRELL
59705, United States Navy

Rear Admiral Jarrell distinguished himself by
exceptionally meritorious service in Korea during the
period August 1950 to October 1951.

As commander of Transport Division II, he
commanded the third echelon Inchon operation during the
most critical stage of the war, successfully landing combat
troops in spite of the heavy enemy shelling. Later, his
profound military knowledge was fully displayed, when, as
Senior-Officer-Present-Afloat at Wonsan, he was
responsible to deploy Infantry Division from Japan to
Wonsan, and when, in December 1950, he commanded task
element redeploying the 10th U.S. and Republic of Korea

Corps from Hungnam. In that notorious operation, the significant evacuation from Hungnam area would have been dangerously hampered but for his drastic initiative and selfless devotion. In addition to these brilliant activities in the field of actual military operations, his outstanding services ever since he was appointed a member of UNC Military Armistice Commission were highly contributable to the cause of freedom and peace.

Admiral Jarrell's undeviating devotion to duty and exceptional achievements will be permanently remembered by Korean people and reflect great credit not only upon himself but also upon the entire United Nations Forces.

A TRUE COPY: (Signed) Syngman Rhee

Order of Military Merit Taiguk

Jarrell Wearing Order of Military Merit Taiguk Medal, June 1954
(U.S. Army Photo by PFC Sage (CB))

The next day, 3 June, 1954, Army General J. E. Hull, Commander in Chief, Far East, sent Jarrell a letter of commendation.

HEADQUARTERS
FAR EAST COMMAND
And
UNITED NATIONS COMMAND

COMMANDER IN CHIEF   3 June 1954

Dear Admiral Jarrell

Upon the eve of your departure from the Far East, I wish to express my personal appreciation for your outstanding contributions to the successes attained by the United Nations and Far East Commands.

While serving as Commander Destroyer Flotilla ONE and Commander Destroyer Flotilla Western Pacific you were responsible for the administration and training of Cruiser-Destroyer Force, U.S. Pacific Fleet units in the Far East Area. Concurrently, as the Senior Naval Representative and later as senior member of the United Nations Command Military Armistice Commission during a particularly tense and trying period, you contributed to the development and perfection of policies which were followed by the Commission in its important negotiations with the representatives of the Korean People's Army and the Chinese People's Volunteers. You were most successful in the performance of these and other duties and thereby contributed materially to the overall assigned mission.

Please accept my best wishes for a pleasant trip home and for every success in your new assignment.

Sincerely,

(Signed) J. E. HULL
General, United States Army

Admiral Jarrell departed Korea in June of 1954 and rejoined his Flag Ship, U.S.S. Hamul, in Japan. On 14 June Jarrell was awarded a second oak leaf cluster to the Legion of Merit by Army General J. E. Hull in a ceremony at Pershing Heights, Tokyo.

The citation reads:

HEADQUARTERS
FAR EAST COMMAND

CITATION FOR THE LEGION OF MERIT
(Second Oak-Leaf Cluster)

Rear Admiral Albert E. Jarrell, 59705, United States Navy, distinguished himself by exceptionally meritorious conduct in the performance of outstanding service as senior Naval representative of the United States Military Armistice Commission, in Korea, from 7 December 1953 to 9 June 1954. Admiral Jarrell's discerning judgment and astute comprehension of the far-reaching strategic and political implications involved were of paramount importance in countering many misrepresentations and evasions with reasoned negotiation, demonstrable truth and logical conclusions. His lucid presentation of the Commission's position regarding displaced civilians, and prominent role in revising policies and procedures governing the operation of the United Nations' component of the Joint Observer Team stationed in the Han River Estuary materially facilitated implementation of the terms of the Armistice Agreement. Admiral Jarrell's exemplary leadership and commendable actions earned the respect and admiration of his colleagues, and contributed significantly to United Nations progression toward world peace, reflecting great credit upon himself and the military service.

This is the third Legion of Merit award for Jarrell. The first was while commanding Destroyer Division 42 in WWII. The "V" Device was attached to show it was for action during combat. The second award was for the period of December 3 – 24, 1950, with Transportation Division 11 during the operations in Korea, also under combat conditions. The second award was a gold star, the Navy's device to show that the award was not the first, and was awarded in lieu of a medal. This third award was a bronze oak leaf, which is the Army's device used to show that the award is not the first. Although the citation says it is a "second oak leaf cluster," it is a second additional award, this one being an oak leaf cluster.

Legion of Merit with Combat "V" and
Gold Star and Oak Leaf Cluster

General Hull Presents Admiral Jarrell the Army's Oak Leaf
Cluster to the Legion of Merit Medal
(U.S. Army Photo by Sgt Walter W. Platt (SBC))

Having rejoined his command aboard U.S.S. Hamul, Admiral Jarrell departed Yokosuka on 27 June and returned to Long Beach, Hamul's home port. Arrival in Long Beach was on 14 July, 1954.

While Jarrell had been serving as Professor of Naval Science at Rice Institute he had been observing the NROTC cadets and acquiring knowledge of their goals, aspirations, and their motivation for joining the Naval Reserve Officer Training Corps.

During his own long service in the Navy he had seen many changes, and observed how the officers and men had changed as the Navy had changed. During the time he was stationed in Long Beach aboard Hamul he wrote an article, "The Vanishing American Naval Officer," which was published in the September 1954 edition of the *United States Naval Institute Proceedings*, in which he laid out his thoughts. They were quite radical for a Flag Officer to publicly expound.

When Jarrell submitted the article for publication he suggested that the following statement be included at the beginning:

> This article is written for young officers and
> young men who want to be officers, and
> parents whose sons desire a naval career

Admiral Jarrell's article describes how the Navy has changed. Prior to, and even into World War II, Navy discipline and Navy morale were high. Each officer and enlisted man knew his job, worked hard and long hours, and was proud of their elite organization. There was mutual respect between the officers and men. Retention and reenlistments were high. During the War, the size of the navy was greatly increased and the ranks were filled with Naval Reserve Officer Training Corps officers and patriotic men who enlisted because of the National cause. The new officers and men were trained by the "old salts" and performed well during the War. Following WWII a tremendous number of personnel, who were trained and doing a fine job, left the Navy to resume their civilian jobs. Very few stayed on and made the Navy their career.

In Jarrell's opinion, post-WWII the quality of the officers, and consequently the men, had deteriorated, resulting in less than acceptable operations. The old policy of Navy officers serving sea duty for several years before advancement was gone. Some never went to sea. "The genuine salt today is a rarity." A number of changes had taken place that contributed to this. Officer pay could not compete with civilian pay; an officer commanding a fleet loves his job and it is his chosen profession, but, "...his pay will be about that of the vice-president of a small bus company." Many men who attend Annapolis or NROTC do so with no expectation of making the Navy a career. Low pay, reduced benefits, a critical press, and a civilian leadership that belittled the services all played a part.

The Navy's pride and discipline was largely a result of its *Articles for the Government of the Navy*, the traditional "Rocks and Shoals," which were the basis for law and order on the sea. They specified the behavior of the officers and men, and were very specific. The old saw, "The Captain goes down with his ship" exemplifies this concept. The Captain is responsible for the operation of the ship and is held responsible, possibly along with others, if an accident should occur. Likewise, if a ship is to sail on a particular date and time, it is understood that any sailor who missed sailing with the ship will be held accountable, no excuses. Everyone knew the rules, the rules were strict, most everyone followed the rules, and this kept pride and discipline high.

In 1951 the Uniform Code of Military Justice replaced "Rocks and Shoals." UCMJ was largely based upon civilian court systems and provided for civilian attorneys and, under UCMJ, the Court of Military Appeals consisted of three civilian judges. All of a sudden the strict code of the Navy was replaced by a more lenient court. The captain whose ship may have run aground could use a civilian attorney who might argue that he was asleep at the time and had no responsibility, while the "Rocks and Shoals" would have maintained that the captain did not properly train the men under him. The sailor who missed his ship's sailing could argue that he didn't know the sailing date, which would be very hard not to know. In Jarrell's view, the UCMJ resulted in a sloppier operation of the Navy, requiring more lawyers and legal staff to keep up with the paperwork and appeals. Even worse, in his observation, "Maintaining professional discipline today is a rather tough problem." Under "Rocks and Shoals," a Court-martial "was a highly professional though sometimes soul-trying procedure. We all knew that if we ever relaxed in holding a commander accountable, we would soon have irresponsible officers in command." Under the UCMJ a slick attorney may be able to divert the focus away from the actual facts of the case and get an acquittal based on some other irrelevant information.

Admiral Jarrell was a professional naval officer who loved the Navy and wrote the article in an attempt to bring to light the problems that he saw. When he submitted the article to the *Institute* he wrote, "Frankly, I doubt that my article will attract much attention and I shall not be disappointed if you reject it. It is the kind of article that, if published, would be read by those who agree with me and therefore don't need to read it, and would not be read by those who really should read it."

He couldn't have been more wrong. The Chief of Naval Operations, Admiral Robert Carney, wrote Al, "My personal congratulations to you on the fine Naval Institute article on the Vanishing American Naval Officer. These things need to be said – and reiterated. It took courage, for it will not be popular in many circles. I shall urge the Secretary [Secretary of the Navy, Charles Thomas] to read, mark and inwardly digest."

The article was well received and Jarrell received a tremendous number of positive letters. Many NROTC professors told him that they were going to use the article in their classes. The publisher, United States Naval Institute, wrote on October 4, 1954, "It may interest you to know that this article has caused more comment than any other article we have published in the Proceedings in years. Practically all of these comments are favorable and we are receiving requests from numerous Naval activities for permission to reprint it for local use." Once again, Jarrell succeeded, this time even beyond his own expectations.

One day, Lewis brought a little bunny home to the "H" Street home. He kept it for a few hours before our dad found out about it and told him to get rid of it. Lewis cried that the pet store where he got it had told him that the sale was final and there were no returns allowed. Dad barked, in his most commanding voice, "I don't care what you have to do, but you can not have that rabbit." Somewhat later, Dad discovered that there was now a kitten in Lewis' room. Again, "I told you, No Pets!" Lewis replied that he wasn't told there would be no pets, but that he had to get rid of the rabbit and it didn't matter how. So he traded it for a cat. Admiral Jarrell, our dad, priding himself on his command of language and logic, conceded that that was, indeed, what he had said, and allowed Lewis to keep the cat. The family negotiated on a name for the new member, and Dad suggested "Regal," a name the cat wore for the next 23 years.

In all of the previous cities that we had lived, we had always rented our homes, not knowing how long we would be in any particular place. Coronado was a nice town and our folks thought that it might be the place for them to set roots when retirement time finally comes around. On weekends, and whenever he could get away, Dad would drive from Long Beach to Coronado and house-hunt with Mom. They finally found the right house, on Adella Avenue. In late September and early October the move was made from "H" Street to the new home, our home.

CHAPTER 16
THE FINAL COMMANDS

Jarrell remained Commander, Destroyer Flotilla ONE until December 1954 when he received orders to take command of the Amphibious Training Command, Pacific Fleet, headquartered in the Naval Amphibious Base, Coronado, California. Admiral Jarrell relieved Rear Admiral Burton Davis on January 13, 1955. Jarrell would remain in this billet for seventeen months.

Naval Amphibious Base Coronado provided administrative and logistical support to the amphibious forces stationed there, and coordinated training exercises with other military organizations. It was the West Coast home of the Underwater Demolition Team, the predecessor of the SEAL Teams. Training on the beaches adjacent to NAB Coronado would include beach landings using the large Landing Ship, Tank (LST), as well as the smaller LCVP (Landing Craft, Vehicle and Personnel). Naval Construction Battalions (Seabees) would also train on the NAB Coronado facilities. Interservice exercises would often take place at other locations such as the United States Marine Corps Base, Camp Pendleton.

An example of the sorts of training exercises NAB Coronado would be involved in is an exercise, code named "Surfboard," that took place mid-March 1955. This operation would include the Army's 38th Infantry Regiment from Washington State, and it would be in the planning stages for over a year. The premise was that an enemy force had invaded the California coast and had set up a nuclear arsenal in the hills behind San Simeon, a small town 100 miles north of Santa Barbara. The Army would be in command of the operations once the troops hit the beaches, and they would storm the beaches and work inland to neutralize the enemy. Admiral Jarrell would be in command of the ships, and would pick up the Army at Puget Sound, Washington, transport them to Southern California, deliver them to the beaches, and then recover the troops and take them back home.

Admiral Jarrell's flagship for this exercise was U.S.S. Mount Olympus (AGC-8). Olympus, along with the necessary troop transports and landing craft, sailed to Puget Sound to pick up the Army and all its equipment, including tanks and other vehicles. From Washington the ships sailed to a point off the beaches at Coronado and held a practice landing to familiarize the Army with the amphibious landing procedures. Sailing to San Clemente Island, offshore San Diego, exercises were held with live fire from ships, aircraft and artillery. Submarines were used to simulate an attack on the ships. The final stage was to conduct the landing operation at the beaches near San Simeon, which went well. Following the exercises, the Army troops and equipment were returned to Washington State.

Quite often in conducting operations of the magnitude of Surfboard things can go wrong. Part of the exercise is to overcome unexpected events and learn from them so that they are not so much of a problem in actual combat. During Surfboard two planes collided, and civilian vessels encroached on the area and had to be avoided. The crew's training and professionalism kicked in and the incidents were dealt with. Of a more vexatious nature were two stories that a reporter filed with his paper.

Invitations were sent inviting news reporters to accompany U.S.S. Mount Olympus on the exercise. A number of reporters accepted and boarded the ship in San Diego on 18 March. One of them was Mr. Jerry Root of the *Monterey Peninsula Herald*. The stories that Mr. Root filed about the exercise were rather derogatory toward the Navy and made it look like the navy personnel were bungling fools, didn't know how to do their jobs, and couldn't do anything without permission from the admiral. A sampling of the two stories:

Wednesday, March 23, 1955

"Life Aboard The Mt. Olympus, or How Snafued Can You Get?"

- "As far as the newspapermen aboard her for Surfboard were concerned, the Olympus might as well have done its communicating with smoke signals and Boy Scout flags."
- "The ship is yours they said... Communication facilities were ample and all news copy would be expedited."
- A number of times Mr. Root emphasized his being told repeatedly that communications were not a problem.
- A number of times Mr. Root expressed their (implying all the reporters) displeasure at communications being delayed and costly.
- Mr. Root said that communications could not be completed for a number of reasons including his using the wrong form, the receiving station was not available, or the message had to be censored by the commander.
- Mr. Root wrote, "Get the message off? The officer looked alarmed. 'We can't get a message cleared until after the movies. That's standard procedure.'"

In summary, the first story posted by Mr. Root was replete with stories of the ineptitude of the ship's complement.

Friday, March 25, 1955

"Submarines Stalk Surfboard Task Force in Black Pacific"

- Mr. Root mentions that word of two ships being "sunk" in the exercise was announced by the commander "diffidently," and the apparent collision course of a "pip" 10 miles away was reported by the commander in a way that "He didn't appear concerned."
- Mr. Root wrote, "The ship that was going to ram us was now 10 miles away. The commander said it had the right of way and the convoy would have to change course. He said he would wait a while before waking the admiral. A lieutenant watching the radar said, 'Here's a new one.' We waited but no immediate response from CIC [Combat Information Center]. I waddled outside, climbed down two decks and burst into CIC. A group of officers were huddled around a table. A sailor watched over their shoulders. 'What's that pip?' I asked him. 'Oh, hell, it's an island,' he said, 'they had it doing three knots.'"

The two articles garnered a lot of attention by the Navy brass. Reports were written by a number of the cognizant commanders, and Jarrell, being the senior officer, wrote the following two memos.

19 APR 1955

From: Commander Task Force TWELVE
To: Commander FIRST Fleet

Subj: News Items of Monterey Peninsula Herald

Ref: (a)   Superintendant, U.S. Naval Postgraduate
                    School ltr Ser A7-1(992) of 24 March 1955

Encl: (1) Five photostatic copies each of press items written By Mr. Jerry Root under dates of 23 and 25 March 1955

1.   Reference (a) was addressed to Commandant Eleventh Naval District and Commandant Twelfth Naval District, with a copy to Commander FIRST Fleet. It expressed concern over a Monterey Peninsula Herald press item dated 23 March 1955, and made inquiry regarding any information of a mitigating nature that might be available.

2.   Although Commander FIRST Fleet has already addressed a personal letter to Rear Admiral MOOSBRUGGER regarding the item of 23 March, which letter accurately reflects my own views, I believe that my own experiences with Mr. Root, the writer of the article, should be presented. I also enclose photostatic copies of another article prepared by the same writer.

3.   Mr. Root and his photographer came aboard my flagship 18 March and departed 21 March. I greeted them and had a long and pleasant conversation. I learned that Mr. Root, before embarking, had been informed that he could transmit press copy and photographs free of charge. It was carefully explained by Commander MORGAN, my Public Information Officer, that exclusive press releases could not be so transmitted; such transmissions would violate existing instructions, which avoid competition with private enterprise, and "playing favorites." The majority of reporters understood our Naval instructions and the reasons behind them. Mr. Root was informed that general press releases, available to all press sources that desired them, were released free of charge. He also was informed that the desires of the representatives of the press would be given

utmost consideration, compatible with my operational traffic requirements.

4.   I believe that Mr. Root was pleased with his reception, and fully understood and was fully satisfied with naval requirements, which I could not violate. At any rate, he and his photographer gave me the impression that they were pleased; they did not leave the ship, but remained aboard during the rehearsal, the firing demonstration, and the assault. During a part of the firing, I provided the photographer with a helicopter; during the assault, I was requested to provide a boat for the first waves, and complied, although Mr. Root and his photographer changed their plans and went in with the beachmaster prior to the assault. This was a distinct favor on my part. I saw both of these representatives and chatted with them on several occasions during their three day visit. I also inquired several times of my Public Relations Officer regarding their welfare. As an item of associated interest, two lieutenant commanders relinquished their lower bunks to Mr. Root and his photographer.

5.   Under the circumstances, it was inconceivable to me that Mr. Root could be displeased. As a guest, I feel that if he had any cause for dissatisfaction, he should have informed me. I made myself fully available. In fact, I was present in Flag Plot during the mid-watch submarine episode, the only time that I saw Mr. Root late at night, although I was present during all submarine contacts.

6.   I consider the articles to be obviously false to an informed reader. For example, why would Mr. Root state that he "climbed down two decks and burst into CIC?" CIC is five decks below Flag Plot, is clearly marked regarding

non-admittance of unauthorized persons, and Mr. Root had been informed regarding restricted areas. Furthermore, I have inquired of the senior officer on watch at the time of Mr. Root's self-asserted entry, and this officer states that he has no knowledge of such entry. Also, Mr. Root stated to Commander ROBERTSON, senior officer on watch in Flag Plot, "I am going to bed." Mr. Root then left Flag Plot. If Mr. Root did actually "burst into" my CIC as he states, then he is guilty of wanton disregard of oral instructions and bold-lettered warning signs, as well as colossal abuse of my hospitality.

7.   Mr. Root's statement that his copy would have to be censored by me is deliberately false. Shortly after he came aboard, I personally explained to Mr. Root that there would be no censorship; there definitely was none. On one occasion, my Public Information Officer pointed out to Mr. Root that one of his releases contained a word that had no meaning, since the word was not to be found in the dictionary. Did Mr. Root wish to send the copy as presented? Mr. Root did not, and he made a statement to the effect that he could not understand his own error.

8.   If I had violated my instructions and sent Mr. Root's exclusive copy gratis, and if I had given precedence to his copy over my operational traffic, it may be possible that Mr. Root would not have written abusive articles. Of course, Mr. Root was given consideration that was given to other reporters, and in addition he received other assistances, such as the helicopter, because of my desire to be helpful.

9.   I doubt very much that I could have done anything that would have prevented Mr. Root from writing derisive

articles. He must have written them for one or both of the following reasons:

    a. To attempt to attract reader interest by posing as a writer well versed in naval tactics and life aboard ship; and, employing his own obvious knowledge, to add humor to his articles by ridiculing the Navy's performance during PACTRAEX 55P. (actually Mr. Root showed little knowledge of naval life; my watch officer gave him much assistance).

    b. To attempt to undermine the public's confidence in the ability of the Navy to fulfill its missions in national defense.

10.   While I would prefer to consider Mr. Root's articles as nothing more than a display of a perverted sense of humor, by an inept writer posing as a professional, I cannot disregard the possibility of subversion as a motive. Mr. Root displayed considerable skill in deceiving me; I had believed that he was pleased with his treatment aboard ship; his deceit must have been planned. Although I doubt that Mr. Root's articles would influence an informed reader, the majority of his readers probably are not very well informed on naval subjects. The average teen-ager, for example, might read the articles with admiration for Mr. Root's discerning mind, and decide against enlisting in such a "slap-happy outfit" as the U.S. navy.

11.   I shall not in this letter tear down, bit by bit, Mr. Root's statements. However, in the article of 23 March, Mr. Root appears to speak for all newspapermen aboard MOUNT OLYMPUS when he states, "As far as the newspapermen aboard her for SURFBOARD were

concerned, the OLYMPUS might as well have done its communicating with smoke signals and Boy Scout flags." Insofar as I know, other newspapermen did not share this view. The use of the radio-telephone was not suggested by Mr. Root, as he infers, but by my Communication Officer. The alleged statement that "We can't get a message cleared until after the movies" is a ridiculous and untruthful item of reporting. Regarding the plane collision, instead of being tight-lipped, I personally interviewed the injured pilot as soon as he was brought aboard, to insure that he was in fit condition to talk, then personally authorized an interview. Furthermore, I personally informed Mr. Root of this within about five minutes after the pilot reached sick bay.

12.   I fully recognize the importance of maintaining freedom of the press. However, I do not confuse freedom with license. Freedom requires the acceptance of responsibility and accountability. In a separate letter I shall submit a recommendation regarding Mr. Root.

(signed) A. E. Jarrell

The follow-up letter with Admiral Jarrell's recommendation was very brief:

CONFIIDENTIAL   19 APR 1955

From: Commander Task Force TWELVE
To: Commander FIRST Fleet

Subj: Mr. Jerry Root – recommendation for investigation

Ref: (a) CTF 12 ltr Ser 871 of 19 April 1955

1.   It is recommended that Mr. Root be investigated regarding possible subversive activities.

                                        (signed) A. E. Jarrell

Admiral Jarrell had observed, on numerous occasions over the years, actions by reporters, politicians, and diplomats that he thought were contrary to the best interests of the United States. Upon reading the two articles by Mr. Root, he sensed that there was more to the story than just a reporter on assignment. However, there is no evidence that any action was ever taken on Jarrell's recommendation. It is worthwhile to note that at age 31 Mr. Root was not a seasoned reporter, and subsequently moved on to work for other Bay Area newspapers. But one fact should not be overlooked: Whatever reason Mr. Root had for writing the articles in such a disparaging tone, it created an uproar in the naval commands that cost time and money to remedy.

In June-July 1955 the Amphibious Training Command hosted the Indian Platoon of the 57th Special Infantry Company, United States Marine Corps Reserve, from Albuquerque, New Mexico. The men were training in marksmanship at the Marine Corps Rifle Range at Camp Matthews, near La Jolla, California. All members of the platoon were Native Americans, and at the end of the training a number of the officers involved in their training were given the title of Honorary Chief of the New Mexico Indian Nation. Admiral Jarrell was one of those receiving his Chief's headdress in the ceremony, which included Native American dances.

Admiral Jarrell – Chief Big Man
(Depot Photographic Service, MCRD San Diego)

Military assistance by Naval Amphibious Base Coronado extended worldwide. Admiral Jarrell traveled in September 1955 to Taiwan, Vietnam, and Thailand to inspect their capabilities and to make recommendations for improvement. This travel included inspections of ships to determine sea worthiness, observing amphibious exercises, and determining the level of proficiency in

English to evaluate what the effectiveness of United States instructors would be.

Admiral Jarrell and his staff would travel extensively giving talks and seminars to all branches of the military services, focusing on the role of the United States Navy in amphibious assaults. He found that the audiences were much enlightened and more respective of the efforts the Navy put in to these actions.

*　　*　　*　　*　　*

In May 1956 Admiral Jarrell received new orders to report to the Naval base in Yokosuka, Japan, to assume the duties of Commander Fleet Activities (ComFltActs) Yokosuka. Fleet Activities Yokosuka (FAY) is the name given to the naval base located adjacent to the city of Yokosuka, Japan, at the inlet to Tokyo Bay. The base was the largest in the western Pacific and could facilitate almost every task that might be required to support and repair ships of the fleet.

Our family left Coronado in mid-June 1956 and drove to San Francisco where we would board the steamship President Cleveland for the trip to Yokohama. We were accompanied by our two family pets: Spiffy, the little dachshund, and Regal the cat. We arrived in Yokosuka July 1 and took up residence on-base in a home on Halsey Road, on Edwina Hill. My sister Joan, who had completed one year of college, took a year hiatus to experience the Japanese culture. Lewis was in high school and attended Yokohama American High School in Yokohama. I started eighth grade in Yokosuka and, the following year, attended "YoHi."

Admiral Jarrell assumed command of Fleet Activities Yokosuka on July 1, and held a press conference on July 2. The Japanese press corps were very impressed with Jarrell as evidenced by this translated excerpt of the 3 July, 1956, newspaper, *Kanagawa Shimbun* (Kanagawa Newspaper) in Yokohama:

The ComFltAct of Flag Rank started his work on 2 July, 1956 and held a press conference at 1000.

Unlike his predecessor, RADM JARRELL is an admiral who is amiable and, at the same time, a statesman.

At the press conference mentioned, the Admiral started his talk with his first visit of Japan as an Ensign almost 30 years ago. Ball game was held between US team aboard a US vessel and All-Star team of Japan. "Loser was the US team," said he, sufficiently impressing press men with his pro-Japanese sentiments.

Referring to question of labor, he stated that "he was not considering to effect any change in the existing labor situation, since same sum of budget of last year had been allotted for the new Fiscal Year, which starts as of 1 July, 1956," well sweeping off the force reduction jitter existing among certain quarters on the station.

Numerous Japanese citizens were employed on the Navy base, and word of impending cuts had them concerned. In addition, policies and procedures for awarding contracts to vendors who would provide on-base services were not being strictly adhered to. Admiral Jarrell quickly took action to get on-track to repair the relationships with the Japanese communities.

Jarrell immediately began to work with the Japanese, and his policies had a positive impact on Japanese communities and industries. Examples of his first month in office:

12 July – He and Ann attended Yokosuka Chamber of Commerce Tea Ceremony.

12 July – Attended the launching of M.S. Pacific Pioneer by Uraga Dock Shipyard.

14 July – Attended the Memorial Ceremony for Commodore Perry's landing in Japan, held by the Mayor of Yokosuka.

18 July – Toured the *Kanagawa Shimbun* newspaper plant in Yokohama.

24 July – Entire family attended the traditional opening celebration of the Sumida River in Tokyo.

25 July – He and Ann attended a show in Tokyo with Mr. M. Azuma , Managing Director of N.K.K.

27 July – Authorized Uraga Dock Company to use a small part of unused space adjacent to Yokosuka for a casting shop.

31 July – Authorized the use of two Navy boats to provide safety watch for an annual swimming race across Tokyo Bay.

3 August – He and Ann attended a dinner party at the home
of the mayor of Yokosuka, Y. Umezu.

Admiral Jarrell received an invitation from the Japanese
government to allow three teenagers from the naval base to
participate in a Japanese archery event known as yabusame. This is
a centuries-old ritual originally started in order to keep the samurai
archery skills honed. Riding horses, the archers would gallop down
a straight course while standing up in the stirrups. They would pull
an arrow from the quiver, nock it, and fire the arrow at a small
target or ball. Each pass would have three targets. The ritual
leading up to the contest is steeped in tradition and religion. The
first rides down the course are performed by three young boys
dressed in the traditional garb and on horses galloping at full
speed. Each "Purification Boy" makes two passes down the course.
The purpose is to chase away any evil spirits that might be in
attendance. The invitation to Admiral Jarrell was to offer this
honor to three American boys. Jarrell's son, Henry, was one of the
boys who accepted the invitation.

I and the other two boys practiced on weekends for several
weeks in the Emperor's stable grounds in Kamakura, Japan. We
would walk to the train station in Yokosuka, get off at Kamakura,
and walk down the dirt roads to the stables. On the day of the event
we and our families were driven to the Meiji Shrine in Tokyo
where the ritual was to be held. The three of us were taken to a
building on the Emperor's grounds where we were decked out in
traditional samurai dress by a number of young women, who
constantly giggled at something they found terribly amusing. At
the venue, the three of us mounted our horses and awaited our turn
to ride. I was last to make the run, and remember a handler
whipping the horse's flank to get him to run. Standing up in the
stirrups and loosely holding the reins, as we had been taught, I

managed to complete the course without falling off. The three of us were told that, having participated in this capacity of the ritual, we were now honorary sons of Emperor Hirohito.

Admiral Jarrell's Son Henry Participating in Yabusame, 1957

The relationship with the Japanese people that Admiral Jarrell fostered continued during his tenure as Commander Fleet Activities Yokosuka. Social events and assisting industries in need were not the only items he considered important. In August 1956 Jarrell arranged a tour of FAY for several employees of *Bokyo Shimbun Sha* (Anti-Communist Newspaper). They expressed gratitude for the tour, and the Editor, Michio Asanuma, proudly told Jarrell that "I can say with pride that our paper is the oldest anti-communist paper in Japan that is launching anti-red drives and fighting for annihilation of Communism." This was right up Jarrell's alley, as he had been a staunch opponent of communism his entire life.

Another example of Admiral Jarrell's diplomacy was when a sixth grade girl wrote him a long letter thanking him for the privilege of going on a base tour and seeing how clean the streets were, and how large the ships were. The student, Reiko Sugawara, wrote, "I felt more and more grateful for the fact that America was protecting our country with all these giant ships." Jarrell, never neglecting to respond to any communication, wrote back:

4 January 1957

Dear Reiko-san,

I received your letter. I can not read Japanese so I had it translated into English. I appreciated your writing me such a fine letter.

We Americans at Fleet Activities, Yokosuka will always welcome visitors. We would like our Japanese friends to know how well we are taking care of their base here.

With best wishes for your happiness and success,

Sincerely yours,

(Signed) A. E. Jarrell

Miss Reiko Sugawara
Class 1, sixth year
Sakamoto Primary School
Yokosuka City

Even a young girl in the sixth grade was treated with respect, and Jarrell made it a point to let her know that it was <u>her</u> base, not his.

Admiral Jarrell continued his policy of building relationships with the Japanese people by attending their local functions and by inviting Japanese to attend American functions and celebrations on the Navy base. His largesse included allowing local industries who had emergencies that would severely impact their companies to use Navy facilities if Navy regulations and availability permitted. On two occasions local shipbuilding companies had emergency need of dry dock facilities, and Jarrell arranged for the use of Fleet Activities Yokosuka dry docks to be made available to them.

Admiral and Mrs. Jarrell, with Daughter Joan, Attend Japanese
Festival
(Official U. S. Navy Photograph)

During his tenure as Commander Fleet Activities Yokosuka my dad had occasion to make an official Naval visit to a city in the northern Japanese island of Hokkaido. During his trip he visited with the mayor of a local town and introduced himself and his staff. The conversation went in many directions and the subject of hunting bears came up; bear hunting in Hokkaido was a big event. My dad told me how the conversation went, and laughingly said that when he asked the mayor how the bear season had been, the mayor replied through an interpreter, "Very good. Hunter get 23 bear and bear get 4 hunter." Dad seemed to think that it was a fair way to hunt.

*   *   *   *   *

On 14 May, 1957, Admiral Jarrell received orders to "detach from duty as Commander, Fleet Activities, Yokosuka, Japan, and... proceed to Seoul, Korea, and report... for duty as Commander, Naval Forces, Korea." He was going to spend a year in the "Land of the Morning Calm."

Prior to 1 July, 1957, the naval forces in Korean and Japanese waters came under the command of Naval Forces, Far East (NavFE). By July 1957 NavFE was abolished and reorganized into Commander Naval Forces Japan (CNFJ) and Commander Naval Forces Korea (CNFK). CNFK is responsible for the support of all naval forces on the Korean peninsula, as well as additional duties concerning the other military branches, United Nations, and the Armistice. Admiral Jarrell had the daunting task of creating and organizing the new Command and integrating it into the various operations already underway in the region. Jarrell was the first Commander, Naval Forces Korea.

His orders notified him that he would be performing collateral duties, and ordered him to report to:

Commander in Chief, United Nations Command, for additional duty as Commander, Naval Forces, United Nations Command;

Commander, U.S. Forces, Korea, for additional duty as Chief, U. S. Navy Advisory Group, Republic of Korea Navy, and Navy Advisor to the Republic of Korea Navy, and Commander, Naval Component Command, U. S. Forces, Korea;

Senior Member, United Nations Military Armistice Commission, for additional duty as Naval Member, United Nations Military Armistice Commission.

This was not going to be a cake-walk.

Admiral Jarrell was relieved 15 June, 1957, as Commander Fleet Activities Yokosuka, by Captain Kemp Tolley. Prior to his detachment, he made several trips to Korea to prepare for the task that lay ahead. His headquarters would be in Seoul, but he would be traveling extensively to Chinhae where a naval base was being constructed, to Pohang where training takes place, as well as the various ports of entry where naval ships might be stationed.

With the family residing in Yokosuka and no dependent housing available in Korea, the family remained in the Halsey Road house on the naval base during the time Jarrell was in Korea. Joan traveled back to California, where she began her sophomore year at the University of California Santa Barbara.

Jarrell flew to Korea 28 June and assumed the duties as Commander Naval Forces, Korea on July 1, 1957. On the same date, he reported for additional duty as Naval Member, United Nations Military Armistice Commission.

Also on July 1, Admiral Jarrell reported for additional duty as Chief, U. S. Navy Advisory Group, Republic of Korea Navy, and Navy Advisor to the Republic of Korea Navy, and as Commander, Naval Component Command, U. S. Forces, Korea.

In a newspaper article published in Seoul, Korea, on 7 August, 1957, Admiral Jarrell's responsibilities were summarized:

ROK Naval Forces Expand Under UN

A growing component in the overall strengthening of United Nations forces in Korea is the naval service of this water-boundaried country.

Commander of the Naval Forces, Component, United Nations, Korea is Rear Admiral Albert Jarrell of the United States Navy.

Admiral Jarrell also is commander of United States Naval Forces, Korea, an alternate member of the UN Command Military Armistice Commission and Chief, U.S. Naval Advisory Group, ROK Navy. He came to Seoul with his 10-officer staff when the UN headquarters in Korea was moved to the city July 1 of this year.

The main function of the UN naval headquarters in Seoul is planning and cooperating with the growing Republic of Korean Navy and Marine Corps.

The office maintains advisory groups, which send men in an advisory capacity with units of the ROK naval and Marine forces. Recently, advisors accompanied the two ROK branches on operation "Lucky Tiger," an amphibious assault maneuver.

The ROK Navy was only the Coast Guard in 1946, with no planned organization or methods of training. Some attempt was being made to resolve this when the conflict with North Korea began.

During the conflict, ROK officers and enlisted men were trained on American ships and in naval bases in the United States. The "on-the-job" training under great stress provided a nucleus of American-trained ROK naval and Marine personnel, and now the Republic has its own academies for training with the United Nations advisors.

During the past few years, the ROK naval force has been increased and now has a destroyer escort as its largest ship. Other ships include mine sweepers and patrol boats, as well as craft for amphibious operations.

Much of Admiral Jarrell's work would involve diplomatic relationships with various countries that had a presence in Korea. Jarrell had on-going communications with various Chinese (Nationalist Chinese – Taiwan) officials such as the Commander-in-Chief, Chinese Navy, Admiral Liang Hsu-chao, and other high-ranking officers. The British Embassy officials and diplomats of other countries were also routinely communicated with, and often Jarrell would arrange social events when visitors arrived in Korea.

A great deal of the focus of the communications and visiting were related to fighting the scourge of communism, particularly with the Nationalist Chinese, who were forced out of mainland China when the Communists took over that country. Anti-communist sentiment was very high in Korea, China (Taiwan), and Japan, and various entities, both governmental and civilian, were concerned and active in the fight against communism.

After the Armistice was signed refugees continued to stream into South Korea. The UN Military Armistice Commission, of which Admiral Jarrell was Senior Member, had to deal with this influx of displaced people, and to ferret out the communist infiltrators that might be with them. The Korean people controlled some of the communist agents by taking action on their own, to the dismay of the Communist.

Admiral Jarrell found the negotiations with the Communists to be very frustrating. In every meeting they would be rude, demanding, and vulgar. They made a point of insisting on one-upmanship. Their side always had to have higher ranking officers or the more important officials. Jarrell once told about a particular meeting where the Communists were being particularly vulgar. Jarrell and his entourage stood up and left the building, saying that they would not sit for that kind of behavior. He said that the Communists were shocked! No United Nations delegation had ever done that before; they had just sat and taken the abuse.

Members of UN Military Armistice Commission Leave Meeting
12 Feb 1958
F-R: Admiral A.E. Jarrell, General V.L. Zoller,
Brigadier J. W.Tweedie
(U.S. Army Photo by SFC W. R. Bradford)

Jarrell also was dismayed by the lack of progress and the amount of money the United States was spending for the UN negotiations. In his records was found a carbon copy of a satirical story describing how the situation in the armistice negotiations might look two decades later. The story most probably was written by him as the satire and style was definitely his, and it certainly reflected Jarrell's thoughts at the time.

98TH FINAL DRAFT PRELIMINARY PROGRESS REPORT

MUNSAN, KOREA, DECEMBER 18, 1981 – A new wave of cautious optimism developed today among UN Armistice representatives. An eventual settlement in the somewhat prolonged prisoner of war question seems not too distant, an unidentified, un-named spokesman said.

Cause for the renewed hopes, the first of this year, was a faint hint from Peiping that the Chinese were thinking about considering a move to permit the UN preliminary peace conference liaison sub-delegation to offer for general debate a resolution to give thought to placing on the agenda a discussion of the possibility of obtaining a qualified Chinese agreement to take under advisement the question of allowing an appeal by the sixth-echelon UN Special Issues negotiating team to soften the Communist ban against leaving a conference room once a session has been called to order. This issue has plagued the talks for the past 17 years.

Meanwhile, representatives of Communist Great Britain, Communist Australia, and the forty-eight neutral nations supervising the peace, arrived in Panmunjom today for next week's dedication of the magnificent new 189 story Preliminary Peace Talk Tower. Upon arrival in Munsan-ni Base Camp they issued a statement charging U. S. "war mongers" were threatening the peace and urged a more cooperative attitude toward the demand that the UN side begin reporting arrivals and departures of pointed flag staffs shipped into and out of Panmunjom, first brought up

by the Communists back in 1953. A preliminary
investigation is still being conducted.

Forty-eight star General Sterling Flitty is expected to arrive
from Washington tomorrow. He is U. S. President
Willawaw's personal representative and, together with the
United Nations Chief Peace Negotiator Rattly Boon will
represent the UN side at the dedication ceremony.

The new home of the Preliminary Peace Talks was erected
by the United States at a cost of $62,583,371,223,945.31. It
replaces the old 88 story preliminary tower built in 1957. It
is equipped with the latest atomic facilities for processing
UN concessions. It also has a special shop for tempering
UN optimism with caution and a beauty parlor where up to
220 faces can be saved at one sitting.

Yesterday nine star General J. B. C. Jones, formerly Far
East Affairs expert and currently personnel officer for the
gigantic UN scratchpad reclamation base at Pusan, awarded
the Military Order of Superhuman Patience to SFC John
Doe of Southport, Indiana, the last remaining member of
the original UN truce team of 1951. SFC Doe is shortly
retiring at the age of 73.

In Tokyo, 38 star General P. Carpenter Bags, American
Defense Department Comptroller representative, reported
that UN expenditures in the 29 year-old Korean temporary
peace had mounted to $420^{18.25}$ to the 48 supervising
Neutral Nations, 20^4 to the Custodian Forces, and 4^{18} for
operation of the MAC. Of the expenditures all but
$34,819.15 have been American dollars. In Washington
today President Willawaw denounced critics who charged
the Korean Peace is expensive. "We have supported the
peace since 1952 and we shall go on supporting it," he said.

"What do people want to do – lose the peace?" President Willawaw also lashed out at persons who contend keeping the peace is too costly. He said more money has been spent by Americans on living in the last 29 years than has been spent on the peace.

The author of this "Report" written in the 1950s probably didn't dream that the morass of the Armistice would still be unchanged more than half a century later. In the story the inference that Great Britain and Australia had become communist countries is based on the Russian master plan to first take over Asia and then move to Western Europe and, ultimately, control the entire world.

The Korean Navy had about 75 ships consisting mostly of amphibious craft. Almost all of these were docked at the naval base at Chinhae. Additional, smaller bases were located at Inchon and Pusan. The U.S. Navy Advisory Group, of which Jarrell was the Chief, was involved in almost all aspects of running the Korean Navy. Prior to the Korean War, Korea had only a Coast Guard, so the training and experience of operating a navy had to be acquired. U.S. Navy advisors worked with the Koreans in the shipyards, Naval Academy, and various on-shore support facilities, and advisors also spent a great deal of time aboard the Korean ships while at sea.

The Korean Navy is modeled after the United States Navy, even to the style of uniform. The U.S. Navy Advisors were having a great impact on the betterment of the ROK Navy. Being in the Korean Navy was not easy or profitable; the discipline was well enforced and the pay was minimal, but there was no lack of volunteers. The Koreans wanted to protect their country from communism and to remain a Republic.

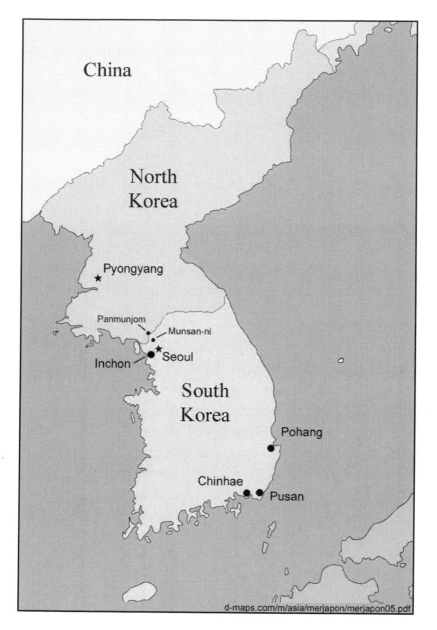

Important Korean Facilities

On December 20 our dad, after being away for nearly six months, began six days leave and flew back to Yokosuka to spend

Christmas with the family, returning to Korea December 27, 1957. He visited the family again on leave from 27 February to 3 March, 1958.

On 17 March, 1958, Dad returned to Yokosuka for a medical procedure on his right knee to remove cartilage that had been a chronic problem for most of his life. His knee issue may have originated as far back as his college or high school days when he was active in sports. His knee problem notwithstanding, he continued to play tennis his entire life.

The Bureau of Naval Personnel had notified Jarrell on 10 March, 1958, that his new orders were to report to the Commander in Chief, Pacific Fleet, to assume duty as Commander, Training Command, Pacific Fleet, in San Diego, California.

President Syngman Rhee bids Farewell to Admiral Jarrell
(Office of Public Information, ROK Photo)

*　*　*　*　*

Admiral Jarrell was relieved as Commander, Naval Forces Korea, on 14 June, 1958, by Rear Admiral Eugene B. McKinney, and flew from Chinhae, Korea, to Yokosuka that evening. From then until June 26 our family made preparations to depart Japan and return to our home in Coronado, California. We boarded American President Lines steamship SS Hoosier Mariner (in 1959 renamed President Buchanan) in Yokohama June 27 and arrived Los Angeles July 8, driving to Coronado the same day.

During the two year absence, my parents had made the Adella Avenue house a rental property. In an effort to make the process of renting the house as convenient as possible for themselves, Mom and Dad had hired a property management agency to oversee it. Upon returning to the house Dad commented, "I would board it up rather than rent it again in the future."

Jarrell reported for duty as Commander, Training Command, Pacific Fleet, on 17 July, 1958.

The Training Command office was located at the U.S. Fleet Sonar School in San Diego. It had a flag mess (high-ranking dining area) in which Admiral Jarrell could entertain foreign flag officers, local consular officials, and commanding officers of foreign ships undergoing training or visiting San Diego.

In August 1958 Admiral Jarrell and the Korean Chief of Naval Operations, Vice Admiral Jeung Kuk Mo, discussed the impending acquisition of four LSTs (Landing Ship, Tank) by Korea, and the subsequent training of the crews in the Southern California area. Jarrell commented, "We will see that the ships leave here ready for operations." On 12 March, 1959, Admiral

Jarrell wrote to the Chief of Naval Operations, Admiral Arleigh Burke, that "I just thought that you would be interested personally in knowing that our Korean friends rank, in shakedown and other training, at about the top. We have just completed in shaking down the last of four Korean LST. They have done as well as I knew they would; this, in spite of the fact that, for reasons of economy, they have been operating with only two thirds of a normal crew."

Admiral Jarrell continued receiving mail from Koreans and Americans who he had cultivated a relationship with during his tour in Korea. All wished him well in his new assignment and expressed gratitude for his invaluable services while he was in Korea. As was his policy, Jarrell responded to every letter he received.

A few months after assuming command of the Training Command, Pacific Fleet, Admiral Jarrell was contacted by *Navy Times* newspaper and asked to provide some biographical details for a piece they do for senior officers who report for a new assignment. Jarrell complied, and the piece was run in the January 13, 1959, issue of *Navy Times*.

Navy Times, 13 January, 1959

Navy training includes virtually every aspect of Navy life, particularly aboard ships. Training Command observers often are aboard vessels and can recommend appropriate training to ensure combat readiness and efficient operation of the ships of the Navy.

Routine deployments of ships always include multiple drills for damage control, general quarters drills and gunnery practice. There is little time to relax while at sea.

As one would imagine, when tasked with such a high level of responsibility, things may not go right and being contacted at any time of the day or night is to be expected. When a late-night call came in to our house, it was the responsibility of us kids to answer the phone and screen the calls. Dad didn't want to be interrupted in his sleep unless it was absolutely necessary. One night, in the wee hours of the morning, the phone started ringing. I was hoping my brother would answer it, so I ignored it. It kept ringing, and in those days a phone would not stop ringing until the caller gave up. My brother, apparently, expected me to answer it, which I didn't want to do. Finally, I gave in and opened my bedroom door to go to the phone and heard my father stomping down the hallway, and for the first time in my life, and the last time in my life, I heard my father cuss: "Damn it!" Turns out the call was for him.

The Navy Training Center, San Diego, routinely offered classes and seminars to top-level leaders in countries throughout the world, most often to NATO (North Atlantic Treaty Organization) and SEATO (Southeast Asia Treaty Organization) countries. In those classes the world situation would be analyzed and studied to better understand the military and political implications of events.

Seminars would often include speakers from corporations involved in the defense industries. San Diego had numerous defense companies that participated, such as Convair-Astronautics and Ryan Aeronautical, as well as companies located elsewhere like Chance Vought Aircraft, headquartered in Dallas, Texas. Those companies were more than helpful in presenting information that was unique to their industry, and they provided renowned and highly qualified speakers.

Other branches of service would routinely take advantage of Navy training and would reciprocate by providing instruction and seminars in areas of their expertise. The Air Force Air Research and Development Command worked closely with Admiral Jarrell, as well as elements of the Army and Marine Corps. In Japan, operating out of Itazuki Air Base, the United States Air Force worked with the Navy's Fleet Training Group to provide services for intercept, target acquisition, and simulated air attack exercises. The inter-service cooperation benefitted both the Navy and Air Force, and maintained an avenue of communication that brought the services closer for future operations.

The Commander of the Peruvian Pacific Fleet, Rear Admiral Gustavo Mathey, on 13 November, 1958, notified Admiral Jarrell that he wished to award him the Peruvian Cross of Naval Merit in appreciation for the outstanding training given to their navy. Jarrell replied on 18 November, "It will be an honor and a privilege to receive the Peruvian Cross of Naval Merit. I certainly do not deserve this decoration, since it has been a continuous pleasure to be associated with you and the Peruvian ships. However, I appreciate your thoughtfulness, and that of your government, with which our country has always enjoyed friendly relations."

The awarding of the medal was made November 23 at the North Island Naval Air Station in San Diego. Pursuant to Navy regulations, Jarrell forwarded the medal and citation to the Bureau of Naval Personnel (BuPers) where it would be held by the Department of State until such time as he could legally accept it. The possession and wearing of foreign decorations by American Navy personnel must be authorized by the Department of Navy and Department of State. Regulations clearly state which medals may be accepted but not worn on the uniform, and which may be worn and the order in which they must be displayed on the uniform. If the medal had not been previously approved by the Navy, the recipient would transfer it to BuPers until such time as permission is given.

As the Commander, Training Command, Pacific Fleet, Admiral Jarrell had the overall responsibility for all of the subordinate training commands throughout the Pacific Fleet. Fleet Training Centers were located at strategic points where personnel could receive detailed instruction and training on subjects and procedures that would be difficult or impossible to teach aboard ship. Fleet Training Groups would be responsible for training of officers and men assigned to the various ships and bases throughout the Pacific. The activities under Jarrell's command were: Fleet Training Group, San Diego; Fleet Training Center, San Diego; Nuclear Weapons Training Center, Pacific; Fleet Sonar School, San Diego; Fleet Air Defense Training Center, San Diego; Fleet Training Group, Pearl harbor; Fleet Training Group, Western Pacific; Fleet Gunnery School, San Diego; Fleet Training Center, Pearl Harbor; Fleet Training Group, Subic Bay; Pacific-Fleet Photo-triangulation Group. To sum it all up, Jarrell commented to the Deputy Chief of Naval Personnel in March of 1959, "As you know, the Training Command exerts a direct influence on fleet readiness..."

In late March 1959 Jarrell embarked on an extended visit to the facilities located at Pearl Harbor, Hawaii, Yokosuka, Japan, and Subic Bay, Philippine Islands. The purpose of the trip was to inspect the facilities and procedures, and to discuss problems or needs that the local commanders had. The trip had to be planned well in advance, as the Military Air Transport Service (MATS) flights were difficult to book in advance. VIP flights were not available to some of the destinations, so Jarrell tried to acquire a dedicated plane for the trip. As Jarrell put it, "I doubt that it would be good for the prestige of the Navy for me and my inspection team to arrive in the Philippines, utilizing a regular flight, for the purpose of conducting a full dress military inspection." Jarrell eventually was able to secure the use of the Commander Seventh Fleet airplane, and did not need the services of MATS.

In May of 1959 Jarrell traveled to the Armed Forces Special Weapons Project (AFSWP) at Sandia Base, New Mexico, just outside of Albuquerque. His orders stated that the trip required a security clearance up to Top Secret, which Jarrell had. Jarrell took with him Captain Bailey, the Commander Nuclear Weapons Training Center, and other key officers in his command. AFSWP was a military agency created in 1947 with the responsibility for all aspects of nuclear weapons under military control. (At the time of the trip, AFSWP was transitioning into the newly established Defense Atomic Support Agency - DASA.) The meeting Jarrell attended was to brief him and the other officers on improving the general knowledge of safety measures for special weapons. Part of the briefing was a tour of Manzano Air Force Base, code name "Site Able," a location in the Monzano Mountains used for nuclear weapons storage. Admiral Jarrell echoed his boss, Admiral Herbert Hopwood, Commander in Chief, Pacific Fleet, when he wrote that, "...if more persons are familiar with the handling of special weapons, better security would follow." He was committed to expanding the special weapons training and security in the Navy's Training Groups and Training Centers.

*   *   *   *   *

On 31 July, 1959, Admiral Jarrell forwarded his "official request for early retirement" to Rear Admiral Paul H. Ramsey, Chief of Staff, Commander in Chief U. S. Pacific Fleet. On 5 August the request was forwarded to the Secretary of the Navy with the recommendation of approval of the request. Admiral Jarrell's request for retirement follows:

31 July, 1959

From: Rear Admiral Albert E. Jarrell, U.S. Navy, 059705
(Commander Training Command, U.S. Pacific Fleet)

To: The Secretary of the Navy

Via: (1) Commander in Chief, U.S. Pacific Fleet
(2) Chief of Naval Personnel

Subj: Voluntary Retirement, request for

Ref: (a) ALNAV No. 34
(b) BUPERS INST 1811.1A

1. Having completed 38 years' active service, it is requested that I be transferred to the Retired List of the Navy, effective on the first day of October, 1959.

2. It is realized that the requested effective date of retirement does not allow for the normal time required for processing, outlined in reference (b). However, my request for a very early retirement is caused by item (H) of reference (a), which was received this date. Item (H) is quoted as follows:

"Effective 1 November, the authority to advance officers on the retired list by reason of having been commended for performance of duty in actual combat will be repealed. Officers who retire on 1 November or later will not be advanced to higher grade for this reason. The last advancements, under present law, of officers retiring voluntarily will be on 1 October."

3. Honorary advancement on the retired list is of very great personal importance to me in connection with future plans.

4. The report of my retirement physical examination will be forwarded to the Chief of Naval Personnel (Pers-B52) at the earliest possible date.

5. If it is not practicable to effect my retirement in time to receive honorary advancement on the retired list, it is requested that this letter be cancelled.

(signed) A. E. Jarrell

Copy to:
BUPER (Advance copy)

On 23 September, 1959, the Secretary of the Navy, William B. Franke, wrote to Admiral Jarrell and informed him that his wishes to retire effective 1 October 1959 were amenable to the Department of the Navy. In addition, the results of the retirement physical showed that Jarrell's chronic knee problem had progressed to arthritis, which was also evident in his shoulder. In this regard, Jarrell was deemed to have a twenty percent disability and would be placed on the disability retirement list effective 1 October, 1959.

When my dad told me of his retirement plans. I asked him if he was going to have a huge retirement parade. He replied that all those officers and men had better things to do on a weekend than march for one person who is retiring. That's the kind of leader Dad was: the men were very important to him.

The Chief of Naval Operations, Admiral Arleigh Burke, wrote Jarrell a personal letter regretting Jarrell's retirement, but wishing him well.

CHIEF OF NAVAL OPERATIONS

19 September 1959

Dear Al:

On the eve of your retirement, I join the whole
Navy in sending you our best wishes for your future
health, happiness and success. You have made an enviable
reputation in this splendid Navy of ours and your many
friends and shipmates will have bright memories due to
your efforts. I know that you, too, as you look back
over your years in the Navy, will have nostalgic memories
of the people with whom you have served, the people in
foreign countries whom you have met and assisted, and
the many interesting places where you have been.

You have truly rendered distinguished service to
your Navy and your country. Your contributions will long
continue through the example which you have set for others
to follow. A sterling combat record as a destroyer
division and squadron commander during World War II reflects so well your valor and courage. Again, during the
Korean action TransDiv ELEVEN performed superbly under
your keen leadership and fighting, aggressive spirit.

As a flag officer you have confidently and expertly
executed your assignments with wisdom and resourcefulness.
You gave unstintingly of your versatility and enthusiasm
in sensitive positions of great responsibility in the Far
East, and through your cooperation, diplomacy and tact,
you have strengthened the will of men and helped them to
remain free. Yours has, indeed, been an illustrious and
fruitful career, and we will sorely miss you for we have
learned to lean heavily on your counsel.

Best of luck and Godspeed to you.

Sincerely,

ARLEIGH BURKE

Rear Admiral Albert E. Jarrell, USN
Commander, Fleet Training Command, Pacific
c/o U. S. Fleet Sonar School
San Diego 47, California

On 1 October, 1959, the day Rear Admiral Albert
Edmondson Jarrell retired from the Unites States Navy, after thirty
eight years of faithful service to the Country, Vice Admiral Jarrell
was no longer on active duty. On this day, a letter from the

Secretary of the Navy, William B. Franke, summarized Jarrell's service career.

THE SECRETARY OF THE NAVY
WASHINGTON

1 October 1959

My dear Admiral Jarrell:

It is with sincere regret that I note your transfer to the Temporary Disability Retired List. The termination of your active service will be a distinct loss to the Government of the United States.

In recognition of your outstanding performance of duty as Engineering Member of the U. S. Naval Mission to Brazil from February 1941 to February 1943, the Government of Brazil conferred upon you the Decoration and Diploma of the National Order of the Southern Cross (Official). The Commander-in-Chief, United States Atlantic Fleet commended you for the valuable contributions you made to the efficiency of the Destroyer-Destroyer Escort Shakedown Group operations from March 1943 to February 1944. During this period, you assisted in the formulation of policies and doctrines which enabled that newly-formed group to assume an operational status and to accomplish its assigned objectives in a timely fashion.

You were awarded the Legion of Merit with Combat "V" for exceptionally meritorious conduct while serving as Commander, Destroyer Division FORTY-TWO in action against enemy forces in the Southwest Pacific Area. In supporting the Aitape-Humboldt Bay, Biak, Noemfoor, Sansapor, Moratai, and Leyte operations, you directed your division with skill and tenacity. The President of the United States awarded you the Navy Cross for extraordinary heroism while serving as Commander, Destroyer Squadron FIFTY-FIVE and of the screen of detached groups which served as Gunfire and Covering Forces, in action against the enemy in the vicinity of Okinawa from March to May 1945. You aggressively maintained the fighting efficiency of the officers and men of your command at a high peak throughout this hazardous period, and your unfaltering decision, cool judgment, and resolute fortitude in the face of continual peril reflected the highest credit upon you and the Naval service.

As commander of Transport Division ELEVEN, you were awarded a Gold Star in lieu of the Second Legion of Merit with Combat "V" for exceptionally meritorious service during the amphibious operations at Wonson, Samchok and Hungnam, Korea from 3 December to 24 December 1950. You continued to perform commendably as Chief of Staff to the Commander, Destroyer Force, U. S. Atlantic Fleet, and as Professor of Naval Science at The Rice Institute, Houston, Texas. While serving as Commander, Destroyer Flotilla ONE and as Commander, Destroyer Flotilla, Western Pacific, you set standards that will be difficult to emulate. I also note with pleasure that you were awarded the Oak Leaf Cluster in lieu of the Third Legion of Merit for distinguished and meritorious conduct in the performance of outstanding service as Senior Naval Representative of the United Nations Military Armistice Commission in Korea, from 7 December 1953 to 9 June 1954.

Carrying out all your assignments with alert initiative and dedication of purpose as Commander, Amphibious Training Command, U. S. Pacific Fleet; as Commander, Fleet Activities, Yokosuka, Japan; and as Commander, Naval Forces, Korea, you gained the admiration and respect of all with whom you served. During your tour as Commander, Training Command, Pacific you have met the challenges of complex and ever-changing training demands with uncommon administrative ability and superior leadership. During this successful tour of duty the Peruvian Government presented you the Peruvian Cross of Naval Merit.

Your performance of duty throughout your career has been uniformly excellent. May it be a source of great pride and satisfaction to look back upon a job "Well Done."

Sincerely yours,

(signed) W. B. Franke

Vice Admiral Albert Edmondson Jarrell
U. S. Navy, Retired
Commander, Training Command
U. S. Pacific Fleet
c/o Fleet Sonar School
San Diego, 47, California

CHAPTER 17
RETIREMENT

Having been commended for his outstanding performance while under fire in combat, per the existing regulations Dad was elevated to the rank of Vice Admiral on the day of his retirement.

Vice Admiral Jarrell (Ret) slipped into retirement quite seamlessly. He continued to play tennis, and increased his reading of various magazines and newspapers to analyze their positions on politics. He had a longstanding view that the media would almost always report news in a fashion that suited their purposes rather than honestly reporting and letting the readers interpret the details for themselves. He often commented to me that in order to get the true, unbiased story on the news he had to subscribe to *Intelligence Digest*, a periodical published in England. He kept in touch with his past friends and cohorts, and reached out to become involved in state and federal politics.

Dad's knee continued to bother him, and he and Mom decided to move to a drier climate that might give him some relief. In the center of San Diego County is the small town of Ramona where the humidity level would be comfortable for him almost all year. San Diego, on the other hand, can occasionally be muggy from July to October. Mom and Dad retained a contractor who built a ranch style house on an acre of land on Eleventh Street in Ramona. The house on Adella Avenue was sold, and the day I completed my junior year at Coronado High School in the summer of 1960, the move to Ramona was made.

I completed my senior year at Ramona High School, class of 1961. I had talked to my dad about a career in the Navy, but was advised that with my nearsighted vision I wouldn't be able to attend Annapolis and become a line officer. I thought that entering the Navy as an enlisted man might be a problem for me because of my dad's long career and the possibility of resentment or the appearance of favoritism, so instead I enlisted in the Air Force. I have always believed that it was the best decision for me, and that had I gone straight to college I would probably have had a hard time of it.

Dad would spend hours at the dining room table with his Corona typewriter banging out letters and articles. Most of the letters were to newspapers, mostly the *San Diego Union* or *Tribune*, but often to the local *Ramona Sentinel* paper or the *Escondido Times-Advocate*. The letters invariably would have something to do with world affairs, communism, Korea, or the Panama Canal, all subjects he was well versed in.

Jarrell was also involved in civic assistance organizations such as the Ramona Community Chest, which years later became part of the United Way organization. He was the Ramona coordinator for American Field Service, an international youth exchange program. Jarrell was a member of the Ramona Kiwanis Club and was active in finding Southern California speakers to make presentations at their weekly meetings.

Jarrell volunteered to be the umpire and scorekeeper for the Ramona Little League Association, was an original member of the Ramona Historical Society, and founded the Ramona Taxpayers Association. Ann also was involved in community activities with her membership in the Ramona Women's Club and the Intermountain Republican Women's Federation.

As a director of the California Republican Assembly, Jarrell was instrumental in defining the Republican political platform. He also was a member of the California Republican State Central Committee and the San Diego County Republican Central Committee, where he served as Precinct Chairman for the 80th Assembly District. Al was instrumental in reorganizing the 500 precincts of California's 80th Assembly District.

In the early 1970s Jarrell worked with John Stull, who would become the California 80th District Assemblyman and later State Senator. Jarrell served as Stull's Honorary Chairman and would represent him in venues where Stull's schedule would not allow him to attend. Jarrell was campaign director for two additional California Legislature races and two campaigns for U. S. House of representatives. All were successful.

Never fond of paying taxes that would be wasted on nonessential projects, Jarrell became the president of the Ramona Taxpayers Association. One of his pet peeves was that he paid lower property taxes when he had lived in the upper class city of Coronado than he did in the rural area of Ramona.

After a series of routine periodic medical examinations, the Navy determined that Jarrell's knee disability was not going to improve and, on 30 April, 1964, notified him that he was being transferred from the Temporary Disability Retired List to the Retired List.

Jarrell continued to stay in contact with his friends in Japan, Korea and China (Taiwan). No only did they exchange Christmas cards every holiday season, but they continued to communicate on a social level. A number of his friends went out of their way to meet with him when they would be in the Southern California area on business.

In March of 1962 the results of a Gallup poll caught Jarrell's eye, resulting in a letter to Dr. George Gallup. At issue was a poll that showed Americans were strongly against the admission of Outer Mongolia to the United Nations. A few months later, per a deal worked with Russia, Outer Mongolia was admitted to the UN and a new Gallup poll coincidentally showed President Kennedy's approval rating to be considerably improved. Jarrell, with his vast network of contacts, knew of no organizations or individuals who supported the admission of Outer Mongolia, but did know of vigorous opposition to their admission. Since no other events had taken place to change the public's mind regarding President Kennedy, his rise in the poll numbers got Jarrell to question the validity of the poll. He asked Gallup to explain his methods, particularly how he creates the polling lists, and if he has any financial backers who might lobby him in some fashion. He ended his letter with, "Polls are a popular subject for conversation. It seems rather strange that I never have heard anyone state that he had been polled by your organization; nor have I ever heard anyone state that he has knowledge of anyone else being polled." Jarrell never received a reply.

Gallup's silence prompted Jarrell to write to the Editor, *San Diego Union*. He included his letter to Gallup and gave an example of somewhat devious questioning. In a recent poll Gallup asked the question of, 1) which candidate in the party that you do <u>not</u> support would best help the candidate in <u>your</u> party, and 2) which candidate in the party you do <u>not</u> support would serve best if elected? The point Jarrell was trying to make was that the way a question is posed could affect the way the results are published, depending on the agenda of the pollster. Jarrell referred to an experience he had in Mexico with a pollster when he served there.

"Several years ago I had some experience in Mexico with a poll conducted by Dr. Lazlo Radvanyi. Based on my conversation with him I reached the conclusion that it is extremely difficult to conduct a public opinion polling system that is completely free of prejudice and external influence. Mature, free people have opinions. Most of them are voters. Dr. Radvanyi informed me that paid, mature [poll] workers were not as reliable as unpaid college students, too young to vote." Jarrell did not place much stock in polling results.

Admiral Jarrell never did think that the United Nations was a worthy organization. He gave a speech to the Intermountain Republican Women, Federated (San Diego County), in the early 1960s in which he made that known. The group gave a press release to the *Ramona Sentinel* newspaper in which it said that Jarrell did "not consider the United Nations to be altogether an evil organization." Reading that, Jarrell fired off this response to the newspaper: "In my speech I said, 'I consider the United Nations to be the greatest threat that ever has confronted our nation.' I also said, 'The American fighting man is an American, motivated by patriotism; he is not an internationalist.' By no stretch of the imagination could any part of my speech have been taken to infer that the American fighting man is willing to fight with the United Nations under any conditions."

Jarrell based his dislike of the UN on his own personal observations before and during the Korean War and the Armistice, and on the myriad questionable or malevolent actions that that body had executed. The Korean War was a prime example. The UN initiated the "police action" to stop the war, but only 15 members participated. About three fourths of the members refused to participate (the so-called neutral nations). One of the original UN members, a permanent member of the Security Council, Russia, worked with Communist China to plan and initiate the communist aggression! So, of course Jarrell was not pleased with the United Nations. His position on the Korean War was that had we not been a member of the UN we would have won the war in short order instead of it dragging on in Armistice negotiations for, at the time, thirteen years (now approaching 70 years).

Jarrell was particularly concerned about a huge movement within our own government to disarm the US and give the UN more military power. To accomplish this, the Arms Control and Disarmament Agency was formed under President Kennedy's administration. This was authorized by Public Law 87-297 enacted September 26, 1961. The United States Department of State published Publication 7277 entitled, "Freedom from War, The United States Program for General and Complete Disarmament in a Peaceful World." Included in the First Stage of implementation was "U. N. Peace-keeping powers would be strengthened." Included in Stage Two would be the reduction of armed forces and "Establishment of a permanent international peace force within the United Nations." Finally, in Stage Three, "States would retain only those forces, non-nuclear armaments, and establishments required for the purpose of maintaining internal order; they would also support and provide agreed manpower for a U.N. Peace Force." Admiral Jarrell found this to be abhorrent.

Many politicians, primarily on the left, found the concept of turning our military over to the United Nations to be quite appealing. Jarrell found Senator Thomas Kuchel to be particularly noteworthy in this regard. Kuchel gave a speech in which he accused those who did not support his views to be right wing extremists and "Fright Peddlers." Jarrell wrote to Kuchel and expressed his displeasure. Kuchel wrote back but Jarrell was unconvinced of Kuchel's sincerity in expressing concern over disarmament. Jarrell again wrote Kuchel and concurrently sent a letter to the *Escondido Times Advocate* newspaper saying, "In his

'Fright Peddlers' speech, published in the *Times-Advocate*, Senator Kuchel made it clear that he favors the New Frontier efforts toward disarmament (PL 87-297). He made it equally clear that his stand is eminently correct, in as much as most of his opposition comes from 'fright peddlers,' also known as 'right wing extremists.' There are many people who disagree with Senator Kuchel who are not extremists, but are very concerned about the failure of our country."

Dad talked to me often about the many dishonorable wars that took place following WWII. World War Two, according to him, was fought for patriotic reasons, not only by the United States but by the other allies. Although the United States entered into combat later than the British, it was a fight to defend our freedom and prevent the invasion of Axis powers. Had we not entered the war, Britain most certainly would have fallen and the next country in line could very well have been the United States. Virtually all American citizens were involved in one way or another, either by contributing to the war effort through the labor force, donations, or War Bonds, or by reducing non-essential consumption of food and materials. But the wars that followed, Korea (1950-53) and Vietnam (1964-75), were, according to my dad, fought for reasons that President Eisenhower called the Military-Industrial Complex, or more accurately, the Military-Industrial-Congressional Complex. In his view, there was no compelling strategic reason to fight those wars other than to accomplish goals separate from national security. Industry providing war materials made huge profits from the war, and politicians passing huge appropriation bills made huge political capital.

My dad told one story about a US plan to bomb Chinese supply lines that were running war materials into North Korea to fight against the UN forces. Corporations in one of the UN allies fighting the war happened to be selling raw materials to China, which were then being used, in part, to manufacture the Chinese war materiel. If the finished goods were prevented from reaching North Korea, China might possible quit purchasing the raw materials. Through the United Nations, pressure was exerted on the US to abandon the plan to bomb the supply routes. In this example, the Military-Industrial Complex overruled the battle commanders for reasons having nothing to do with winning the war.

Jarrell spent hours involved in various issues that concerned him, banging away at his typewriter, meeting with like-minded people, and speaking at organized events. He would read various newspapers and magazines and shoot off a letter if he thought a commentator was spouting something un-American or progressive. Taxes were a constant thorn in his side, as he thought that there was no accountability and no justification for new, higher taxes. He summarized his thoughts in a tongue-in-cheek letter published in the *San Diego Union* in August 1962:

One Party To Earn, The Other To Spend

Pursuant to persistent requests of many friends, I have decided to be the standard bearer of a new political party. We have agreed that, first, our party must have a name that will have a strong appeal.

It is common knowledge that our country is short on sophisticates and long on SOBs. The name that we have chosen, the USOB Party, obviously will draw the support of all Unsophisticated SOBs, and there are legions of them.

We are in the process of drawing up a platform. To make it easy to understand, we have decided to restrict it to just one plank. This will call for a continuation of high taxes for the opposition, and no taxes at all for our party members. We are going to collect all of the tax money and do all of the spending.

Our main difficulty may well be that everyone who has been paying taxes for others to spend will want to join our party and get some of the gravy. We can't permit this because somebody has to pay taxes and we are against paying them ourselves. We therefore are in favor of continuing the two-party system, one party to work hard and pay taxes and the other party, our party, to collect and spend.

With only half the voters paying taxes, and with our understandable desire to get our hands on all the tax money possible, we are considering an eight-day week so that the opposition will have more time to work and earn money. Also, and this is important, the eight-day week will provide our majority party members with eight days of leisure instead of only seven. Of course we may have to use some of this longer week to devise new methods to spend money.

A. E. Jarrell
Ramona

It is good to know that Albert Jarrell had a sense of humor.

In 1969 Jarrell was the Chairman of Citizens to End Campus Anarchy, fighting to stop the influx of radicals to the universities. One focus was to prevent the rehiring of Herbert Marcuse, a Marxist professor who reportedly was the first protester to occupy the University of California San Diego administration building, which was organized by his student, political activist

Angela Davis. The efforts of Citizens to End Campus Anarchy were unsuccessful.

In the late 1960s Mom and Dad's faithful dachshund, Spiffy, passed away and was laid to rest in the Sorrento Valley Pet Cemetery in San Diego. Spiffy had traveled more than the average American, having been to Houston, Coronado, Japan, back to Coronado and then to Ramona. Regal, the cat, remained and gave my parents his total affection. It was mutual.

My dad was satisfied with the environment of Ramona, California, but he was frustrated by the governmental actions over which he had no control. A major problem for him was the constantly increasing property taxes with no measureable improvement in infrastructure. He once told me that the taxes were being used to build marble government buildings containing lavish artwork. A slight exaggeration, perhaps, but the message was clear: government wastes money. Dad had friends who were retired Admirals who, on their government retirement pay, could not afford to pay the constantly increasing property taxes and were forced to leave the state. (It wasn't until 1978 when "Proposition 13" was passed that the property tax emergency was alleviated)

* * * * *

In 1972 Mom and Dad made the decision to move to Sedona, Arizona, where they built a home in the Chapel Bells subdivision south of the city. They and Regal, the cat, made the move.

Jarrell immediately became involved in civic affairs, volunteer work, and politics. He became a Republican precinct member and was elected a member of the State Republican Executive Committee in 1974. Admiral Jarrell served as president of the Sedona-Coconino Taxpayers Association and was later the chairman of its Legislative Committee. Never wanting to have an idle moment, he was a member of the board of Sedona Healthcare Services, Inc., vice chairman of the Coconino Health Planning Council, and a member of the Executive Committee of the Northern Arizona Health Planning Council.

A major national issue that occupied Jarrell's attention at the time was the Carter administration's plan to give the Panama Canal back to Panama. Jarrell had researched the legalities of the United States' possession of the Canal and, working with legislators, had incontrovertible evidence that we could (and should) hold on to it. Jarrell and innumerable citizens worked tirelessly to change minds within Carter's administration and to convince scores of legislators that the plan was not advantageous to America's national security, but the Torrijos-Carter Treaties were signed and the Canal Zone would be gifted back to Panama.

Admiral Jarrell entered the political arena himself, for the first time in his life, in July of 1976. Coconino County was primarily a Democratic district and Republicans didn't field a candidate in the 1974 race. Jarrell believed that the conservatives of the county should have a conservative to vote for in the election. He ran as a candidate for the office of State Senator from the 2nd Legislative District. As the papers reported, "He didn't win, but he put up a valiant fight, befitting a man with his history and background." I later asked him how he felt about losing. Dad replied, "I'm fine with it. My opponent and I share similar views and beliefs and I am sure he will do a good job."

Even in politics my dad cared for the people he touched. Two things he told me have stayed in my mind. The first was that he would not ask for money, but if someone volunteered a donation he would accept it. The second was that he made sure that the campaign bumper stickers he gave out had an adhesive on them that would allow easy removal from the bumper. He said that supporters should not have to use knives and solvents to remove a political campaign sticker off of their car.

ALBERT JARRELL
for
STATE SENATOR

District 2   Republican

1. No gun controls — "except for criminals".
2. Speedy trial and punishment for crimes committed with a deadly weapon.
3. Cost of government should increase no faster than the population.
4. One of the most important functions of government should be the encouragement of industry, private enterprise, and individual responsibility.
5. For economy, private enterprise should handle energy problems.
6. A sound education should be available for all.
7. Public servants are just that — not your masters.
8. Land use — local or state control.

Al strongly favors:
1. More promotion of the tourist industry.
2. Increase of energy production by removing federal controls, and encouragement of private enterprise. Arizona can greatly increase its energy production, probably to self-sufficiency, by construction of nuclear & solar plants.

If elected to the State Senate:
1. Al would be able to devote full time to the office.
2. Would make frequent visits to the district.
3. Would work for passage of the County Charter Bill (County Home Rule).
4. Would try to resurrect the proposed joint resolution of the Arizona Legislature which called on the U.S. Congress to balance the national budget. This resolution easily passed the Arizona House, which is controlled by Republicans; but when it reached the Senate, which is controlled by Democrats, it was so extensively amended that it was rendered meaningless. Al cannot understand why both houses of our Legislature should not agree on a strong resolution demanding that Congress balance its budget. Every unbalanced budget means more inflation.

LET'S KEEP DOWN THE COST OF GOVERNMENT — AT ALL LEVELS!

Albert Jarrell For State Senate Committee
3 North Leroux, Room 211
Flagstaff, Arizona 86001   Tel. 779-2356
Larry Davis, Campaign Chairman
Joe Burke, Finance Chairman

Jarrell's Campaign Brochure

Regal, the cat who had traveled from Coronado to Yokosuka, Japan, back to Coronado and then to Ramona and Sedona passed away in 1976 at age 23. Dad had purchased a gravesite at the pet cemetery in Sorrento Valley, San Diego, at the same time that Spiffy was buried there. He bundled Regal up and drove him to San Diego for burial, where he rests today.

Among Dad's many interests was the United States' apparent inability to win a war post-WWII. He talked to me about this on numerous occasions, and a good part of the problem, as he saw it, was that war was too profitable for too many people. Because of his position in the upper ranks during the Korean War, and his involvement with high ranking officials from the various nations involved, he saw that many military decisions were being tempered by political pressure. Many of the speeches he gave to various organizations after his retirement had to do with this topic, along with the problems of communism and socialism encroaching into our societies.

Jarrell read an editorial in the April 4, 1975, issue of *The Wall Street Journal* titled "Saigon's Collapse" in which the writer expressed that the blame for how the Vietnam War was ending should, to a large extent, fall on the shoulders of the Saigon government. Jarrell disagreed, writing to the *WSJ* that "You blame the Saigon government too much, the United States too little." His argument was that the Paris Agreement on Vietnam resembled the Korean Armistice Agreement and both were flawed. In Vietnam the agreement authorized the enemy to keep 300,000 troops in South Vietnam, which Jarrell said "are conditions that a conqueror might impose on the conquered."

Jarrell went on to say, "We should have learned a lesson from our Korean fiasco, but we didn't. Syngman Rhee begged us to let him win. 'If you don't let us beat the communists, they will one day beat you. Just let us win.'" Jarrell saw the same policy being used in Vietnam and thought that the US should have supported the South Vietnamese with advisors and military support, but American troops on the ground, and turning it into our war, was a big mistake.

Jarrell said that an interview with the Shah of Iran by *U.S. News and World Report* in 1961 made the message clear. Jarrell summarized: "The Shah questioned the advisability of an anti-communist regime's loyalty to the United States in view of what happened to the Polish and Yugoslav exile governments during World War II, the Chinese Nationalists, the Republic of Korea, South Vietnam, the Congo, and Laos. The Shah explained that past experience has shown that when confronted with a communist challenge the United States abandons its anti-communist friends and either partitions the threatened country or insists on a coalition government with the communists included."

Dad had given up tennis a few years after moving to Sedona, and had given up cigar smoking while still in Ramona. He considered himself to be in pretty good health, which was confirmed by Navy doctors during his routine physicals. In March 1977 Mom and Dad traveled to San Diego where they both had a physical examination at the Balboa Naval Hospital. While in San Diego, they saw their new two-week-old grand-daughter, Jennifer Kay Jarrell, while spending some time with my wife Claudia, our two-year-old son Alan, and me. The report of the physical examinations, dated 1 April 1977, gave both Mom and Dad a clean bill of health.

My parents attended the state convention of the Arizona Federation of Republican Women in Flagstaff, Arizona, in late April. Upon returning home on April 23, Dad sat in his favorite chair and Mom handed him a cold beer in a German mug that they had picked up on a trip to Europe. Mom was walking back to the kitchen when Dad made an agonizing sound. When she turned, he was clutching his chest and fell to the floor. She called a paramedic who lived in the neighborhood but he could not reach the house in time to save him. Vice Admiral Albert Edmondson Jarrell, a twentieth century Vasco da Gama, had passed away at age 75.

Lewis and I drove overnight from San Diego to Sedona. Joan, who was in Mexico at the time, made her way to Sedona as quickly she could. In Dad's desk was a letter in which he wrote that he wished to be buried in his Navy uniform, the uniform of the country and service that he loved so much. Always planning ahead, Dad had left detailed instructions for Mom and us regarding what needed to be done.

Dad was buried in the family plot in Shadowlawn Cemetery, LaGrange, Georgia, on 27 April, 1977.

The Sedona newspaper gave Al a front-page eulogy listing his history, awards, and accomplishments. They published personal comments by those who knew him:

"Jane Welton, past president of the Verde Valley Republican Women, said, 'It is impossible to estimate the number of contributions to this community made by Al Jarrell. He was always more than willing to lend himself and his ability on behalf of any worthy cause. Those of us who worked with him are going to miss profoundly his wise counsel as well as his enthusiasm.'

"Maleese Black, president of the Keep Sedona Beautiful committee and community worker, said Jarrell was 'one of the most devoted volunteers this town has ever had.'

"Vince Manka, a past president of the taxpayers association, said, 'Al and Ann were one of the greatest couples in Sedona. Normally you don't expect a military man and his wife to be but that's the kind of people they have been.'

"Charles Andrews, another past president, said, 'Al was a real fair, open-type person... We are going to miss him a lot. He would stand up and face anybody...'"

I once asked Dad what was the hardest job he ever had to do. His answer was, "I don't think I ever worked a day in my life. Everything I've done has been a pleasure." In our conversations over the years he never talked about his eventual death, living each day to the fullest and doing the things he loved. But had he been asked, he probably would have said that he would prefer to die suddenly, either by medical emergency or in combat. To die a slow, lingering death by cancer or dementia would have been anathema to him.

It has become popular to refer to the men of the World War II era as being the "Greatest Generation," and that appellation might well be applied to Al Jarrell. But he would be the first to argue that he was only doing what had to be done, and men and women of all the ages have done great things. Early explorers – both land and sea, Revolutionary War, Civil War, Spanish-American War, Astronauts, Gulf War. Every generation has people who step forward to do the hard things that have to be done. Those who know little of history may pick one group that they think should stand out, while not being aware of, or forgetting, all the others.

Mom was asked to return to San Diego with Lewis and me but said that her friends and interests were in Sedona and she chose to stay. A year later, I was returning to San Diego from a business trip and decided to swing through Sedona to talk Mom into moving back with me. The moment she opened her door and I stepped inside she said that she wanted to go back with me to live in San

Diego. It turns out that even though she had performed volunteer work in Sedona, and been involved in a myriad of civic activities, the real catalyst for all of her associations and interests had been Al. With him gone, the constant activity dissipated and living in Sedona was no longer for her.

Mom drove back to San Diego with me and arranged for a realtor to sell the Sedona house. She bought a nice ranch style home in my neighborhood and lived in San Diego until she passed away on 3 May, 1992, at age 86. Ann, too, was buried in the Jarrell family plot, next to her beloved Albert.

ABOUT THE AUTHOR

Although Henry Jarrell was born in Georgia, he only spent a few months there. As a Navy dependent his formative years were spent in a different city and different school virtually every year. Most people would think that this was a bad thing, but he got to travel to many places and meet new people. Besides, for him this was the norm.

After graduation from High School, he joined the Air Force and became a jet engine mechanic. Upon discharge he was hired by a San Diego company that made gas turbine engines and packages, and remained with them until retirement. Through the years he worked in a number of departments including assembly, test, field service, service engineering and project management. Along the way he earned a degree in microbiology which, although not directly related to his field, opened many doors of opportunity.

Most of his work was detail oriented and involved writing technical reports and instruction manuals. He hopes that this book does not read like a dry engineering study.

Henry appreciates all reviews, and welcomes comments and error notices at hejarrell@gmail.com.